VICTORIAN ENGLAND'S

BEST—SELLING AUTHOR

*

'Tis fifty years since! Lo! The Sower had birth,
Who cast the great seeds of democracy forth,
The people rejoiced at the newness of deeds
And welcomed the bosoms that rose 'midst the weeds.

He spake as he marched o'er the hard, thorny field,
To the toilers therein who their misery revealed,
"O! Men of my country, the day dawn is nigh,
When all who oppress ye and chain ye must die.

"The shams of the centuries must be dethroned
'Ere the bonds be dissevered 'neath which ye have groaned;
Down! Down! As the wreckage of things that are wrong
They shall go if ye strive with the strength of the strong!"

'Tis fifty years since! Lo! The Sower today
Beholds the vile weeds slowly passing away,
And better and nobler fruition appears
To gladden his soul at his sowing of years.

Still true to the mission he bore at his birth!
Still giving his light to the poor of the earth!
He stands as once stood the grand prophet of old,
Who doom and disaster to Jewry foretold!

No faltering! No wavering! Still fearless and brave!
He thunders his truths 'gainst the men who enslave,
Believing that Victory—a hundred years hence—
Shall come to the Sower of fifty years since.

William Allan, M.P. 'Reynolds's the Sower',
Special Supplement to
Reynolds's Newspaper, 27 May 1900

VICTORIAN ENGLAND'S

BEST–SELLING AUTHOR

The Revolutionary Life of G W M Reynolds

To Kats
Lots of Love,
Stephen S. Basdeo
xox

Stephen Basdeo and Mya Driver

With a Foreword by Rebecca Nesvet

(and on behalf of Mya!)

PEN & SWORD
HISTORY

AN IMPRINT OF PEN & SWORD BOOKS LTD.
YORKSHIRE – PHILADELPHIA

First published in Great Britain in 2022 by
PEN AND SWORD HISTORY
An imprint of
Pen & Sword Books Ltd
Yorkshire – Philadelphia

ISBN 978 1 39901 572 1

Typeset in Times New Roman 11.5/14 by
SJmagic DESIGN SERVICES, India.
Printed and bound in the UK by CPI Group (UK) Ltd.

Pen & Sword Books Limited incorporates the imprints of Atlas, Archaeology,
Aviation, Discovery, Family History, Fiction, History, Maritime, Military, Military
Classics, Politics, Select, Transport, True Crime, Air World, Frontline Publishing,
Leo Cooper, Remember When, Seaforth Publishing, The Praetorian Press,
Wharncliffe Local History, Wharncliffe Transport, Wharncliffe True Crime and
White Owl.

For a complete list of Pen & Sword titles please contact
PEN & SWORD BOOKS LIMITED
47 Church Street, Barnsley, South Yorkshire, S70 2AS, England
E-mail: enquiries@pen-and-sword.co.uk
Website: www.pen-and-sword.co.uk

Or

PEN AND SWORD BOOKS
1950 Lawrence Rd, Havertown, PA 19083, USA
E-mail: Uspen-and-sword@casematepublishers.com
Website: www.penandswordbooks.com

Contents

Victorian England's Best-Selling Author: The Revolutionary Life of G.W.M. Reynolds

Reynolds's Political Instructor (1849–50)

Acknowledgements

I (Stephen) would like to thank all members of my family for all the support they have given over the years, as well as my former supervisors Rosemary Mitchell and Paul Hardwick. I am sure you knew I would return to Reynolds after my brief stint in medieval literature! Thank you also to Jessica Elizabeth Thomas. who has transcribed a lot of Reynolds's early writings from the 1830s and 1840s, and made them available on an open access website. I am eternally indebted to Dr Rebecca Nesvet, a fellow penny blood scholar, who has given me countless pieces of advice and has proofread my work on numerous times before now; just in case I have never expressed my thanks for your friendship properly by now, I do so here. Also to Rachael Gillibrand, who, as a non-specialist, read some of these chapters to make sure they made sense to a person unacquainted with Reynolds—thank you.

Other more 'official' notes of thanks go to the good people at the journal *Law, Crime and History,* for allowing me to republish one of my academic journal articles on Reynolds in this book (chapter four).

Unless otherwise stated, all images are from my (Stephen Basdeo's) collection, but where other images from external bodies have been used, some with prior permission, our thanks again go to you, and you are listed in the image credits.

Mya (Driver) would also like to thank her mother, Jamila, who helped out on some of the transcriptions of *Reynolds's Political Instructor*.

A final thank you goes to the good people at Pen and Sword: Jonathan Wright, the production team, and my editor!

(Reynolds scholars—a small but growing community though we are—you're all mentioned in the preface!)

Foreword

'Serious about Joy': G.W.M. Reynolds in His Time and Ours

Rebecca Nesvet

'The poets are the trumpets that sing men to battle', the Romantic poet, Percy Bysshe Shelley famously wrote in 1821, 'and the unacknowledged legislators of the earth'. It was Shelley's belief that writing can motivate mass movements and transform society. However, it was not Romantic-era poetry chapbooks, written primarily by university-educated people and sold to men and women of leisure, that communicated radical ideas to the mass public of the early industrial age.

The two literary media that did in fact accomplish this feat were illustrated popular fiction and print news. No one exploited the potential of those media to disseminate radical ideas and political self-awakening to Victorian working-class people more effectively than George William McArthur Reynolds (1814–79). He was once widely read, not only in England, but also across Britain and the Victorian empire, and simultaneously revered and reviled. He was personally involved in democratic politics, but now is hardly taught in colleges and universities and never at UK (age 16) GCSE examination level. In very literal ways, Reynolds is an 'unacknowledged legislator of the world'.

In Shelley's conception, poetry, or creative writing intended to transform the broken world benevolently, is not merely practical: it is also prophetic. The poet is a poet because they question some of the more deluded assumptions and biases that permeate their society, and explain clearly why readers should, too. In some ways, this conception of poetry is deeply problematic: no one really stands outside their world and time. Various forces conspire to prevent us from seeing the water that surrounds us in what Toni Morrison has called the 'fish bowl' or 'structure that transparently (and invisibly) permits the ordered life it contains to exist in the large world'.[1] And yet, Reynolds was as embedded in the Victorian fish tank as any of his contemporaries, but he saw, more clearly than his canonised competitor Charles Dickens, through a few of the paradigms in which he swam.

As Basdeo and Driver point out in the book you are about to read, in Reynolds's earliest publication, he argues that the Gospels do not relate a unitary, linear history of the life and ministry of Jesus; an idea that remains capable of antagonising people today. In an era when the feminist Mary Wollstonecraft was still largely vilified or dismissed even by radicals, Reynolds argued that women were capable of reason, political participation, and, if educated like men, of every other intellectual activity from which his society barred them. His conviction that universal education can inform just, intelligent, universal political participation, was central to the political struggles that transformed and modernised Britain. In my country, the United States, knowledge of the necessity of educational equity for genuine democratic rule and vice versa informs gerrymandering, voter intimidation and obstruction, systematically unequal schooling, redlining, and the school-prison industrial complex. While some of Reynolds's creeds are now vindicated in Britain and elsewhere, others have yet to be realised, in part because of how widespread, if unspoken, is the belief that they are true.

Reynolds also deserves attention as an entertaining, engrossing storyteller. As the critic Rob Breton has recently pointed out, the success of Reynolds and other penny press authors and entrepreneurs demonstrates that in the 1830s-60s, radicalism itself was far more popular than historians and literary critics have been willing to acknowledge.[2] It is also important to note that, as Basdeo and Driver refreshingly clarify in this book, Reynolds did not pursue radical print primarily for its commercial value, and his career-long achievement in entertainment was never really about escape from social reality.

'Joy is political', wrote New Zealand author A.J. Fitzwater, recent winner of the prestigious Sir Julius Vogel award for excellence in the popular fiction genres of science fiction, fantasy, and horror.[3] 'This is not a new idea', Fitzwater explains:

> All marginalized populations have found ways to continue despite the spirit being under duress, the body under threat, their words suppressed, their future in jeopardy. We tell

joyful stories in times of fear to light the way in the dark, to document that history, to model the voices that need to be heard and the bodies that need to be seen, and to simply say *no,* you will *not* take our joy from us.[4]

The 'industrious millions' of Reynolds's Britain were no exception. From the 1840s when the serial parts of his radical romp *The Mysteries of London* first began to appear through the 1890s and beyond—when the *Mysteries* remained in print, as popular literature, around the world—this work and others by Reynolds disseminated joy, in spite of the critics who argued that workers have no right to leisure. The popular fiction and nonfiction writing that Reynolds composed or edited is, to quote Fitzwater again, radically 'serious about its joy'.[5]

Little River, Wisconsin

August 2021.

Notes

1. Toni Morrison, 'Playing in the Dark', in *Literary Theory: An Anthology,* ed. by Julie Rivkin and Michael Ryan (Malden, MA: Blackwell, 2004), 1011.
2. Rob Breton, *The Penny Politics of Popular Fiction* (Manchester: Manchester University Press, 2021).
3. A.J. Fitzwater, *The Voyages of Cinrak the Dapper* (Minneapolis: Queen of Swords Press, 2020), 1.
4. Ibid.
5. Ibid., 2.

Timeline of Major Events in the Life of George W.M. Reynolds

1814   Birth of George W.M. Reynolds on 23 July.

1816   Birth of Edward Reynolds.

1818   Birth of John Dicks

1823   Death of Reynolds's father, George Reynolds, on 28 January. Reynolds is enrolled as a pupil at Norton Knatchbull Grammar School.

1828   Reynolds is enrolled as a cadet at the Royal Military Academy, Sandhurst.

1830   Death of Reynolds's mother, Caroline Reynolds, on 13 September.

1832   Reynolds's tract *Errors of the Christian Religion Exposed* is published. He briefly meets Eugène Sue in Paris in March.

1833   Edward Reynolds is enrolled at Sandhurst.

1835   Reynolds begins working at the Librairie des Etrangers in Paris. He receives £400 inheritance on 23 July, and he marries Susannah Pierson on 31 July. Publication of *The Youthful Imposter*.

1836   Birth of Reynolds's son, George Edward, on 20 January.
Publication of Reynolds's *Songs of Twilight*.
Purchases the *Paris Advertiser* from Charles Renouard, but declared bankrupt by a French court a few months later.

1837   Returns to England, takes up residence in a one room lodging in Bethnal Green, becomes editor of the *Monthly Magazine*, and begins the serialisation of *Pickwick Abroad; or, The Tour in France*.

1838   Birth of Reynolds's daughter Blanche on 23 February.
Publication of *Alfred: The Adventures of a French Gentleman*.

1839   Publication of *The Modern Literature of France*.
        Briefly incarcerated in the Queen's Bench Prison for debt, applies to Royal Literary Fund for Financial relief.
        Publication of *Grace Darling*.

1840   Birth of Reynolds's son, Alfred Dowers, on 22 March.
        Subject to a bankruptcy order.
        Becomes a teetotaller on 16 May and begins editing the *Teetotaler*.
        Publication of four full-length novels: *The Last Day of a Condemned*; *Sister Anne*; *Robert Macaire*; and *The Steam Packet*. Also published in *Teetotaler* were *Noctes Pickwickiane*, *A Drunkard's Tale*, and *Pickwick Married*.

1841   Quarrels with fellow teetotallers and resigns from *Teetotaler* in September.
        Publication of *Master Timothy's Bookcase*.

1842   Birth of Reynolds's son, Edward on 26 January.
        Publication of *Master Timothy's Bookcase*.

1843   Publication of *A Sequel to Don Juan*.

1844   Living at King Square, Goswell Street.
        Birth of two children: Frederick (20 May) and Theresa Isabella (exact date unknown).
        Begins the serialisation of the first series of *The Mysteries of London*.

1845   Becomes editor of the *London Journal*.

1846   Living at Powell Street West, Goswell Road.
        Begins serialisation of the second series of *The Mysteries of London* and *Faust: A Romance of the Secret Tribunals*.

1847   Leaves the *London Journal* and establishes *Reynolds's Miscellany*.
        Publication of *The Parricide; or, The Youth's Career of Crime* and begins serialisation of *Wagner the Wehr-Wolf* and *Days of Hogarth*.
        Susannah publishes *The Household Book of Practical Receipts* and *Gretna Green*. Both Susannah and Reynolds's novels are criticised by the *Daily News* in November for their immorality.

1848   Reynolds embraces Chartism and speaks at three political rallies.
        Reynolds faces bankruptcy in August and John Dicks pays off his creditors.

Birth of a daughter: Joanna Frances.

George Vickers and George Stiff establish a rival to *Reynolds's Miscellany* named *Reynolds's Magazine*.

Publication of *The Coral Island, or the Hereditary Curse* and *The Pixy; or, The Unbaptized Child* and begins serialisation of *The Mysteries of the Court of London*.

1849   Reynolds embarks on a speaking tour through Scotland, Ireland, Northumbria, West Yorkshire, and Derbyshire. Elected to the executive body of the National Charter Association and to executive body of National Parliamentary and Financial Reform Association (NPFRA).

Susannah Reynolds establishes the short-lived *Weekly Magazine*.

Establishes *Reynolds's Political Instructor*.

Begins the serialisation of *The Bronze Statue; or, The Virgin's Kiss*.

1850   Splits from the NPFRA after a disagreement with Thomas Clark. Also purchases holiday home at Herne Bay where first-born son George Edward dies in September.

First issue of *Reynolds's Weekly Newspaper* on 5 May.

Begins serialisation of *The Seamstress* and *Pope Joan*.

1851   Begins serialisation of *The Necromancer* and *Mary Price: Memoirs of a Maid Servant*.

1852   Begins serialisation of *Kenneth: A Romance of the Highlands*; *The Massacre of Glencoe*; and *The Soldier's Wife*.

1853   Birth of two children: Ledru-Rollin and Louise-Clarice. Begins a campaign against army flogging and Reynolds's books are banned among the army.

Begins serialisation of *Joseph Wilmot: Adventures of a Man-Servant*; *Rosa Lambert; or, the Memoirs of an Unfortunate Woman*; and *The Rye House Plot*.

1854   Begins serialisation of *May Middleton: The History of a Fortune*.

1855   Begins serialisation of *Ellen Percy: Memoirs of an Actress*; *Agnes; or, Beauty and Pleasure*; *Omar: A Tale of the War*; and *The Loves of the Harem: A Romance of Constantinople*.

1856   Birth of daughter Emily Reynolds.

Begins serialisation of *Margaret: The Discarded Queen* and *Leila: The Star of Mingrelia*.

1857   Pierce Egan the Younger joins the *Reynolds's Miscellany* firm as a permanent writer, a position he occupies for the next two years.

       Begins serialisation of *Canonbury House; or, The Queen's Prophecy*; *The Young Duchess*; and *The Empress Eugenie's Boudoir*.

1858   Death of Susannah Reynolds in October.

       Marriage of Blanche Reynolds to William Eadon; Theresa Isabella marries Archibald Douglas Lamb; Frederick Reynolds marries Florence (further details unknown).

       Reynolds is successfully sued by Ernest Jones for libel.

       Publication of *Empress Eugenie's Boudoir*.

1859   Birth of Reynolds's first grandchild, Kate Eadon.

       Begins serialisation of final novel: *Mary Stuart*.

1861   Birth of grandchild: Charles Eadon.

1862   Birth of grandchild: Ellen Eadon.

       John Dicks establishes *Bow Bells*.

1864   Birth of grandchild: Gertrude Eadon.

1865   Becomes a leading member of the National Reform League.

       Marriage of Joanna Frances Reynolds to Arthur Lamb in August.

       Birth of grandchildren: Frank Eadon, Frances E. Lamb, and Edith Lamb.

1866   Birth of grandchildren: Hilda Eadon, Frances E. Lamb, Edith Lamb.

1868   Birth of grandchild: Florence Lamb.

1869   *Reynolds's Miscellany* is discontinued and staff transferred to *Bow Bells*.

1871   Birth of grandchild: Eva Blanche Lamb.

1873   Louise Clarisse marries Adolphus J. Bell.

       Birth of grandchild: Isabella J. Lamb.

1875   Ledru-Rollin Reynolds marries Marian Rees. Marriage of Kossuth-Mazzini Reynolds to Harriet (further details unknown).

1876   Birth of grandchild: George E. Lamb.

1877   Reynolds suffers a stroke leaving him paralysed down one side of his body.

       Birth of grandchild: Dudley Reynolds.

1879   Reynolds dies on 19 June and is buried in the catacombs of Kensal Green Cemetery.

1881   Death of John Dicks.

Theresa Isabella emigrates to the United States.

Alfred Dowers Reynolds dies alone and bankrupt in New Zealand.

Birth of grandchild: Vera Reynolds.

1884   John Dicks publishing firm begins reissuing Reynolds's novels as part of the 'Standard English Novels' series.

1886   Birth of grandchildren: Cyril Reynolds, Gladys Reynolds.

1894   Death of Edward Reynolds.

1900   Future Prime Minister of the United Kingdom, Ramsey MacDonald, writes the first biography of Reynolds for the *Dictionary of National Biography*.

1920   Death of Theresa Isabella in New York.

1963   Publication of Louis James's *Fiction for the Working Man*, the first book to highlight the importance of Reynolds's life and work to modern historians.

Preface

In presenting this work to the world, I shall not make its preface a vehicle for the intrusion of elaborate remarks and tedious comment ... on that public whose favour and support I have now again to solicit.

George W.M. Reynolds,
Songs of Twilight (1836)

If readers ever find themselves on Harrow Road in the Royal Borough of Kensington and Chelsea, London, they will be in the vicinity of Kensal Green Cemetery. They might then take a moment or two to find the entrance—an imposing neoclassical arch with iron gates—enter it, and perhaps spend some time quietly contemplating some of the names on the gravestones they encounter.

The cemetery is like a 'who's who' of Victorian literature and history. Many of the period's leading lights are enjoying their final rest there. Of those interred there, the names of such 'Eminent Victorians' such as the socialist Robert Owen, Thomas Hood, Isambard Kingdom Brunel, the authors Anthony Trollope and William Harrison Ainsworth, will likely be familiar to any student of Victorian culture.

Although I am personally a big fan of the novelist Harrison Ainsworth's works, if I were there myself my attention would be directed to finding the grave of another man who is the subject of this book: George William MacArthur Reynolds.[1] Aged 64 when he passed away, Reynolds is one of the most interesting characters in Victorian literary history, and the author of what was probably the period's biggest-selling novel: *The Mysteries of London* (1844–48), published in four volumes, which reportedly sold over a million copies.[2] These novels were like the soap operas of their day: serialised in weekly penny numbers, they gave readers an insight into the corrupt world of the aristocratic upper classes, as well as the seedy side of low life among the criminals who haunted London's courts and alleys.

Reynolds wrote many more novels; a grand total of 58 full-length novels, numerous short stories, poems, and essays flowed from his pen. Yet I only became acquainted with Reynolds when I was completing my MA dissertation in 2014, which focused on Victorian crime and penny fiction. My supervisor, Prof. Heather Shore, suggested that I look up an author named George W. M. Reynolds and his novel *The Mysteries of London*. In what some might call fate, two days later I noticed on eBay a lovely four-volume first edition set, printed by G. Vickers, containing all the illustrations. At £40 they seemed like a bargain, so I snapped them up and immediately set about reading them.[3]

To say that Professor Shore's reading recommendation made me a little poorer would be an understatement; after having read *The Mysteries,* I wanted more, so I began to track down first editions of Reynolds's works including *Alfred* (1839), *Faust* (1845–46), *The Mysteries of the Court of London* (1849–56). As I write this in 2021, I have just about collected all the originals of Reynolds's novels (I am still looking for original copies of two of his novels: *Margaret, the Discarded Queen* and *Leila, The Star of Mingrelia*—I do have reprints of them, but reprints just are not the same as getting hold of first editions so, readers, do get in touch if you ever come across these in a bookshop).

Although I have read most of the above, either as part of my research, or just for fun, I do keep coming back to his *Mysteries.* I am interested in the history of crime and in particular portrayals of organised crime in fiction. I find that Reynolds had quite a sophisticated view of organised criminals' *modus operandi,* which correlated (approximately, though not perfectly) with modern criminologists' definitions of the 'organised crime'.

While many Victorian writers often presented their characters as irredeemably criminal, often two-dimensional, characters, Reynolds however humanises his criminals and encourages the reader to feel sympathy with them. There is not a person who reads *The Mysteries of London* and does not feel for the plight of the 'Rattlesnake' growing up as a labourer in the mines, or even the Resurrection Man who wanted to live an honest life but is told that 'society has condemned you'. A point which I intend to make in an academic monograph I am currently writing on the subject of organised crime in popular literature, is that the biographies which Reynolds gave his criminal characters anticipate that famous phrase: 'society gets the criminals it deserves', which was unusual in an era when poorer people were often written off as part of an irredeemable and ever-growing 'dangerous' or 'criminal class'.

Reynolds has become famous in our family at least. My parents, having been intrigued by his novels, decided that once or twice a week we would gather and listen to me reading *The Mysteries of London*. My parents loved it. Soon we worked through all four volumes of Reynolds's masterpiece. It is therefore an honour to write a history book on this man, and the experience of doing so has been extra special because my niece, Mya Driver, has assisted me in this endeavour by transcribing all of the primary source material contained in this book.

Mya and I had three aims in putting this book together. The first was to offer readers the first book-length biography on Reynolds together, with a discussion of his major works; in writing of the ensuing biography, however, I am indebted to several scholars before me who have conducted research into Reynolds's life and works such as Louis James, E.F. Bleiler, Dick Collins, Jennifer Conary, Rohan McWilliam, Ian Haywood, Maha Atal, Sophie Raine, Stephen Knight, Mary Shannon, and Chris Anderson. The research of these scholars has enabled me to recount Reynolds's life, and in this book I have also provided new insights into his life.

The second aim in compiling this book was to counter an accusation that was levelled against Reynolds while he was alive, which has been uncritically repeated by some modern historians. This is the charge that Reynolds was a charlatan, whose support for progressive and democratic causes was never genuine, and that he only became a democrat to sell more novels. I believe this to be an unfair accusation. As readers will see in the ensuing biography, the evidence speaks for itself: Reynolds expended much time and effort in agitating for universal suffrage, and his activities as a political activist certainly did his literary career no favours.

The final aim of this book was to provide a resource for scholars by including all of the articles that Reynolds wrote for his newspaper *Reynolds's Political Instructor*, and Mya Driver has completed a wonderful transcription of these fascinating pieces which have long been out of print.

Stephen Basdeo
July 2021

Victorian England's Best-Selling Author

The Revolutionary Life of G.W.M. Reynolds

Stephen Basdeo

Thomas Paine has turned the youth's brain: Reynolds's Early Life and Schooling

> In the secluded and picturesque churchyard of Eythorne near Dover, there are many tombstones with inscriptions announcing that that they are 'sacred to the memory' of some departed scions of a family bearing the name of REYNOLDS. Yeomen in the olden time … For many generations they seem to have pursued 'the even tenour of their way' until at length some of them began to seek spheres of employment and emolument elsewhere….
>
> *Reynolds's Miscellany* (1859)

The village of Eythorne, near Dover, in the late eighteenth and early nineteenth centuries was, much like today, a very quiet place. Situated in the middle of hilly open country, much of which belonged to the Earl of Guildford,[4] the village was but a small hamlet with a public house. In this village lived one John Reynolds, a yeoman farmer.

The life of a yeoman farmer in the eighteenth century was not an easy one and their social and economic status declined. It is true that, if yeomen owned property or land worth over 40s, they might be entitled to vote in parliamentary elections. But their business model—growing food for subsistence and selling the surplus on the open market—seemed increasingly outdated in a century that saw the rise of bourgeois capitalism. Many yeomen farmers simply could not compete with wealthier, often aristocratic landowners. The result was that many of them lost their homes and their land in the face of competition. Perhaps the same happened to the family of John Reynolds, for records show that he later lived town of St Clements, maybe having moved there in search of work due to its proximity to Sandwich, one of the Cinque Ports on the Kent Coast (some records give Eastry as the place of John Reynolds's residence; the proximity between St Clements and Eastry probably means that the family settled somewhere in between the two parishes).[5]

It was while living in St Clements that John Reynolds met a widower named Mary Munro *née* Sayer, whom he married, on 13 September 1769, in the local parish church. Mary bore five children: George, born on 2 February 1769; Mary, baptised on 2 February 1770; Elizabeth, baptised on 11 July 1771; and two other boys named William and John, whose birthdays and baptismal dates remain unknown.[6]

It is the firstborn George Reynolds whose life is of most interest. Little is known of his life apart from the fact that he was a post-captain in the Royal Navy. This was a courtesy title given to an officer who had been promoted to the rank of captain but had not yet been given command of his own vessel. Post-captains generally received only half pay owing to the fact that they did not often see active service; by the time that George Reynolds attained the rank of post-captain in the early nineteenth century the major naval campaigns of the Napoleonic Wars were over. So, post-captain George Reynolds certainly would not have been rich and he never got the chance to distinguish himself in battle. In fact, George Reynolds is noteworthy only because, on 23 July 1814, he and his wife Caroline welcomed their firstborn child—a son, whom they named George, after the father. It is this George, who was given the middle names of William MacArthur, who is the subject of this book.

Captain Reynolds and his family lived in the Parish of St Clement, Sandwich, in the county of Kent. Although St Clement is a small town the house in which the family lived, and for how long, remains unknown, although the family were still living in the town when Edward Reynolds was born in 1816.[7]

Biographers in the early twentieth century simply asserted that Reynolds 'attended Dr Nance's school' in Kent. For those wishing to know more about Reynolds's early life this casual statement has made research difficult, for there was never a school that was *owned* by a Dr Nance or bore his name. In actual fact Reynolds—which is how George William MacArthur will be referred to hereafter—was educated at the Norton Knatchbull School. The school was the brainchild of a local landowner named Sir Thomas Knatchbull who, from philanthropic

3

motives, wanted to establish a 'free' grammar school on his land for the benefit of local boys. Thomas Knatchbull died before his scheme took but the projected school was provided for in his will. When Knatchbull's nephew, Norton Knatchbull, inherited Thomas's estate, he carried out his uncle's wishes and established the school. From a simple schoolroom with two adjoining buildings—which is now home to the Ashford Museum—the new grammar school, was expanded during the eighteenth century to accommodate boarders.[8]

The reputation of many public and grammar schools was in decline during the Georgian period. Recalling his days at Westminster School, the memoirist William Hickey (1749–1830) remarked that when he was fourteen years old he and his fellow school boys often visited taverns and brothels. In 1797, the lads at Rugby School rose in revolt against their schoolmaster because he fined them over their riotous actions outside the school. In 1818 a rebellion by boys at Eton grew so serious that local militia had to be called in to quell the riot. Unruliness was further fuelled, no doubt, by the fact that the boys were often left alone overnight. No wonder that Henry Fielding's Parson Adams in *Joseph Andrews* (1742) remarked that such schools were 'the nurseries of all vice and immorality. All the wicked fellows whom I remember at the university were bred at them'.

We might infer that school life at the Norton Knatchbull School was similar to that described by Fielding. When a new headmaster, Dr Stephen Barrett, was appointed to the position in 1762. Nevertheless, at least the new headmaster certainly had the knowledge to teach the syllabus, which in all grammar schools in the seventeenth and eighteenth centuries consisted of the works of Ancient Roman and Greek authors, as well as rhetoric and grammar. Barrett originally hailed from the North Yorkshire village of Kildwick, but went on to receive his MA at Oxford College, Oxford. Barrett counted among his friends literary luminaries such as Samuel Johnson and Edward Cave, founder of the *Gentleman's Magazine*.[9] It was Barrett who oversaw the expansion of the school. Under his leadership the school, whose fees were relatively cheap at 15s per quarter, began waiving fees for boys whom the local parish had decided were deserving of charity and an education. The poorer boys were not boarders like the other fee paying lads but would have lived at home with their families.

After Barrett's retirement one Dr Stoddart took the reins of the school and there is surviving testimony of what school life was like under

Dr Stoddart from the recollections of another former pupil who attended the school in the early nineteenth century. The school week lasted from Monday morning until Saturday morning and the boys were made to study late into the evening. On Saturday afternoon the 'day' boys would have gone home to their parents while the boarders stayed in dormitories. Discipline seems to have been, in at least this lad's case, rather lax:

> I remember once during my time at Dr Stoddart's on a fair day in Ashford all the boys were admitted into the town (at other times we were confined to the school yard, that being our place for playing), when with five or six other boys we procured a vast quantity of rotten eggs; and with one of these beautiful odoriferous combustibles, I threw it at Mr Chas. Stoddart, our second master, who wore spectacles, and hit him in the glass eye while reading a letter … at evening studies the Doctor was fully prepared to proceed to action, using a table well stored with the birch. He commenced from the senior boy down to the junior, telling us if we did not deserve it then, we should before the week was out.[10]

The child in question here was Thomas Knatchbull, a distant descendant of the original Knatchbulls who founded the school. He relates other instances of unruly behaviour among the youths the under Dr Stoddart's charge, for which they were always given a sound caning. In spite of children's unruliness, and the seemingly necessary beatings he had to administer, in 1868, when Augustus John Pearman wrote a history book about Ashford, Stoddart was remembered by the local inhabitants as someone who was always kind to pauper children.[11] After the departure of Dr Stoddart, Dr Thomas Nance took the reins as head of the school.

Reynolds's father died, when he was just seven years old, on 28 January 1823.[12] A few months later Reynolds's mother enrolled him at Nance's school. It is not known whether Reynolds was simply a day attendee or a boarder. Given the fact that his parents were hardly rich (although they were not destitute) and lived local, it is more likely that he was a 'day' boy.

What Reynolds was taught at school can be known from other sources, for luckily we have some testimony from Dr Nance himself.

There was about forty scholars registered at his school and they would have been taught the standard grammar and public school curriculum of the period: Greek, Latin, and rhetoric. There was minimal effort to provide the boys with a practical education to equip them for life in an industrial society, which appears to have annoyed several parents according to Nance himself.[13] It seems that parents in Ashford wanted their children to be taught more practical subjects that would allow their children to get on in the world and the school entered a period of decline, evident by the fact that fewer pupils were progressing on to university.[14]

Reynolds remained at Nance's school until 1828. Then, at the urging of his godfather Dr Duncan MacArthur and his grandfather (on his mother's side) Purser Dowers, the now fourteen-year-old Reynolds was enrolled as a cadet at the Royal Military Academy, Sandhurst, with a view to becoming an officer. MacArthur and Dowers probably hoped that young Reynolds would become an officer like his father had been.

It may surprise the modern reader to learn that at nineteenth-century Sandhurst cadets were also encouraged to refine their creative instincts. The reason for this, so Sir Alexander Hope remarked in 1817, it was better for the officer corps to have gained a wide range of skills and interests in the sciences and humanities rather than to be filled with young men who had only been taught drilling and mathematics.[15] The curriculum at Sandhurst was therefore much more varied than those found at the public and grammar schools. The subjects taught to cadets at Sandhurst when Reynolds attended combined 'general education' subjects with those of a more military focus: higher mathematics, the Attack and Defence of Fortresses, drawing, Latin, German, and modern history.[16] Cadets at Sandhurst were also expected to become fluent in French. After all, French in this period was the *lingua franca* and a fluency in French served Reynolds well in later life. It was probably at Sandhurst, with the college's emphasis on creative and technical subjects, that Reynolds discovered his passion for writing.

Sadly, in the summer of 1830, Reynolds's mother Caroline died. Shortly afterwards, on 13 September 1830, Reynolds's grandfather withdrew the now sixteen-year-old George from Sandhurst.[17] There are many possible reasons why Reynolds's grandfather might have withdrawn him from Sandhurst. Dick Collins notes that Reynolds's archival record simply says that he was 'withdrawn by friends', and that this meant either one of two things: poor academic performance, or that the tutors had deemed him to be unsuitable for military life.[18] It is unlikely that Reynolds was a poor scholar because much of his early writings reveal him to be a cultured and refined man, familiar with both the classics and the great works of English literature. He probably did hate the military life, however; contempt for naval figures was expressed in Reynolds's first full-length novel titled *The Youthful Imposter* (1835), in which the villain of the story is Lord Fanmore, a tyrannical and deceitful naval officer.[19]

Perhaps there was another reason why Reynolds was withdrawn from Sandhurst: although his family was never destitute, an education at Sandhurst was expensive and would have cost a parent or guardian about £50 per year (fees at Sandhurst were often subject to negotiation depending on how educated a prospective pupil was and what classes they needed to take). The college also recommended that pupils had a further £50 per year in readiness for maintenance expenses. The boys would have needed to purchase their own uniform as well. Both young George and his brother Edward were in line to receive inheritance money. George was due to receive £400 from his mother when he turned twenty-one in July 1835. Both Reynolds and Edward were due to receive £2,400 each from their father's estate, but neither of them would receive this money until Edward had turned twenty-one years old.[20] For Reynolds, this meant that he could not access his father's money until 1837. In the meantime their grandfather, who appears to have had no assets and little very money of his own,[21] had to make do with £1,000 for the boys' maintenance and education.

The £1,000 provided in the will for the boys' maintenance sounds as though it was a lot of money but the cost of the boys' education would soon have depleted it, especially when it is remembered that Edward's education also had to be provided for. There are in fact records for an Edward Reynolds at Sandhurst, which is *probably* Reynolds's brother, who attended the college between 1833 and 1837.[22] A four-year stint at Sandhurst for Edward would cost £200 in fees alone, while Reynolds's fees for his two-year tenure would have amounted to £100. That is, before the boys' guardians even began to consider their maintenance costs. Dr MacArthur and grandfather Dower probably reasoned that they might as well take Reynolds out of Sandhurst if he hated military life, as it was expensive. Besides, Reynolds was due to inherit a small bit of land while Edward would not, so it would have made sense for MacArthur and Dower to focus on Edward's education.

Edward spent much longer in education than Reynolds. A later commentator declared that Edward went on to study 'at one of [England's] great universities'.[23] No further details of Edward's education are known and it is not even known when Edward attended university. Although we do not know which university Edward attended, however, it can only have been one of three: Oxford, Cambridge, or maybe the University of London which was founded in 1836.

Records fall silent for Reynolds until 1832 when, at the age of eighteen, his first publication appeared: *The Errors of the Christian Religion Exposed*. Printed by the radical publisher, Richard Carlile—who published cheap editions of Paine's *Rights of Man*—Reynold's book, as its title implies, contains a debunking of all the 'errors' that Reynolds had found in the New Testament, especially the idea that Jesus's coming was foretold in the Old Testament. It was also an affirmation of his newly-adopted Deist beliefs:

> I am now eighteen years old, and till within this year have been a firm believer in Christianity. My father and my mother, both of whom are now dead, were also of the same creed, and the whole of my surviving relatives also are what they call Christians. About a year ago I began to be sceptical. People may wonder how I came to muse on this matter so young, and with so little experience; but truth may be descried from fallacy even by a youth, and an infant child can distinguish the luminous mid-day from the deep shades of night. When I first began to grow sceptical with regard to revealed religion, I read Paley's Evidences, Tomlin's Theology, Hugo Grotius, and many other works over again attentively. All these, however, only served to convince me that the Christian creed and system must rest on a very brittle foundation, if they wanted such elaborate and numerous works to support them.[24]

Deism is hard to define but in short, it is an ideology which posits that a Supreme Being created the universe and imparted to humankind the gift of reason. However, it rejects the idea of revelation from God, holds that God does not reveal himself to anybody, and that he *never* intervenes in human affairs. For Deists, the Bible and the idea of revelation is therefore of very little importance, because in their view, the tales contain just as much truth as the Greek myths.

The first major work to outline the tenets of Deism was Edward Herbert's *De Veritate, Prout Distinguitur a Revelatione, a Verisimili, a Possibili, et a Falso* (1624) ('On Truth, as it is Distinguished from Revelation, the Probable, the Possible, and the False'). It was a methodology for the investigation of truth and a scheme of natural religion, the latter of which a person could only realise through empirical observation of the world around them. These ideas were expanded upon by intellectuals such as John Toland and John Locke. The writer from whom Reynolds received his understanding of Deism, however, was Thomas Paine (1737–1809), a leading intellectual in both the American and French Revolutions. In his day, Paine was most famous for having written *Common Sense* (1776)—which undoubtedly convinced large numbers of American colonists of the need for separation from Britain—and *The Rights of Man* (1791). Although feted by American and French radicals for his ideas on democracy, Paine became infamous after publishing his *Age of Reason* (1794–1807) in which he argued that,

> I believe in one God, and no more; and I hope for happiness beyond this life.
>
> I believe in the equality of man; and I believe that religious duties consist in doing justice, loving mercy, and endeavouring to make our fellow-creatures happy.
>
> But, lest it should be supposed that I believe many other things in addition to these, I shall, in the progress of this work, declare the things I do not believe, and my reasons for not believing them.
>
> I do not believe in the creed professed by the Jewish Church, by the Roman Church, by the Greek Church, by the Turkish Church, by the Protestant Church, nor by any church that I know of. My own mind is my own church.
>
> All national institutions of churches, whether Jewish, Christian or Turkish, appear to me no other than human inventions, set up to terrify and enslave mankind, and monopolize power and profit.
>
> I do not mean by this declaration to condemn those who believe otherwise; they have the same right to their belief as I have to mine. But it is necessary to the happiness of man that he be mentally faithful to himself. Infidelity does

not consist in believing, or in disbelieving; it consists in professing to believe what he does not believe.[25]

This had an electrifying effect on young Reynolds, who openly admitted that Paine's works were a major influence on him when he wrote *Errors of the Christian Religion Exposed*:

> I am not ashamed to own that it was the *Age of Reason* that first opened my eyes to the errors in which for seventeen years I have hitherto lived regarding my God; and having avowed this, I am well aware the remark many people will make when they peruse this volume: "Oh! that infamous Thomas Paine—his frivolous and unfounded work has turned the youth's brain." But no; I defy any living soul to refute Paine's arguments. I have read answers to them, and attempts at refutation; but none succeed—all sink to the ground.[26]

A disdain for organised religion and its representatives—bishops, priests, and parsons—remained with Reynolds throughout his life. He had special aversion for the bishops who sat in the House of Lords. 'Sycophant bishops and hireling clergymen' was one phrase he used to describe them in 1850.[27] Several of his future novels featured scheming, good-for-nothing clergymen who, one way or another, oppress the virtuous members of society or who were outright perverts.

Other aspects of Paineite ideology had an influence on Reynolds, especially Paine's republicanism. Paine argued that the sole function of government should be to safeguard the natural rights of the people, and that the people were entitled to overthrow their governments when they felt their rights were being infringed upon—much like the Americans and the French had done in 1776 and 1789, respectively. Paine's *Rights of Man* was actually a riposte to Edmund Burke's *Reflections on the Revolution in France* (1790). In his book, Burke was highly critical of the French Revolution and predicted that radical change, and a complete rupture with a nation's traditions and institutions meant that any new society emerging in France would end in disaster and mob violence. Unlike France, so Burke thought, Britain had one of the best constitutions in the world because it had experimented with different forms of government, including absolute monarchy and republicanism.

10

The result of these tried and tested methods of government had resulted in the creation of the 'glorious institutions' of constitutional monarchy, lords, and commons. Among other arguments Burke made was that social stability resulted when society was governed by a hereditary aristocracy.

Throughout his life, Reynolds wrote several critiques of Burkean constitutionalism and his first criticism of Burke came in the form of a poem titled 'Lines on Edmund Burke' that appeared in *Pickwick Abroad*, one of his early novels:

> If I only were half so great as Xerxes,
> I'd rule the nation with a righteous hand;
> But not on despot principles like Burke's. His
> Reflections upon France none understand.
> Ha takes a proposition, then he shirks his
> Own chosen thesis, which himself had planned.
> Through ev'ry page invariably there lurks his
> Venomous hatred of a mighty land;
> And when he enters on the theme, he works his
> Arguments on grounds where none can stand.
> His soul is far more grov'lling than the Turk's; his
> Logic resembles houses built on sand;—
> But fifteen hundred pounds a year were stronger
> Reasn'ing than common sense; and so we'll chide no longer.

Further criticisms of Burke followed in the 1850s when Reynolds founded a newspaper. The following passage gives an example of Reynolds's acerbic wit:

> The bravado about "our glorious Constitution" is one of those despicable fictions and scandalous frauds by means of which so many Englishmen are gulled, duped, and hoodwinked relative to the rottenness and corruption of their institutions. By persuading men that they are really free, it is so easy to gratify their vanity and induce them to hug the chains of slavery.[28]

Any working-class Englishmen who thought they were 'free' under this constitution, thought Reynolds, were simply deluded. What was needed, was a written constitution such as the one America enjoyed. This constitution, as Reynolds would later argue, should be based upon the principles of the French Declaration of the Rights of Man and Citizen which was adopted by the French in 1789. The French Revolution of 1789–1815 was not the last revolution that would occur in France. There was another revolution in Paris in July 1830. This revolution resulted in the overthrow of King Charles X and the accession of King Louis Phillippe—of whom Reynolds initially approved—who would rule as a constitutional monarch. Reynolds described this event in glowing terms as 'an insurrection having for its object the working of a great and glorious change in the liberties of a mighty people'.[29]

The only further information that historians have for Reynolds's life during the early 1830s is some testimony, of dubious veracity, which alleges that Reynolds became something of a rogue. In 1848, the Home Office, because of Reynolds's later high-profile reputation as a political activist, compiled a dossier on him. The papers included, among other details that were plainly untrue,[30] a testimony from Captain Walmer Vincent who alleged that Reynolds committed 'every species of fraud and immorality'. The same dossier also includes an accusation that Reynolds had run up a huge bill at Long's Hotel in London, had attempted to pay the bill with stolen jewellery, and had narrowly avoided transportation to Australia.[31] We can discount this unfair testimony that impugns young Reynolds's character. A case of jewellery theft would have been dealt with at the Old Bailey, yet in the Old Bailey's records Reynolds appears nowhere. In the Old Bailey's archives there is indeed a nineteen-year-old thief named George Reynolds who was imprisoned for theft, but this George Reynolds gave his profession as a plasterer, he did not steal jewellery, and neither did he run up a huge bill at Long's Hotel.[32]

The truth is that we shall never know how Reynolds spent the time between the publication of *The Errors of the Christian Religion Exposed* and the early 1830s, when he moved to France. France, especially its capital to which Reynolds journeyed, held many attractions for him. Indeed, the country was a hotbed of revolutionary sentiment, and it is understandable that a young Reynolds, an admirer of Thomas Paine and the French constitution, would have wanted to experience life across the channel. It is in Paris that we next join Reynolds to trace the beginning of his career as a bookseller and professional writer.

Reynolds Abroad; or The Tour in France

At length we arrived in the neighbourhood of Paris; and when the lofty domes and spires of the sovereign city met my eyes—child infant as I was——I leapt with delight ... And now—as indeed I have done heretofore—I must frequently fill up those blanks, which would otherwise necessarily occur in the course of my early history.

> George W.M. Reynolds,
> *Pickwick Abroad* (1837–38)

Know ye the land of the great and the brave,
    Whose heroes are mighty to conquer and save;
Where dwell the undaunted, the bold, and the free
    O this is the nation for love and for me!

> George W.M. Reynolds,
> *Alfred* (1839)

The city of Paris during the 1830s was a city that in some respects was thoroughly 'medieval'. Still encircled by walls and checkpoints, young Reynolds would have had to pass through these before entering the city, showing his papers to officers who manned the gates on the way in. The grand medieval cathedral of Notre Dame was falling into disrepair and viewed by many Parisians, so Victor Hugo remarked in *The Hunchback of Notre Dame*, as 'a shabby relic' of an unenlightened pre-revolutionary past. The somewhat dilapidated cathedral towered over an assortment of baroque and neoclassical government buildings and mansions. Alongside such edifices were the 'bohemian' quarters where the artists and writers lived and the Rue Neuve-Saint-Augustin, which was the area that Reynolds chose to reside.

13

Paris was the perfect place to visit for anyone who wanted to experience a life of salons, semi-inebriated political and philosophical discussion, and late-night theatre visits. As William M. Thackeray recalled of his youthful days in Paris: 'What young Englishman that visits it, but has not determined, in his heart, to have a little share of the gayeties that go on—just for once, just to see what they are like?'[33] Amidst the genteel façade, however, were areas like the Cité where the destitute lived, containing poor quality dwellings packed into a number of labyrinthine courts and alleyways in which a stranger would not want to lose his way. A contemporary French author described this region of the city as containing,

> Murky-coloured houses, which were lighted within by a few panes of glass in the worm-eaten casements, overhung each other so closely that the eaves of each almost touched its opposite neighbour, so narrow were the streets. Dark and noisome alleys led to staircases still more black and foul, and so perpendicular that they could hardly be ascended by the help of a cord fixed to the dank and humid walls by holdfasts of iron.

It is not known where Reynolds originally settled in Paris, but it was in this city of contrasts that he decided to make a life for himself.

The exact date that Reynolds moved to France remains unknown. However, Reynolds was in Paris by March 1832, for in that month he briefly met a French author whose works would have a profound impact upon his later writings. The author was Eugène Sue. In an unpublished account of his travels in France (a manuscript which is now lost but an extract of which was later published), Reynolds recalled:

> I was walking one day in the *Rue Croix des Petits Champs* in Paris when a publisher of some standing in that fashionable city when I saw two gentlemen approaching, arm in arm. Just as they came within a couple of yards, one of the gentlemen, and my friend, the publisher, took their hats of simultaneously, and at the same moment I heard my friend whisper behind me: *C'est Eugene Sue.*—*"It is Eugene Sue."* ... He certainly was, for his size, one of the most athletic figures I ever saw; and I could easily fancy

that that he had climbed a hundred times to the mast head in his former profession as a seaman ... He appeared to me to be a West Indian, born of European parents, for his complexion is darker than even that of a Spaniard, and his hair black as jet ... when I met him on the above occasion, he was then about eight and twenty or thirty. He must now, therefore, be about forty-two, or forty-four: an age at which Rousseaux had done but little, and the author of "Clarissa" nothing whatever.[34]

The extract was published much later than 1832, in 1847, and it was probably embellished with the benefit of hindsight. Although Reynolds appeared quite taken with Sue in the above extract, in his *Modern Literature of France* (1839) Reynolds was not so impressed. He stated that while Sue was undoubtedly a talented writer, 'his imagination is only rich in inventing and stringing together a host of improbabilities, occasionally bordering upon monstrosity'.[35]

There is, however, more certainty about the events of Reynolds's life from 1835 onwards, much of which has been illuminated by Jennifer Conary. Records show that Reynolds was working as a bookseller at the Librarie des Etrangers, based at 55 Rue Neuve-Saint-Augustin in Paris, which was owned Charles Renouard.[36] Renouard was an author in his own right, although much of his output consisted of publishing French language summaries of the works of Kant and Hegel between the 1820s and 1840s. Renouard of course had the time to pursue his intellectual interests; he did not actually manage the Librairie des Etrangers but left that job to an Englishman named George Bennis. The bookshop was not only a bookshop but functioned as a circulating library and a publisher of books and periodicals. One of the periodicals published by the Librairie des Etrangers was the *Paris Advertiser*, of which Reynolds would later become the editor.

At some point during his time in Paris Reynolds met a young woman named Susannah Frances Pierson, who was to become his wife. The details of their initial meeting remain unknown. Neither was it known why Susannah was in Paris at the time, nor what her social background was. Susannah never publicly divulged many details about her early life. Looking back in the year 1840, Susannah simply wrote that she had 'passed the greater portion of her life upon the continent. [She] left England early, and .... [resided] in France, Switzerland, and Belgium'.[37]

Susannah appears to have been a fellow radical and an aspiring writer, much like Reynolds, and in June 1835 Reynolds applied to the British Embassy in Paris for permission to marry the then seventeen-year-old Susannah. The embassy could not grant a marriage license, however, because Reynolds was unable to provide proof of parental consent to it, or even proof of Susannah's age. The young couple therefore decided to side-step the embassy and went directly to the Anglican church of St Michael, Rue d'Aguesson, where they had the banns published. As no one came forward to object to the proposed union—probably because, as Collins states, there was no one who knew the couple well enough in Paris to offer any objection—then permission was granted them to marry. Reynolds and Susannah were then married by Bishop Matthew Henry Thornhill Luscombe on Friday 31 July 1835.[38]

Indeed, it was unlikely that any of the people in attendance would object to the marriage. Reynolds's brother Edward was there to witness the ceremony. It is possible that Edward was not just visiting, but had joined Reynolds and had lived and worked with him in France,. However, if the implication that Edward had been university-educated is true, then perhaps he had been visiting Reynolds briefly. Also in attendance, was a personal friend of Reynolds's named James Brooke Irwin.[39] Irwin was probably a friend from Reynolds's school days at Sandhurst, and was, much like Reynolds, born into a military family.[40] Another woman was present at the ceremony, one Miss Emelie Fouequet, who was perhaps a friend of Susannah's from the time she spent in France.[41]

Reynolds's and Susannah's wedding was therefore a small affair without much fanfare. Indeed, the reason for the small ceremony is potentially explained by the fact that Reynolds and Susannah likely needed to get married in a hurry. The couple were married in July 1835. Their first child, George Edward, was born just six months later on 20 January 1836.[42] To support his new family, Reynolds received the £400 inheritance money from his mother in the month that he got married.

Under the Librarie des Etrangers's imprint, George Bennis published Reynolds's first novel, *The Youthful Imposter* in two volumes in 1835. Reissued in 1847 under the title of *The Parricide*, it tells the story of young James Crawford who, in collaboration with a fraudster named Stanley Arnold, plots to defraud wealthy Londoners of their money.[43] The novel was Reynolds's attempt to capitalise on the popularity of a genre that had caused a sensation back in England: the 'Newgate Novel'. Named after Newgate, the infamous London gaol, the heroes of these novels were usually criminals, from the eighteenth or early nineteenth centuries. The birth of the genre was marked by the appearance of Edward Bulwer Lytton's *Paul Clifford* (1830), the story of an eighteenth-century highwayman whose deeds in the novel served as a social commentary on the moral degradation of the destitute working classes who were forced to turn to crime in order to survive. Bulwer Lytton followed up *Paul Clifford* with the fictionalised tale of the life of the murderer Eugène Aram in 1832, while William Harrison Ainsworth made contributions to the genre in the form of *Rookwood* (1834) and *Jack Sheppard* (1839).

Reynolds's *Youthful Imposter* caused 'a sensation' in Paris when it was first published, and one reviewer predicted that the novel would enjoy success in the United Kingdom because

> There is a good moral to be extracted from the work ... his language is fluent, easy, and often beautiful; his powers of description cannot be for a moment questioned; and, as a French Review very justly remarked, he has few equals in the truth of dialogue. Arnold is an original character, as original as Falkland in "Caleb Williams;" and in saying this, although we say much, we do not say too much. We have no doubt but that Mr. Reynolds will one day shine conspicuously as a literary character: his work affords ample proofs of a deep scientific acquaintance with the most abstruse authors, with the various sectarian opinions of philosophers in all ages, with ancient and modern classics ... He has many peculiarities of style, is somewhat pedantic in the precision of his grammatical exactitude, and is occasionally guilty of irreligious allusions. Still he has written a good novel—a novel that will lay the foundation of his future fame—a novel that must ever be perused with the sincerest delight.[44]

It was quite a coup, indeed, for Reynolds to be spoken of in the same breath as William Godwin, the author of *Caleb Williams* (1794). Godwin, father to Mary Shelley, was one of the most famous philosopher-novelists of the late eighteenth century. The sentiments in the above review chime with the opinion of at least one modern literary critic.[45]

Nineteenth-century publishers certainly thought Reynolds's novel was a worthy investment. A London edition was printed by Longman in 1836,[46] and it was quickly pirated by an American publisher in Philadelphia.[47] Reynolds's sensational novel was also translated into French by A.J.B. Defauçonpret under the title of *Le Jeune Imposteur*.[48] But not everyone in the 1830s agreed with the above assessment, as the following remarks in *The Monthly Review* illustrate:

> The author commends his work to the "tedious hour of some love sick maiden or amorous youth;" consisting, as he says it does, of "the lucubrations of one who has boldly set forth into the world to vary the sameness so incidental to modern novels." In truth, it is only suited to the melancholic or the foolish; while its bad taste and outrageous improbabilities are even too much for love-sick maidens and amorous youths.[49]

When the novel was reissued as *The Parricide* in 1847—by which time Reynolds had made a name for himself as the author of certain scandalous novels—it was almost unanimously condemned. Sophie Raine has unearthed several reviews of the reissue from various periodicals and her findings make for amusing reading. With the pompous moralistic tone common to a lot of Victorian literary commentary, *The Pilot* accused Reynolds of 'corrupting' youthful readers with his 'pernicious' content.[50] *The Nottingham Review* remarked that 'we do not deny that Mr Reynolds is a man of considerable talent, but judging from the "Parricide" we should say of mean ambition, and sorely perverted taste'.[51] The *Leeds Times* declared that while Reynolds was a talented writer, the novel 'minister[ed] to a morbid taste in the people, which ought rather to be checked than pandered to'.[52]

Another newspaper, the *Liverpool Mercury*, condemned the *Youthful Imposter* for portraying crime 'too liberally'. The newspaper even implied that the novel was autobiographical, having speculated that as a youth Reynolds himself had probably committed some of the crimes detailed in the novel.[53] It might be the accusation from this newspaper, written in 1847, that was responsible for another one of the untruths in the Home Office dossier written the following year, which alleged that Reynolds had been a criminal in his youth. As we have seen, in the dossier, Captain Walmer claimed that Reynolds had once pretended to be a gentleman's servant to defraud someone, which is what happens in the novel. The same testimony also alleges that while in France, Reynolds had regularly cheated gambling men out of their money by using loaded dice, and these kinds of scenes do occur in *The Youthful Imposter*.[54]

But Reynolds was in his element in Paris and he made the acquaintance and 'friendship of the most eminent authors of France'.[55] We might surmise that the authors he referred to here were the aforementioned Eugène Sue, as well as Paul de Kock and Victor Hugo, whose works Reynolds later translated. The artist and illustrator Gustave Doré was also one of Reynolds's acquaintances.[56] Reynolds formed acquaintances with publishers such as Louis-Claude Baudry who, since 1815, specialised in reprinting English works for the British expatriate community. The 'reprinting' work carried out by Baudry's firm—as well as Baudry's rival Galignani—however, was little better than piracy. The English press took a dim view of the actions of these continental 'pirates':

> The numbers of English residents in France are so rapidly increasing [...but] an abominable piracy ever since the last Revolution has enabled Messieurs Baudry and Galignani to reprint standard English works, and sell them at the ridiculously cheap rate of five francs a copy ... piracy and plagiarism have been the means of raising Galignani and Baudry from the humble stations of petty and obscure booksellers into that of great and important publishers ... the piracy continues as before; and the two Parisian monopolists laugh at threats, opposition, or remonstrance ... In Brussels, Mr Wahlen pursues the same piratic game, and circulates throughout Belgium and Germany upwards of seven hundred copies of every new and interesting work. Thus three foreign publishers supply to their English public, all over the continent, three thousand two hundred copies of new books.[57]

The same article lamented the absence of international copyright agreements which allowed foreign publishers to print English works without ever paying a penny in royalties to either the authors or the original British publishers.

Between writing a full-length novel and working at Bennis's bookshop, it is a wonder that Reynolds found the time for undertaking other projects. In doing so, however, he did have to be on his guard against those 'native and exotic swindlers'. Jennifer Conary has highlighted the case of one particular swindler named John Wilks who tried to con Reynolds out of his money.[58] Wilks, the managing editor of the *Paris Literary Gazette*, approached Reynolds in the autumn of 1835 with the prospect of founding a new literary magazine for the English expatriate community in Paris. The new magazine would be titled *The London and Paris Courier*. Reynolds was initially open to the idea of investing in the project. After all, Reynolds had the money—he had recently received his inheritance. But then one of Reynolds's acquaintances warned him off the project by pointing out that Wilks had previously defrauded investors. When Reynolds searched through old newspapers to ascertain the truth of the matter he found that his friend's warning was all too true. Reynolds immediately pulled out of the investment.

Wilks was angry, and in the 27 October 1835 issue of the *Paris Literary Gazette,*[59] he published a notice saying lamenting the fact the *London and Paris Courier* had not yet begun its publication 'but for the non-completion of a contract to supply the caution-money, entered into by an Englishman'.[60] A few days later, Wilks launched legal proceedings against Reynolds for breach of contract. On 30 November 1835, the judge dismissed the case, and Wilks was ordered to pay Reynolds's legal costs.[61] With the court case concluded, Reynolds decided to tell his side of the story in a specially published *Circular* where he exposed Wilks's past crimes to the whole expatriate community.[62] Wilks had been well and truly embarrassed, and his name among the English community in Paris was mud. He fled Paris, taking with him all of the money which other investors had stumped up for *The London and Paris Courier*, and also all of his *Paris Literary Gazette* employees' wages with him.

Reynolds did have his eye on what looked like a safer investment: the purchase of the Librairie des Etrangers from its owner, Renouard, with which would also come the proprietorship of the *Paris Advertiser*. Bennis had left the firm in October of 1835, and Reynolds's purchase of the business was concluded in January 1836. The lease of the property at 55 Rue Neuve St Augustin passed to Reynolds. There were other literary magazines published by the Galignani firm, who had a near monopoly on English language periodicals in Paris, but Galignani's were 'cut and paste' jobs that merely reprinted content from periodicals back in London.[63] But once Reynolds bought the *Paris Advertiser*, he also became its editor and turned it into a magazine that offered *original* content for English-speaking readers. He published two pieces of short fiction in this magazine. 'The Gypsy: A Tale'[64] appeared in February 1836, and 'The Guardian' appeared in April of the same year.[65] Reynolds also politicised the *Paris Advertiser*, giving it a radical bent, whereas Galignani's periodicals avoided politics as much as possible.[66]

Under Reynolds's stewardship, the Librarie des Etrangers continued as a combined publisher, bookseller, and circulating library that printed and sold English language texts to British expatriates. Reynolds also acted as a literary agent, arranging the import of English language texts into France, and thereby making an effort to combat the literary piracy of the Galignani and Baudry firms.[67] Sales of 'official' books imported from London and sold through Reynolds appear to have been relatively high.[68] Books were subsequently published under the joint imprint of G.W.M. Reynolds and the Librairie des Etrangers. It is not known how many books were subsequently published by Reynolds. Thus far, historians have only located only two works that list Reynolds as publisher: a reprint of Captain Marryatt's *Rattlin the Reefer*, printed in 1836; and Catherine Gore's *Mrs Armytage; or, Female Domination*, also printed in 1836.

Reynolds's fluency in the French language enabled him to make forays into translating the works of French authors into English. His first endeavour was a book of poems titled *Songs of Twilight* (1836), which was a translation of *Chants des Crepuscule* by of one of France's finest poets: Victor Hugo (1802–85). It is easy to see why Hugo's poetry attracted Reynolds's notice. The collection contained poems that celebrated the French Revolution of 1830, as the following lines reveal:

> And France has awaken from stupor profound,
> And the watch-word has rais'd her champions around;
> And the din of their weapons struck loud on the ear,
> As it hearken'd the tread of the cavalry near.
> But the tyrant has marshall'd his warriors vain,
> And his culverins thunder'd again and again,
> For the stones, that the citizens tore from the street,
> Laid the cohorts of royalty dead at their feet;

And their numbers increas'd—for they fought to be free—
And they pour'd on the foe like the waves of the sea;
While the din of the tocsin, that echo'd on high,
Was drown'd in the fervour of liberty's cry!

The young Victor Hugo's political philosophy must have accorded with that of the young Reynolds, although in later life Reynolds became quite critical of the French political party with which Hugo was associated: *Le Partie de l'ordre* (The Party of Order). In 1850, Reynolds declared that this party 'consists of the most infernal miscreants that ever disgraced the human form'.[69]

However, *Songs of Twilight* attracted very little notice in England or France. One magazine that reviewed it was the *Athenaeum*, one of the period's leading literary magazines. The *Athenaeum*'s review criticised Reynolds for offering 'dilutions' of Victor Hugo's poetry rather than translations:

> *Songs of Twilight, translated from the French of Victor Hugo, by George W.M. Reynolds*, author of 'The Youthful Imposter.'—Though the verse of Mr Reynolds be smooth and his language carefully chosen, the pamphlet before us must be pronounced to contain dilutions, and not versions, of Victor Hugo's poems. In his preface, indeed, the translator owns as much. He need not be told that, if there be one thing above another for which the writers of *la jeune France* are remarkable, it is for the license of their imagery, and the audacious loudness of their personifications,—these may offer in their difficulty and exaggeration so many reasons why an author should altogether refrain from attempting to naturalize them in our soberer literature; but he is unacquainted with his first duty, if, choosing to make the essay, he emasculates his original, by way of escaping from quaintnesses and individualities.[70]

However, Reynolds's translations of Hugo's songs were reprinted later in the nineteenth century when critical editions of the French author's poems, edited by Isabel Hapgood, were published by the New York Kelmscott Society. Thus, Reynolds's translations were viewed by some later academics as being of high scholarly merit.

Aside from the negative reviews, everything appeared to be going well. Reynolds was now the editor and proprietor of a magazine which was becoming increasingly popular with the Paris-based English reading public. He made a fatal mistake, however, which meant that his purchase of the business was illegal: foreigners were not allowed to own businesses in Paris unless they were naturalised French citizens. Reynold applied to the French government to see if they would retrospectively grant a 'brevet de libraire'—a publishing house licence—but this was rejected on 9 April 1836.[71] Reynolds had to give up the publishing house and he lost all of the money he invested in it. The ownership of the Librarie des Etrangers and the *Paris Advertiser* immediately passed back to Renouard. A French court then declared Reynolds bankrupt, yet it was a bankruptcy with conditions, and did not lead immediately to the erasure of his debts: Reynolds was subjected to a *cession de biens* which meant that he would have to continue making set payments until certain debts were discharged.

Reynolds had learned hard lessons about the unscrupulous nature of businessmen. If Wilks was one of the 'foreign swindlers' in Paris that good Englishmen had to be on their guard against, Renouard was one of the 'native swindlers'. Jennifer Conary points out that Reynolds was still, understandably, smarting about this a few years later. In Reynolds's novel *Pickwick Abroad; or, the Tour in France* (1839), there is the short story of a swindler in Paris named Renard, who is described as 'the most notorious villain in existence' because of 'the way in which he treated a young English gentleman'.[72] Of course, with no right of appeal, the only redress Reynolds had was to cast Renouard as a villain in a novel; as for Reynolds, he returned to England either in the winter of 1836, or the early months of 1837, and sought lodgings in London, which is where we join him in the next chapter.

Taking the Pledge: Reynolds, the *Teetotaler*, and his Early Novels

The opponents of Teetotalism urge that it is too dangerous an innovation, and that society is not yet fitted to receive it. One word will suffice to answer this objection ... Reformation can never be too rapid nor too prompt, when applied to the vices of an age, of a sect, or of a society.

> George W.M. Reynolds,
> *The Anatomy of Intemperance* (1840)

"Vy, Samivel, it's impossible. I'd rather not believe it, Samivel. You ain't no child o' mine to go an' forsvear all kinds o' lush in that oudacious manner. 'Spose it is right to give up drinking, Sammy!"

> George W.M. Reynolds,
> *Noctes Pickwickianae* (1840)

In the eighteenth century, Bethnal Green was a suburb featuring cottages, a high street, and some common land that could be used by people of any social rank to rear livestock and grow food. This was not the case by the early Victorian era, and it is to Bethnal Green, which was then classed as one of London's worst neighbourhoods, that a bankrupt Reynolds and Susannah and their child returned. By the time Reynolds arrived in the 1830s, industrialisation and rapid urbanisation had destroyed the once picturesque village and it was one of the poorest districts of the capital. From 1837 to 1842, 548 extra slum houses were built in this already overcrowded area.[73]

Destitute and needing shelter from the streets, the Reynolds family took up lodgings in a single room in Suffolk Place. Suffolk Place has

24

long since been demolished and no contemporary pictures survive, but it appears to have been a large tenement into which a number of people lodged. In the house that the Reynolds family occupied there were ten other poor families eking out a living;[74] as the census return for 1841 reveals, alongside Reynolds's family there were thirty-five people in total living in the property.[75]

So poor were some of the families living in Bethnal Green, that in the 1840s a preacher named Mr G. Alston remarked that 'Not one father of a family in ten in the whole neighbourhood has other clothing beside his work suit'.[76] The stench must have been horrific. The former patch of common land was now a rubbish tip which was overlooked by the windows of the rickety tenements—the walls of some of these houses were so unstable that residents had propped up them up on the outside by placing beams against them. Other houses, which in the opinion of contemporary philanthropists were little better than 'huts', were built directly over sewage pits.[77] The supposedly 'upmarket' houses and tenements were little better. In their description of conditions in the Bethnal Green tenements a journalist for the *Illustrated London News* remarked that most of the residents in these shaky dwellings lived in 'a state of extreme filth and squalor':

> The miserable rooms are underlet and teeming with inhabitants to an almost inconceivable extent. The water for some fourteen or fifteen houses is frequently supplied from one tap in a dirty corner, where it runs for only a short time every day; and the places are mostly undrained. Add to this the decay of vegetable matter, the occasional evidence of the presence of pigs from adjacent houses which have back yards (these have none), and that sickly odour which belongs always to human beings living in such a state, and the result will represent a score of places extending over Bethnal-green parish for more than a mile in length and half a mile in breadth.[78]

People needed houses to retire to after their hard day's work, working for subsistence wages, and building regulations were lax. The result was living conditions that shocked contemporary charity workers.

Luckily Reynolds soon found employment as the editor of the *Monthly Magazine* which he turned from a fairly small 'c' conservative periodical into one which promoted a radical political philosophy and was unafraid to criticise the ruling class. Reynolds wrote a lot of original content for this magazine which he signed under the pseudonym of 'Parisianus'. Although the first article signed with that pseudonym appeared in March 1837, Reynolds probably took over the reins of the periodical in January of that year, because the lead article in that month's issue is devoted to 'The Approaching Session of Parliament'. In language that is characteristic of Reynolds's later newspaper articles, the article is very critical of the aristocracy, which is a hallmark of Reynolds's later writings.

For a man who became highly critical of imperialism as he matured, Reynolds's first signed article for the *Monthly Magazine* is interesting because he supports French imperialism. During the Napoleonic Wars— essentially the first world war with fighting on every continent—several of France's colonies had been captured by the allies. These territories included Guadeloupe, Martinique, French Guiana, St Lucia, Tobago, the Seychelles, and Réunion. After Britain and Prussia's final defeat of Napoleon at Waterloo in 1815, however, it was agreed at the Congress of Vienna that most of France's colonies would be restored to her, although Britain retained St Lucia, the Seychelles, and Tobago. By 1825, France became more assertive on the international stage and sent a naval expedition to Haiti to demand indemnification for financial losses suffered when Haiti declared independence from France in 1791. By 1830 French forces gradually extended their foothold in Algeria which took 17 years for them to fully subdue. This was the context in which Reynolds wrote his first 'Parisianus' article titled 'Constantina; or, the Importance of its Occupation by the French'. Constantina—modern day Constantine, was a prosperous town located in Algeria. In his article Reynolds declares that it is,

> [His] object ... to demonstrate the absolute necessity which obliged the French to undertake the expedition, not only in consideration of their northern possessions in Africa, but also with regard to their political credit and reputation at home and at foreign courts.[79]

In Reynolds's view, the French capture of the town, with its bustling markets and rich, fertile hinterland, would aid the spread of European 'Civilization' because it would lead to the increased trade in goods from Africa and Europe, and it would also help to dislodge the existing despotic rulers who held sway there. Although he never denounced this article, judging by Reynolds's later writings in the 1850s, he had definitely abandoned support for European imperialism.

Reynolds's support for French imperialism at this early stage was no doubt an extension of the fact that he was a confirmed Europhile. In the same magazine he wrote several articles of literary criticism highlighting the excellence of European literature. The first of these was a series titled 'On the French Poets and Novelists' which began in May 1837. These articles were a response to a piece in *The Quarterly Review* in which the writer alleged that all the works of contemporary French novelists and poets 'abound[ed] with voluptuousness and licentiousness'.[80] *The Quarterly Review* also asserted, somewhat bizarrely, that the 'low' quality of French literature in turn meant that there were more murders in France than in England. Reynolds countered these remarks by offering a sustained defence of the works of Paul de Kock, Victor Hugo—who in Reynolds's eyes was 'the French Walter Scott'—Alexandre Dumas, and Honoré de Balzac. Lamenting his countrymen's prejudice against French people, and Europeans in general, Reynolds wrote two follow-up articles extolling the literature and culture of Belgium and Hungary as well.[81] A revised and significantly expanded version of 'The French Poets and Novelists' was then later published by George Henderson in two volumes as *The Modern Literature of France* (1839). Reynold was making a name for himself, and his rising status was illustrated in the amounts that publishers advanced to him for his books: for the publication of *The Modern Literature of France* Reynolds received £300.[82]

Reynolds also contributed several translations of poetry—mostly of Victor Hugo's works—as well as serialised stories to the *Monthly Magazine*. One such story was 'The Baroness: A Novel', an inheritance drama that began in August 1837 and finished in March 1838. Other short stories included 'The Sculptor of Florence' and 'Mary Hamel: A Tale of the Seventeenth Century'. There are so many forgotten authors whose stories appeared in early nineteenth-century literary magazines; they usually made very little impact with the reading public and mostly served to provide an hour or two of pleasant diversion. Reynolds, however, incorporated many of these stories into a later novel: 'The Sculptor of Florence' and 'The Baroness' both reappeared in *Master Timothy's Bookcase* (1841). However, there were two novels that were first serialised in *The Monthly Magazine* that were so successful they were later published as standalone works: *Pickwick Abroad; or, The Tour in France* (1837–38) and *Alfred: The Adventures of a French Gentleman* (1838).

Modern readers will associate the name of Mr Pickwick with that of Charles Dickens, and it might naturally be wondered why Reynolds has a novel about Mr Pickwick credited to him. Some context is needed here: we have already remarked that copyright law, at an international level, was almost non-existent and allowed for the works of English authors to be pirated in France and vice versa. In the United Kingdom, copyright law did exist, but it hardly offered robust protection to authors. The first copyright law was enacted in the United Kingdom in 1710 and granted ownership of a text to an author. Although the law appeared to favour authors, however, booksellers and publishers got a better deal. The statute granted an author copyright over their works for a period of fourteen years, after which their works passed into the public domain. This meant that any printer could then reproduce a text and not pay a penny to the author. Several court cases during the eighteenth century tested the limits of the 1710 statute, but by the end of the eighteenth century the law still granted authors protection of their works for a time, but pirated and abridged works were also allowed by law.[83] Unfortunately for Charles Dickens, who at this point in his career wrote under the pseudonym of 'Boz', his *Posthumous Papers of the Pickwick Club* (1836) became a victim of its own success. Dickens's work was popular but it was expensive, retailing at 1s per issue, and the three-volume version of the novel printed after its initial print run was 31s 6d. This was expensive at a time when the wages of a male labourer could be as little as 9s per week. Labourers may have been poor, but many of them could read. Yet they could not justifiably spend 31s on a brand new novel.[84]

Just as Dickens was making his mark in the literary world so too were other 'cheaper' publishers, who provided entertainment for the poorer classes. To cater to the demand for cheap entertainment businessmen such as Edward Lloyd—the creator of the 'penny dreadful'[85]—began publishing cheap penny serials. Seeing the success of Dickens's *Pickwick Papers*, Lloyd took the character of Pickwick and published new stories featuring him. From Lloyd's press issued a number of 'Dickensian' works, many of which were written under the pen name of 'Bos'. Such works included *Penny Pickwick, Pickwick in America, Oliver Twiss* (based obviously on Oliver Twist), *Nickelas Nickelbery* (from Dickens's *Nicholas Nickleby*), and *Barnaby Budge* (from Dickens's *Barnaby Rudge*). The historian Ian Haywood points out, however, that these works were not mere plagiarisms, but original works, closer to modern-day fan fiction than outright copies. Dickens was understandably annoyed. He did try, but ultimately failed, to get an injunction taken out against these cheap copies. Part of Lloyd's defence was that the imitations were so bad that nobody in the world could have mistaken them as having been written by Dickens. In hindsight, however, perhaps Dickens should have been thankful to Lloyd's pirate authors, for these works actually helped to propel Dickens's Pickwick character to great heights of fame among a poorer class of readers who would never have been able to afford the original.[86]

Reynolds decided that he too would capitalise on Pickwick Mania by writing *Pickwick Abroad; or The Tour in France*. Reynolds's contribution to the Pickwick craze might be categorised as a picaresque novel—a series of loosely connected tales told in quick succession. Reynolds's Mr Pickwick sets off to France and has a number of adventures, mixing in high society, and even Napoleon makes an appearance.

Reynolds left the *Monthly Magazine* in towards the close of 1838, and *Pickwick Abroad* had not finished its serialisation. The reasons why Reynolds left are not known; perhaps the owners of the *Monthly Magazine* dismissed him because they were worried about Dickens's publishers Chapman and Hall launching a further legal case against them.[87] Although this is ultimately speculation, the timing of Reynolds's departure gives one pause for thought. The publisher who continued Reynolds's serial was Thomas Tegg, who published Reynolds's novel in standalone penny parts of 24 issues.[88] Further episodes continued to appear until September 1839, and Reynolds earned £6 for each issue.[89]

Tegg's payments to Reynolds were a sound investment. As far as reviewers were concerned, Reynolds's *Pickwick Abroad* was one of the better Pickwick tales on the literary market. The work garnered Reynolds respect among reviewers. One reader described it as highly amusing and praised him for the pictures he drew of British and French manners.[90] In echo of this, another reviewer remarked that '[Reynolds's] new adventures of the renowned [Pickwick] club will afford a fund of infinite amusement'.[91]

When *The Monthly Magazine* dispensed with Reynolds's services they discontinued, not only *Pickwick Abroad* but another serial by him:

Alfred de Rosann: The Adventures of a French Gentleman, which began its serialisation in July 1838, and was discontinued in the *Monthly Magazine* in December 1838. When it was discontinued, the Willoughby printing firm decided to issue it as a single volume in 1839. *Alfred* is one of Reynolds's best novels and bears more than a passing resemblance to the yet-to-be written *Les Misérables* by Victor Hugo. The title character, Alfred, is a minor French nobleman, who is wrongly accused of a crime. He is sent to the galleys, but escapes and spends the majority of his life on the run from the police. Along the way, he is taken in by a kind family and offered shelter for the evening, he meets a rogue landlord who very much resembles the Thenardier character from Hugo's novel, and at the end of the novel Alfred finds himself mixed up in the events of the 1830 revolution, much like what happens to Jean Valjean in *Les Misérables*.

Some scholars have alleged that it was also in *Alfred*, in a footnote to its thirty-first chapter which relates the events of the 1830 revolution, that Reynolds claimed to have participated in it. Reynolds does not actually claim this, however, for the part of the story that accompanies the footnote reading *ipso me teste* ('my own witness') reads thus:

> [Alfred] proceeded straight to the Bank of France; and although he was surrounded by the lowest of the low— although he passed through a miserable set of beings, half-naked—half-starved as they were, not a hand was stretched out against the tempting treasure,—not a glance betokened an evil design—not a gesture threatened its security.

Reynolds was here testifying to the orderliness and good behaviour of people during the revolution, a point that he makes over two pages. He is not claiming to have taken part in the revolution. Still, however, it is unlikely that Reynolds was in Paris in 1830, even to witness the good conduct of the revolutionaries. Yet, Reynolds was in Paris by 1832, which is the year that he met Eugène Sue, and in the summer of that year, the Parisian newspapers extensively covered the rebellion of the workers and students on 5–6 June (this is the same insurrection memorialised by Hugo in *Les Misérables*). These were not the only revolutions and rebellion to occur in France at that point. There was a major rebellion in Lyons in December 1831. Further revolts occurred in Lyons in 1832 and 1834. All of these slightly later rebellions were in fact viewed, by some Parisians, as an extension of the revolution of 1830, and perhaps Reynolds, whether intentionally or unintentionally, conflated his recollection of 1832 with his knowledge of the events of 1830.

But to return to the events of the late 1830s: in 1838, Reynolds and Susannah welcomed another child into their family, whom they named Blanche. No doubt much of the money Reynolds earned from writing was devoted to caring for his family, which now numbered four. But in spite of the advances that Reynolds received a lot of this, must have been swallowed up in repayments to creditors from his first bankruptcy. In May 1839, while the serialisation of *Pickwick Abroad* was still ongoing, Reynolds was arrested for debt and placed in the Queen's Bench Prison. He was immediately compelled to apply to the Royal Literary Fund (RLF) for emergency relief. This charity was founded in 1790 to assist destitute authors. Many famous authors had at some point requested relief from the RLF: the organisation has files on Samuel Taylor Coleridge, Leigh Hunt, Thomas Hood, Joseph Conrad, and D.H. Lawrence, to name but a few. Reynolds's case was not unique. To obtain release from his debts, Reynolds requested £20 from the fund in order to apply to the insolvency court for a bankruptcy order.[92] The bankruptcy would have cost £10, so the extra £10 that Reynolds requested must have been to provide for his and his family's immediate maintenance as well.

It certainly took a while for the RLF to deliberate on whether to provide assistance to Reynolds. He was still in the Queen's Bench Prison on 8 August 1839, when he wrote a note of thanks to the RLF for the £15 that they had awarded to him, but also requesting a further £10 aid so he could begin insolvency proceedings.[93] His request for further relief fell on deaf ears. Perhaps the remaining £24 he was due to receive from the final six issues of *Pickwick Abroad* helped him to repay some of his debts, as well as the £350 payment he eventually received for *Alfred*.[94]

Thus Reynolds was not, in the summer of 1839, forced to declare bankruptcy, and he was released from the debtors' prison. He was made bankrupt a year later, however, although the exact details of this remain unknown; his bankruptcy in 1840 is only casually alluded to in further bankruptcy proceedings he faced in 1848. The silver lining in the bankruptcy of 1840, however, was presumably the fact that the *cession des biens* order from a French court was now null and void.

31

Reynolds's experiences in the debtors' prisons, however, shaped his fiction and are most apparent in the novel he wrote in 1839 titled *Grace Darling*. This novel was a retelling of the deeds of a woman named Grace Darling, who, in 1838, became a national hero. She was the daughter of a lighthouse keeper on the Farne Islands who, upon seeing the paddle steamer *Forfarshire* run on to rocks and break in two, rowed out with her father in a small boat to rescue the survivors. Reynolds spoke of Darling in glowing terms in the novel's preface:

> At a period, then, when instances of female heroism are so rare in the British realms, it is with the most unfeigned delight that I have to record one, which, for disinterestedness of motive, and for recklessness of danger in the cause of humanity, is almost without parallel.[95]

Reynolds was not the only writer who sang Darling's praises. She was celebrated in newspapers as the epitome of feminine heroism and virtue. The young Queen Victoria presented a reward of £50 to the Darling family and Grace was also presented with the gift of a shawl and a medal from the Duchess of Northumberland.[96] Other newspapers suggested that a nation-wide subscription should be raised to present the Darling family with a gift.[97] While not wishing to downplay the Darlings' bravery in the 2020s, some of the media coverage became a bit obsessive. And it was not only newspapers who were obsessed. In 1843, the year that Wordsworth was appointed to the position of poet laureate, he wrote a poem celebrating her deed. Adding to the growing Grace Darling 'legend' was the now-forgotten novelist Jerrold Vernon who wrote *Grace Darling, or the Maid of the Isles* (1839), and there were no fewer than four paintings commemorating her deeds.

The real Grace Darling might have acted from disinterested motives, but Reynolds's own contribution to her legend was, just as with *Pickwick Abroad*, an attempt to capitalise on something popular. Grace Darling appears very briefly at the beginning of his novel, when she visits London for the first time and bumps into two of the main characters. The rest of the novel then concerns the adventures of Slapman Twill, Mr Somerville, and the latter's love interest Eliza. At the end, Somerville and Eliza, having embarked on the doomed *Forfarshire*, meet Grace Darling again when she rescues the survivors. Indeed, the fact that Grace

Darling only appears at the beginning and at the end of the novel, might lead the more cynical modern reader to the conclusion that Reynolds had probably already written the novel focusing simply on Somerville and Eliza, before news of Darling's exploits reached London. Then, sensing a golden opportunity to cash in on current events, Reynolds merely inserted Darling into his novel.

One character in *Grace Darling*, named Twill, is incarcerated for debt in the King's Bench, and for these scenes Reynolds likely drew on his own experiences. In spite of the fact that debtors usually had little money about them, prisoners were required to pay an entrance fee into the prisons. They were also required to pay money for their accommodation. The more money that a debtor could pay, then their accommodation would be of higher quality. If you could not pay for your own room, you were placed in the pit with the rest of the truly destitute prison population. On occasion, a debtor might be given the 'freedom of the gate' to enable them to go out and seek work, but most of them had to find some way of paying off their debts from inside the gaol. This often meant that the men in the prison—and the inmates were usually men, because they were heads of their household—had to rely on the income that family members were able to get. Alternatively, charity from outside organisations had to be relied upon.[98]

The absurdity of the debtors' prison system is recorded in *Grace Darling* as Twill 'paid his gate fees and the other little *et ceteras* which were demanded of him'.[99] It is in the debtors' gaol that Twill also meets the Somerville family. Frederick Somerville is incarcerated while his wife Eliza must work all hours in a low-paying menial job, and pawn many of her belongings, to support her husband. Yet Eliza's wages barely cover her husband's accommodation expenses.[100] It was not only paupers who found themselves in debtors' prisons. In Reynolds's novel it is a place where the disgraced members of all ranks meet—fallen noblemen, ruined tradesmen, paupers, are all present—all of whom had some sad story to tell of how they fell into debt. Yet there is a decent sense of camaraderie between the prisoners in Reynolds's novel and several of the inmates, in fact, recount their stories to Twill while drinking with him. Twill, on the other hand, being charitable, paid some of the Somerville's accommodation expenses.

The manner in which the state dealt with debtors needed reforming, and a prominent advocate for this was Charles Dickens. At the age of twelve, Dickens's father was locked up in the Marshalsea prison and young Dickens was forced to work in a factory. But it would not be until 1869 that the government passed the Debtors' Act. This reduced the cost of applying for bankruptcy and dispensed with the routine imprisonment of debtors, although those who had the means to discharge their debts but refused, could still be imprisoned. The same went for those who failed to make payments to the court, so the system became fairer but less harsh on the truly unfortunate.

Grace Darling also reveals another aspect of Reynolds's character: his anti-sexist and anti-racist beliefs. In the novel's preface he attacked Englishmen who 'demand[ed] passive obedience' of their wives. This was at a time when women were often viewed as a physically and mentally 'weaker sex'. Women, even upper and middle-class women, might only receive a very basic education. As one mid-nineteenth century newspaper scoffed: 'of what use is education to the weaker sex?'[101] Yet in contrast to such bigoted views, Reynolds proudly asserted that 'I do not believe that the mind of woman is constitutionally weaker than that of a man: I maintain that if it possessed the same opportunities of development, it would be equally powerful'.[102] He does not appear to have changed his attitude, and in 1848, he encouraged women to take an interest in politics:

> It is a common saying, and as absurd as it is common—"Oh! women have no right to meddle in politics." Women, on the contrary, have as much right as "the lords of the creation" to exhibit an interest in the systems and institutions by which they are governed. For the sake of their children, as well as for their own, they should assert and exercise that right. It is a lamentable delusion to suppose that the intellect of woman is not powerful nor comprehensive enough to embrace such considerations. The intellect of woman is naturally as strong as that of man; but it has less chances and less opportunities of developing its capacity. The masculine study of politics would aid the intellect of woman in putting forth its strength; and we hope that the day is gone by when the female sex are to be limited to the occupations of the drawing-room, the nursery, or the kitchen. We do not wish to see women become soldiers or sailors, nor to work at severe employment: but we are anxious to behold them *thinkers* as

34

well as *readers*—utilitarians as well as domestic economists. And we know of no greater benefit that could be conferred on society in general, than that which might be derived from the influence of the well-developed intellect of woman. Her mind is naturally better poised than that of man: far-seeing and quick-sighted is she;—a readiness at devising and combining plans to meet emergencies, is intuitive with her. Her judgment is correct—her taste good;—and she profits by experience far more usefully than does man. Is it not absurd, then—is it not unjust—and is it not unwise to deny to woman the right of exercising her proper influence in that society of which she is the ornament and the delight?[103]

Some fairly typical 'Victorian' attitudes towards women can still be discerned in Reynolds's proto-feminist declaration, of course: as many Victorian men of his time likewise thought, women were still biologically, although not intellectually, the weaker sex for he states that the work women should do should not be too 'severe'.

Reynolds attacked the 'slavery' of wives to their husbands in *Grace Darling* but he also attacked the slavery of black people as well. In the preface he castigated British imperialists for believing that they had a 'right' to enslave other people.[104] When he was writing in 1839, slavery had only been abolished throughout the British Empire six years earlier. The abolitionists in parliament faced a lot of opposition from what has been dubbed 'The West India Interest'—the plantation-owning classes from the colonies. It is doubtful whether slavery would have been abolished at all, had it not been for the fact that the British government, in order to get the required numbers in parliament, decided to compensate, to the tune of £20 million, the slave owners for the loss of their 'property'. Reynolds's nascent anti-colonialist views would, over the next decade, become more coherently expressed when he established his widely read newspapers.

From the 1850s, several critics levelled many accusations against Reynolds and some of these have been repeated uncritically by modern historians and literary critics. Chief among these allegations is the idea that Reynolds was never a 'genuine' supporter of any cause to which he attached himself—a point that shall be returned to in chapter five. However, one thing which Reynolds can most definitely be praised for, is the fact that, in an era marked by colonialism and racial discrimination, he spoke out against the conventional prejudices of his day. His remarks against slavery above are evidence of this, as is his treatment of Jewish people, for some of Reynolds's novels featured sympathetically-drawn Jewish characters. This won him praise from Britain's Jewish community, who thanked Reynolds for his 'manly defence' of them, and for helping to 'remov[e] the national prejudice'.[105]

For the biographer, the next major event in Reynolds's life is somewhat mysterious. While living in Bethnal Green, Reynolds and Susannah had another son, whom they named Alfred Dowers, born on 22 March 1840. Yet Alfred Dowers is an enigma: there is a record of his birth, and Reynolds and Susannah are listed on that document as his parents,[106] yet by the time of the 1841 census Alfred was not living with the family. One theory might be that, with Reynolds having been made bankrupt in 1840, the couple decided that they could not support another child, so perhaps they put Alfred up for adoption—during the nineteenth century this was an informal process in which the state was not involved.[107] This theory gains extra credence if we consider the fact that, unlike with their other children, Reynolds and Susannah had absolutely no involvement with Alfred Dowers in later life. Or perhaps this is to overthink the matter. After all, the census takers in the nineteenth century had a reputation for being less than diligent: when they turned up at a door, especially at a dwelling like Suffolk Place with over forty people living there, it is unlikely that they went inside to check the details of what they had been told. Even the people interviewed by the census takers could make mistakes: perhaps when Reynolds was interviewed, he neglected to mention his new-born son. The only other record for Alfred Dowers comes half a century later when, after having been made bankrupt, his death in Christchurch, New Zealand, was recorded on 21 October 1886.[108] Whatever the details of his life, Alfred Dowers Reynolds remains a mystery and none of Reynolds's writings shed further light on him.

In the meantime, Reynolds published another novel: *Robert Macaire* (1840). Just like *Pickwick Abroad* before it, *Robert Macaire* was another attempt to capitalise on the existing popularity of a famous fictional character, and like *Alfred* and *Pickwick Abroad*, the novel has a French connection. Robert Macaire was a fictional bandit who first appeared in an 1823 play titled *L'Auberge des Adrets*, written by Benjamin Antier, Jean

Armand, and Alexis Chapponier.[109] Macaire soon became a 'multimedia' sensation in France; new theatrical adaptations, short story spin-offs, as well as cartoons featuring Macaire were published. *L'Auberge des Adrets* also made its way over to London where it toured the 'low' theatres for a time and was then further adapted as a comic ballet at Drury Lane Theatre, with further derivations premiering at the Victoria Theatre.[110]

The Robert Macaire character who featured on the early Victorian stage may have been a comic and romantic figure but Reynolds's character was more realistic. In common with many novels and texts featuring outlaws and highwaymen Macaire is a trickster, and he is involved in the usual episodes one might expect in an outlaw novel—running away from the constables and womanising—but he is also something of a brute or 'semi-heroic', for he does not flinch from committing murder.[111] Thus Reynolds's *Robert Macaire* novel, far from being a good Robin Hood character, is more akin to William Harrison Ainsworth's *Jack Sheppard* (1839).[112] Ainsworth's *Jack Sheppard*, based upon the true story of the boy thief from the eighteenth century, is a true rogue who made the criminal life seem glamorous. And this is the case with Robert Macaire who robs £400 from a publican, cheats an aristocrat out of money at cards, and gets the same aristocrat's daughter pregnant.

The most notable aspect of *Robert Macaire*, however, is that was the first time Reynolds blended a tale of crime with politically radical ideology. Much of this is revealed in some of the songs and poems Reynolds incorporated into his novel such as the one Macaire overhears in a tavern:

> When despots let their subjects seek for just redress in vain,
> The cry will not be stifled by the gibbet nor the chain;
> But loud as if the sounds were born upon the tempest's
> wings,
> It echoes through the palaces and lofty halls of kings.
>
> Though nations long may languish in a lethargy profound,
> At length the voice of liberty must everywhere resound:—
> She, Cadmus-like, has sown the teeth from which an army
> springs,
> To hurl the tyrant from his throne and crush the sway of
> kings.[113]

'I neither quarrel with the song nor with the sentiments', Macaire remarks, 'especially as my own system of philosophy is based on republican opinions'.[114] For all his republican opinions, however, Macaire is not a freedom fighter and never aims to improve anybody's economic position but his own. The manner in which the story ends— with Macaire escaping from the London police and fleeing to France— suggests that Reynolds maybe had in mind a few more adventures for his outlaw hero but which never materialised.[115]

Reynolds received £375 for *Robert Macaire* but the majority of this would have probably been invested in a new project which he would start in the early part of 1840. Perhaps he also had a problem with alcohol which further added to the family's financial woes?[116] On the evening of 13 May 1840 Reynolds, somewhat inebriated, walked past Aldersgate Street Chapel where he noticed that a temperance meeting was taking place. Led by middle-class reformers, some of whom dedicated their lives to 'improving' the manners and habits of the working classes, the temperance movement sought to convince the working people to either enjoy alcohol in moderation or abstain completely from it.[117]

Fired with liquid courage Reynolds entered the chapel. The Rev. Mr Donaldson was delivering a lecture on the virtues and principles of teetotalism—the total abstention from alcohol. Reynolds listened with interest but after the lecture had finished, Reynolds stood up and challenged Donaldson to a debate. Donaldson accepted, and the debate was scheduled to take place a few days later on the 16 May. It seems that Reynolds was very much unprepared for the debate:

> Mr Reynolds began by stating that he came before the audience, labouring under many and signal disadvantages. He had given a challenge which he was induced to consider rash, because he was altogether unacquainted with the principles of the Teetotalers—the arguments they made use of in support of those principles—and the basis on which the fabric of their Association was raised. He had never read a single work, either periodical or complete, upon the subject: he stood before them without knowing what he was about to say; and he should merely open the discussion with a few sentiments upon the subject, — of those sentiments which naturally suggested themselves to him at

the moment. He should commence by observing, that the Teetotalers preached, not against the *abuse* of intoxicating drink only, but also against the *use*. They preached unexceptionable abstinence from all wines, spirits, malt liquors, &C.—a doctrine which attacked the most moderate use of those articles which he (Mr. Reynolds) considered to have become more or less necessary, through habit and hereditary customs, to the people of this country. If the Teetotalers would confine their crusade to a war against the *abuse* of strong drinks, no one would be more willing to join the Association than himself.[118]

Donaldson responded by saying that

[When] Temperance Societies had been first established, they permitted the very moderate use of intoxicating drink. The *use*, however, returned to the *abuse*, and experience in a very short time convinced those philanthropists, who had entered upon the task of reclaiming drunkards, that nothing but a total abstinence would ensure the regeneration of that fallen portion of society. Man is weak – temptation is strong – and he who is allowed to taste one glass, could be readily persuaded to taste a second. This would lead to a third, and the temperance-man would relapse into the drunkard.[119]

The debate continued for an hour and Reynolds was probably looking increasingly red-faced because he was unable to counter the reverend's philosophical points.

Another debate was scheduled for the following week and Reynolds decided not to go on a 'philosophical' attack but to attack the impracticability of teetotalism:

It would therefore be necessary to consider the extent to which the innovations of Teetotalers would reach. What amusements would they supply in a country where the public ones were so dear, as substitutes for the places of entertainments to which the poor flocked? or how would

39

they have the rich pass their evenings? Society was not prepared to receive such sudden changes.[120]

Donaldson had an answer for this as well:

> Mr. Donaldson rose to reply. He said that in any way, either in its abstract sense, or on general principles, he was ready to defend the doctrine of Teetotalism. He had seen so many beneficial effects, resulting from the application of those doctrines to society, that he could not for one moment allow them to be deemed premature in that application. Society, like an individual, could not reform its abuses too suddenly; and if Mr. Reynolds advocated such gradient measures of reform as were practised in the Houses of Parliament, they might all just as well have no reform at all. Where there was any viciousness in society, it was necessary to eradicate it at once, and not let it gangrene by the dilatoriness of the remedy applied. No one could deny the fact, that intoxication prevailed to an immense extent in this country. The peace of families was thereby destroyed,—the jails, the workhouses, and the hospitals were filled with the victims of that terrible vice; the pawnbrokers drove a thriving trade; and the greater portion of the lower classes were literally in rags.[121]

By the end of the debate Reynolds was convinced of the truth of the reverend's remarks. A few days later Reynolds wrote that 'that I consider myself to be acting a far more manly and honourable part by ... confessing that I am beaten by the force of conviction ... and I at once sign the pledge-book of *The London United Temperance Association*!'

Dick Collins surmised that the almost epiphany-like conversion of Reynolds to teetotalism suggests that he had a problem with drink. Whether Reynolds was an alcoholic or not remains unknown, but Reynolds certainly became an evangelist for teetotalism and, to this end, he established a newspaper. Titled *The Teetotaler*, it was edited by Reynolds and the first issue appeared on 27 June 1840, not long after the debates between Donaldson and Reynolds were held in May. The periodical 'supplied the reader with a Miscellany of Literature, conveying amusement, instruction, and morality at the same time'.[122]

Temperance debates were covered in depth and several moralist essays on the virtues of abstinence appeared in its columns. Characteristic of the essays—many of which were probably written by Reynolds—were pieces such as 'A Warning to Drunkards':

> Drunkenness expels reason, drowns the memory, defaces beauty, diminishes strength, inflames the blood, causes internal, external, and incurable wounds; is a witch to the senses, a devil to the soul, a thief to the purse, the beggar's companion, the wife's woe, and the children's sorrow.[123]

A stark warning, indeed! Readers could also avail themselves of the non-alcoholic drinks recipes in the magazine. On the literary side there were poems of various quality, some of which, like the following lines from W.T. Moncrieff, celebrated the virtues of water:

> Give me the stream—the clear—the bright—
> The cool—the chaste—the pure—the free;
> The stream that seeks and loves the light,
> And with the earth shares sovereignty,
> Give me the drink that beauty takes,
> That seeks the sands to cheer the faint,
> With which its thirst Devotion slakes,
> And that springs from rocks to bless the saint!
> Water, water give to me:—
> Water shall my nectar be![124]

Reynolds also wrote fiction for the magazine and decided to enlist Mr Pickwick in the teetotaller cause. In the first issue of the *Teetotaler* there appeared the first instalment of a short story titled *Noctes Pickwickiane*, in which Mr Pickwick and his friend Weller decide to take the pledge:

> *Mr. Pickwick*—Sam, you may give me your opinion of that Madeira which came this morning, if you like.
>
> *Sam*—Can't be done, Sir, as the wery old donkey observed to the costermonger, vich wanted him to trot ten mile an hour.

Mr. Pickwick – Can't be done! and why not, Sam?

Sam—'Cos I've jined them water-drinkin', beer-excludin', moral – reformation, out – an' – out sober fellers as calls 'emselves Teetotalers.[125]

Mr Pickwick decides to join Sam in trying out teetotalism for a few weeks. By the fifth and final instalment Pickwick is a confirmed teetotaller and Pickwick hosts a party at his home for his fellow teetotallers:

Mr. Pickwick. – We will do anything we can to assist those who will sign the pledge-book and try our principles. I bless the day when I embraced the doctrines of Teetotalism. Those of our friends, who have been rather wild, and who did not hesitate to play me a few tricks during my sojourn in France, will now become steady and sedate. This is a happy day, on which you have met at my house to celebrate the signing of some of you. An excellent supper is provided in the next room – with plenty of ginger-beer, lemonade, and iced water. We will see whether total abstinence will impair our intellects.

Sam. – Hooray! Pickwick and Teetotalism for ever! Here's for the triumphs of principle. I'd rather be the walley o' Pickwick vith cold water, than the friend and hale-feller vell-met vith that there drunken lord o' Waterford celebrity. Now, then gen'lemen – there's the supper: make yourselves at home as the Hindoos said to the chaps in the Black Hole of Calcutta.[126]

Noctes Pickwickiane and Reynolds's other *Teetotaler* Pickwick story, *Pickwick Married*, was never reprinted or incorporated into later novels. This suggests that Reynolds did not think them worthy of being published again and the fact that they disappeared

While serving as editor for *The Teetotaler* Reynolds published a standalone tract titled *The Anatomy of Intemperance* (1840) as well as a novel titled *The Steam Packet: A Tale of the River and Ocean* (1840). The novel was an extension of his Pickwick series in all but name as members of a club, headed by Mr Pipfax, journey to France on board a steamship and enjoy comedic adventures on the continent. Although probably of little interest to anyone in the twenty-first century—especially given even the relative lack of interest in Dickens's *Pickwick Papers* among modern audiences—*The Steam Packet* was well-received by at least one reviewer who said that

> Mr Reynolds is a quick observer, a smart describer, and has a happy knack of drawing ludicrous situations and of sketching ludicrous characters. In the persons of the Steam Boat there is not one that is decidedly novel; yet they are brought out so cleverly, and so many laughable incidents are connected with them.[127]

But the most popular serialised tale from Reynolds that appeared in the *Teetotaler* was *The Drunkard's Tale*; after its appearance in the magazine it was then republished as a single volume in 1841 and was serialised again in 1850 (with some minor variations in the title). The early part of *The Drunkard's Tale* was certainly autobiographical, and lends credence to Dick Collins's speculative assertion that Reynolds may have had an issue with alcoholism. *The Drunkard's Tale* begins with an aspiring writer named Victor, who, having inherited a fortune, has absconded to Paris and frequents the French capital's clubs and taverns. While there he met an eighteen-year-old woman named Louise and they get married. Unfortunately for the young couple, Victor was conned out of his remaining inheritance by an unscrupulous writer and publisher, so Reynolds was therefore still justifiably angry about Renouard's actions. The young couple return to England and were forced to live in some of the most disreputable parts of the metropolis. Meantime, Victor's addiction to alcohol spiralled out of control. Arrested for debt and placed in the Fleet Prison, Victor died while incarcerated, 'a grim emblem of a drunkard's failure'.[128] Apart from the anti-hero's death at the end, the novel was essentially a tale of Reynolds's life before he discovered teetotalism.

However, not every short story in *The Teetotaler* had a temperance theme. Reynolds republished some of his earlier short stories from the *Monthly Magazine* such as *The Father: An Episode in the Life of a Nobleman* in his new periodical.[129] Reynolds published this anonymously, however, presumably to give readers the impression that they were getting 'new' content instead of material that was recycled from older magazines.

Susannah Reynolds appears to have taken the pledge, and it was in the *Teetotaler* that her first *signed* literary works appeared. Her output included essays such as 'Intemperance in Woman', in which she castigated her fellow English women for being drunkards. Susannah also published a number of poems in her husband's periodical. These were mainly sonnets and stanzas on various non-temperance subjects like the following:

> When through th' expanse of heav'n the thunders roll,
> And the fork'd lightning flashes o'er the main;
> When the floods sweep the hamlet from the plain,
> And Nature seems convuls'd from pole to pole; –
> And when the forest bends beneath the blast,
> That like the desart-hurricane sweeps by;
> 'Tis then the reminiscence of the past,
> Array'd in terror, meets the sinner's eye;
> While his imagination ponders o'er
> The deeds of former days, and marks the times
> Stain'd with the mem'ry of a hundred crimes,
> For which he ne'er was penitent before, –
> Oh! in such hour, the guiltless martyr's doom
> Were enviable for him who fears the tomb![130]

Susannah also wrote novels herself and in the *Teetotaler* her first signed short story appeared titled *The Galley Slave*. Just like in her husband's early novels there was a French connection in her works: it is a story in which an escaped prisoner seeks refuge with a French peasant family, which is granted, after which the criminal reappears in society a very wealthy man, and becomes engaged to one of the peasant family's relatives.[131]

Reynolds's brother Edward also contributed articles under the pseudonym of 'Gracchus' Another radical at this time, named Samuel Kydd, also wrote columns for other newspapers under the name of Gracchus, but we can assume that *The Teetotaler* articles by Gracchus are from Edward, because Kydd did not join the Reynolds brothers until the 1850s when he started working for a newspaper which Reynolds founded. The assistance of his family—who probably took a greater role in *The Teetotaler* than they are given credit for—meant that, in addition to serving as editor of the journal, Reynolds could focus on what he loved: reading, translating, and publishing French literary works. In 1840, two translations of the works of French authors appeared. The first was a translation of Paul de Kock's *Sister Anne*, the merits of which Reynolds had extolled in *The Modern Literature of France*. The second was *The Last Day of a Condemned*, a translation of Victor Hugo's *Le Dernier Jour d'un Condamné*. As we have seen, Reynolds's ideology had much in common with Hugo's and, like Hugo, Reynolds detested the death penalty. *The Last Day of a Condemned* was a short story written to humanise condemned criminals by portraying the suffering and mental torture experienced by a man in the hours leading up to his execution. Reynolds's translation was never a best-seller in England, but a labour of love, born of Reynolds's commitment to the abolition of the death penalty, something that he continually spoke out against through his whole life.

Yet *The Teetotaler* was not to last. In 1840 the journal enjoyed much success and sold over 10,000 copies per week. By 1841, the circulation had declined to just 3,000 copies per week.[132] After quarrelling with his fellow temperance activists, Reynolds decided to wind it up. Collins attributes Reynolds's decision to begin a new quarrel to a relapse into alcoholism.[133] However, a likelier reason for the quarrel between Reynolds and his fellow teetotallers is the fact that he disliked some activists' religious motivations; his fellow activists were resistant to the idea of forming a national union of all teetotaller organisations; and he disagreed with the fact that other teetotal campaigners seemed all-too-willing to enrich themselves at the expense of the movement's adherents. This can be inferred by Reynolds's 'Farewell to the Public' address:

> Up to its present moment [*The Teetotaler*] *more* than covers its expenses; but an adequate amount of encouragement is wanting, beyond the actual payment of incidental liabilities, to ensure the continuation of the periodical. Circumstances of a different nature also bear their part to induce me to abandon a task for which I have seldom received thanks, the merits of which few have appeared to appreciate, and the termination of which I have for some time contemplated.

I cannot continue to labour in the same cause with men concerning whom fame reports sad tales, and who prefer their own selfish interests to the welfare of the cause. I have now toiled for Union amongst the Teetotalers, with all my soul, and with all my strength; and that prospect is farther off than ever. I see that Teetotalism is made the means of three or four individuals' private emoluments; and that the greediness of the officers of the two great Societies in London to grasp at the loaves and the fishes, has been the source of injury which is almost—if not quite irreparable. I have long beheld with disgust the acrimony which ministers of religion—professors of humility!—have manifested towards those who, though better Christians in *fact* than themselves, do not carry the outward hypocrisy of *appearances* to the same extreme. I have been astounded at those preachers of the Gospel who talk loudly on morality and charity, but who practise "envy, hatred, and malice, and all uncharitableness;"—and I now feel more convinced than ever, that hypocrisy and cant have materially assisted disunion and dishonesty to ruin the prospects of the Teetotal Reformation. These induce me to a retirement from that sphere in which I have sought to be useful; and I cannot say that I leave it with much *regret*.[134]

Thus the magazine ended. Reynolds and Susannah went back to supporting themselves by their literary labours. The end of *The Teetotaler* also marked the end of Reynolds's final comic Pickwick novel, *Pickwick Married*.

After the final issue of *The Teetotaler* and its comic stories had been published, Reynolds's output became more serious in its tone. The year 1841 saw the publication of *Master Timothy's Bookcase*. It is a collection of several short stories he wrote during the 1830s and given unity by having the title character, Timothy, travel through time and witnessing the events related in short stories such as *The Baroness*, *The Sculptor of Florence*, and others, all of which were taken from the *Monthly Magazine*. Although Reynolds reprinted a lot of previous material in *Master Timothy's Bookcase* it appears that reviewers assumed the work was wholly original. *The Era* reported that

Mr Reynolds has turned his literary attention to amplifying Mr Dickens's ideas, or rather carrying them out a little further than that ingenious gentleman himself. The first work we know of Mr Reynolds's is "Pickwick Abroad" and now he has given us "Master Timothy's Bookcase" in imitation of "Master Humphrey's Clock." With the originality which Mr Reynolds possesses and the evidence which all his works have given of rather an extensive acquaintance with the world, we could wish that he had not adopted the idea of any other author but struck an original path of his own ... It promises well, and contains evidence of no common observance of men and manners.[135]

Reynolds was, at this point in his career, a writer whose ideas were indeed rarely original, but as the reviewer pointed out: Reynolds was brilliant at adapting and expanding on the ideas of others. The publisher of *Master Timothy's Bookcase* thought this was a sound investment; the advance of £400 that Reynolds received for this novel from the publisher William Emans must surely have compensated for the loss of his editorial position at *The Teetotaler*.

A further £200 was added to Reynolds's wealth from the advance he received for a long satirical poem titled *A Sequel to Don Juan* in 1843. In emulation of Lord Byron's original *Don Juan* (1819–24) Reynolds's poem is full of innuendo and highly suggestive scenes which would become a feature of some of his later novels:

> The moment that her Grace dropt her disguise,
> And stood in a voluptuous undress,
> Revealing her ripe beauties—Juan's eyes
> Betrayed that joy which eyes alone express.
> A moment did he gaze—and then the prize,
> Self-given, was clasped with fervent eagerness:
> The Hebe Duchess seemed but little coy—
> Another Helen with her Phrygian boy!
>
> Entranced they lay—Juan's head pillowed on
> Her naked bosom, palpitating, warm:
> And, as he lay, his eyes could feast upon

The beauties of that rich voluptuous form,
O'er which an easy conquest he had won,
Without the tears of April or the storm
Of dark December to depreciate
Th' intoxicating joys of that blest state.[136]

This was certainly not 'quality' poetry but it might have raised an eyebrow and provoked a giggle among its readers. The £600 he received in these years meant that Reynolds and his family could move to new lodgings in what was, according to Collins, '[the] distinctly up market' King Square off Goswell Street.

It was here that, in 1844, Reynolds and Susannah had two more children: Theresa Isabella and Frederick. It was the house at King Square that Reynolds was visited for the first time, in 1844, by the publisher John Dicks—who would become an important figure in Reynolds's later life—and he recalled seeing Reynolds working at his craft: 'I found him in a back room, wrapped in a dingy dressing gown, and perched on a stool, writing away like a steam engine'.[137] Reynolds was working on something special when Dicks visited his house in 1844. It was a novel that was to make him famous—or infamous—in the Victorian literary world. It was the story of two brothers, one of whom followed the path of virtue, the other the path of vice. But before we learn more about this novel let us revisit Paris to learn about a novel which, between 1842 and 1843, had thrilled French readers.

In 'the city of strange contrasts': *The Mysteries of London* and the Urban Underworld

> Crime is abundant in this city: the lazar-house, the prison, the brothel, and the dark alley, are rife with all kinds of enormity; in the same way as the palace, the mansion, the clubhouse, the parliament, and the parsonage, are each and all characterised by their different degrees and shades of vice. But wherefore specify crime and vice by their real names, since in this city of which we speak they are absorbed in the multi-significant words—Wealth and Poverty? Crimes borrow their comparative shade of enormity from the people who perpetrate them: thus is it that the wealthy may commit all social offences with impunity; while the poor are cast into dungeons and coerced with chains, for only following at a humble distance in the pathway of their lordly precedents.
>
> George W.M. Reynolds,
> *The Mysteries of London* (1844–48)

> This man [is] a writer of wretched stuff in the form of penny novels, a would-be leader of Chartism, an Editor of periodicals less readable than the *Guardian*.
>
> *Lancaster Gazetteer* (1850)

On 19 June 1842, in the *feuilleton* section of the Parisian newspaper *Journal des Debats*, the first instalment of a new novel appeared. Written by Eugène Sue, who until this point was widely known as a historical novelist, this latest novel was of a wholly different character. The novel was called *Les Mystères des Paris* and, instead of being set in the past as Sue's previous works had been, it was set in Paris during the 1830s. The novel caused a sensation in Parisian society. The circulation of the *Journal des Débats* soared because the novel was a hit with all classes of French society. If a person could not read, it might be read to them by a work colleague or literate family member. Public libraries and reading rooms across France were forced to ration readers' time with the latest instalments. Cafés began charging customers ten sous for a copy. If Sue was a day late in submitting his copy to the editor, it was said that 'beautiful society ladies and chambermaids [were] all in a state of turmoil'.[138] Even Karl Marx, a political scientist who as a rule did not engage in literary criticism, made an exception for Sue's novel and offered an extended critique of it in *The Holy Family* (1844–45).

Although France had a thriving literary scene in the 1840s, Sue's novel was special because it was the first of its kind to shine a light on the crimes, vices, and follies of Parisians in both high and low life. Through the eyes of a man named Rodolph, a mysterious wanderer in the dirty and dingy courts and alleyways of Paris, readers were presented with shocking pictures of depravity: girls of sixteen whom poverty had reduced to prostitution; organised crime figures such as the menacing 'Schoolmaster' and his comrade Bras Rouge plotting their nefarious schemes; and adultery and political scheming among members of the aristocracy. An even more shocking aspect of this novel was that the low-born criminal characters often did the bidding of the seemingly genteel and respectable upper class figures. In Sue's novel the activities of the underworld, and upperworld figures were inextricably connected.

The novel was of course melodramatic. It featured clear good characters and bad ones. As the hero, Rodolphe, made his way through the dark parts of Paris on his self-imposed mission of doing good for the poor and destitute, danger awaited him at every turn. Menaced by the Schoolmaster and his henchmen, at one point Rodolphe is captured, interred in a subterranean vault, and almost dies. Many of the Sue's Parisian 'mysteries' unfolded through the revealing of secret notes. Some of the prominent characters were of 'mysterious' birth. The novel therefore gave birth to an entirely new genre: the urban gothic.[139] Sue took classic gothic motifs that had been a feature of older English-language gothic novels and French-language *romans noir*, but instead of setting his tale in a historical period or in very remote rural areas, as many early gothic novels did, Sue superimposed these motifs onto his stories of life in the modern industrial city.

'Mysterymania' soon spread to Britain where, because there were very few international copyright agreements, a number of translations of Sue's work appeared. There were six English translations of the full novel by 1844.[140] Commenting on the enthusiasm with which the novel was received in Britain, Alfred Crowquill—who provided the illustrations to *Pickwick Abroad* some years earlier—declared in *Bentley's Miscellany* that,

> Mysteries, it appears, are no longer to remain so. Authors …
> start up and show to the world that at least to them there
> never have been such things as mysteries. The veil of France
> is torn from her by a Frenchman, who certainly pays no
> high compliment to his country, by exposing vices of the
> most hideous character, and which are certainly much better
> hidden from both the young and old. The moral to be drawn
> from melodramatic vice and virtue is very questionable.[141]

Crowquill's comment, that some of the 'mysteries' would be 'much better hidden from both the young and old' may at first glance appear like the typical pearl-clutching moralism which inherent in much of the era's literary criticism. But it should be remembered that Sue's tale was one in which, while the hero Rodolphe does do many good deeds, he is a man who is unafraid to dispense summary, and brutal, justice to some of the villains from the Parisian underworld.

Rodolphe was actually the Grand Duke of Gerolstein, and could help the Parisian poor because he could afford to assist them. Yet his exalted rank means that, in some cases, he acts as judge, jury, and executioner. The Schoolmaster attempted to murder Rodolphe, but his plans are foiled, for Rodolphe and his servants got the miscreant completely in their power, and Rodolphe decided to punish him. But Rodolphe deemed it useless to hand over the man to the powers that be. Sue was highly critical of the French justice system. It seemed to him, and indeed many reformers of the time, to be ineffective at punishing criminals, and simply gave them an opportunity to refine their criminal talents in concert with the other reprobates with whom they were incarcerated.

51

Thus, Rodolphe reasoned that giving up the Schoolmaster to the galleys or the guillotine would do no one any good:

> "If on the other hand, you had braved the scaffold – as one having the murderer's only redeeming quality, personal courage – equally little would it have availed with me to have given you up to the executioner. For you, the scaffold would be merely an ensanguined stage; where, like so many others, you would make a parade of your ferocity; where, reckless of a miserable life, you would exhale your last breath with a blasphemy … It is not good for the people to see the criminal cracking jokes with the executioner, breathing out in a sneer … All crime may be expiated and redeemed, says the Saviour; but to that end, sincere repentance is necessary. From the tribunal to the scaffold, the journey is too short; it would not do, therefore, for you to die thus."[142]

Rodolphe therefore began to speak more cryptically:

> "You have criminally abused your strength – I will paralyse that strength; the strongest have trembled before you – you shall tremble before the weakest. Assassin! You have plunged the creatures of God into eternal night – the shadows of night eternal shall commence for you even in this world. This night – in a few minutes – your punishment shall equal your offences. But … the punishment I am about to pronounce leaves you a boundless horizon of repentance … I forever deprive you of all the splendours of creation … Yes! For ever isolated from the external world you will be forced to look constantly within yourself."[143]

Rodolphe did say, however, that the Schoolmaster would be provided for financially, and he placed 3,000 francs in the Schoolmaster's waistcoat. At this point, the schoolmaster was tied to a chair so tightly that he could not move an inch, and a doctor in attendance took the Schoolmaster out of the room. All became silent. Rodolphe's servant, the Chourineur, had no idea what was transpiring in the next room. Then the Schoolmaster was brought back in:

"Blind! Blind! Blind!" cried the brigand, in an increasing tone of agony.

"You are free – you have money – go!"

"But – I cannot go! How would you have me go? I cannot see! Oh it is a frightful crime thus to abuse your strength, in order to–"

"It is a crime to abuse one's strength," said Rodolphe, in his most solemn tones. "And then, what hast thou done with thy strength?"

"Oh death! Yes, I should have preferred death!" cried the schoolmaster, "to be at everyone's mercy, to be afraid of everything! Ah! A mere child can beat me now! What, oh! What shall I do? My God! My God! What shall I do?"

"You have money."

"I shall be robbed."

"You will be robbed! Do you understand these words which you pronounce with so much terror? Do you understand them – you, who have robbed so many? Go."[144]

Rodolphe was not totally unfeeling, however, and he commanded his servant to ensure that the Schoolmaster was cared for by being given a place to stay the night, and he was subsequently placed in the care of an honest and respectable family who live in a rural part of France.

Blinding ceased to be used as a punishment for crimes in Britain and France during the early modern period, and even then, it was rarely used.[145] By the time Eugène Sue was writing, it would have been regarded in both countries as a barbaric punishment. In spite of his novel having been inspired by readings of socialist literature, Sue was not sympathetic to those whom he viewed as *irredeemably* criminal. When, in 1850, Sue was elected to the French Legislative Assembly as the Red Republican and Socialist candidate, he advocated blinding as a means of reforming the irredeemably criminal, or at the very least, placing them in life-long solitary confinement.

Sue's Rodolphe views the righting of the wrongs and crimes of the poor as part of his aristocratic rights and responsibilities. Rodolphe had a lot of sympathy with those whom he views as the 'respectable' poor—that is, those who were deferential to their betters and strove to be virtuous. Hence, there was the sixteen-year-old La Goualese— eventually revealed to be Rodolphe's long lost daughter—who strove to be good in spite of her history as a prostitute, and was a member of the *deserving* poor because she tried to be pure and changes her ways. But Sue also accepted that there were some members of the poor who stood little chance of being reformed, and should, like the Schoolmaster, be cast out from society. Sue's Rodolphe, then, simply wanted to remove from society all of those people who did not conform to his world view.

As Sue's novel was making waves in Britain, Reynolds sought to cash in on the mysterymania, and he began writing *The Mysteries of London* in 1844. Although some of the motifs in Reynolds's *Mysteries* were borrowed from Sue's novel, Reynolds's own tale in some ways surpassed Sue's. Reynolds gave, not only a thrilling tale of the crimes and vices of those in high and low life, but offered thoughtful critiques on the condition of the poor and even hinted that a revolution might be required for the poor to ameliorate their condition. The novel is part-crime literature and partly a political manifesto, and a discussion of it reveals much about Reynolds's attitudes towards the aristocracy and the working classes.

The Mysteries of London, which was serialised in weekly penny numbers by George Vickers—a publisher known for smutty publications— between 1844 and 1848, and eventually ran to four volumes. A scale of *The Mysteries of London*'s popularity—or notoriety—can be gleaned from the words of one commentator who remarked:

> How is it that in quiet suburban neighbourhoods, far removed from the stews of London, and the pernicious atmosphere they engender; in serene and peaceful semi-country towns where genteel boarding schools flourish, there may almost invariably be found some small shopkeeper who accommodatingly receives consignments of ... the "Mysteries of London," and unobtrusively supplies his well-dressed little customer with these full-flavoured articles?

Granted, my dear sir, that your young Jack, or my twelve years old Robert, have minds too pure either to seek out or crave after literature of the sort in question, but not un-frequently it is found without seeking. It is a contagious disease, just as cholera and typhus and the plague are contagious, and, as everybody is aware, it needs not personal contact with a body stricken to convey either of these frightful maladies to the hale and hearty.[146]

With sales figures for each penny issue amounting to approximately 40,000 per week, *The Mysteries of London* has some claim to being the biggest-selling novel of the nineteenth century.[147]

Great Britain in *The Mysteries of London*, as Reynolds imagined it, is a dystopia much as, arguably, Victorian Britain was in real life.[148] Reynolds guided the reader through the social hell that was the modern industrial, capitalist society. It is a society in which a large underclass toiled daily for poverty wages, living in dwellings little better than hovels, while supporting the lifestyles of an aristocratic oligarchy.

The first two volumes told the story of two brothers, Richard and Eugene Markham, whose lives follow wildly different paths. Richard followed the path of virtue and honesty, while Eugène made his fortune through fraud and deceit. While one would expect in such a novel that all went well for Richard, it did not. Although his life looked set to follow that of any normal middle-class Victorian, he was befriended by conmen and, as a result of their machinations, was wrongly accused of a carrying forged notes, and was imprisoned in Newgate for two years. From there, his life spiralled into relative poverty, and he had the misfortune to make an enemy of the sinister Anthony Tidkins, 'the Resurrection Man'.

Reynolds saw society as being divided into three distinct classes: the aristocracy, the industrious classes, and the criminal classes, the last of which was the most fearsome. It was *The Mysteries of London* which was perceived by one commentator in the *Times* as having 'invented' the idea of the criminal underworld:

The supposed "Mysteries of London"' influenced people's belief in 'an underworld of crime and horrors ... and deeds [that] are daily perpetrated in this great city of which no one ever hears.[149]

Reynolds's depiction of how criminals operated was sophisticated and was perhaps informed by the fact that, having spent a good couple of years living in the worst part of the metropolis, he had probably encountered some very shady characters.

The principle villain, Anthony Tidkins, is in many respects a prototype of the modern-day organised crime boss. Tidkins's gang operated as a loose hierarchy, yet there is a sense that Tidkins and his immediate gang were part of a larger network of criminals. Some of the Resurrection Man's associates, for example, include an organisation that went by the name of The Forty Thieves, which meet at regular intervals in the Mint.[150] It is not only with the Forty Thieves that Tidkins had dealings, as readers were also introduced to 'The Old Hag'—a woman who is never called by her proper name—who enticed one of the heroines, Ellen Monroe, into a life of vice. Through the agency of the Old Hag, Ellen became a model for statuary, a sitter for an artist, a model for a bust-sculptor, and a photographer.[151] The fictional Ellen's fate was all too real for many young women whose choice was between starvation and prostitution.[152] At first the Old Hag's activities, which involve dealing with many a young girl as she did with Ellen, seem to have been carried out on an individual level. Yet by degrees Reynolds shows how the Old Hag's activities were interconnected with those of Tidkins.

Modern-day organised crime groups have proven time and again that they are resilient, and Reynolds understood this during his own time: if the head of the organisation, or some of its key members, were killed or incarcerated, the network usually carried on. The reader does not, in fact, encounter Tidkins until chapter twenty-eight, for he was incarcerated in Newgate.[153] Nevertheless, in the early part of the novel, his accomplices on the outside, Bolter and Flairer, expressed their intentions to carry on with the 'jobs' which had been planned by Tidkins before his arrest.[154]

Tidkins, the Cracksman, and their partners in crime Dick Flairer, Bill Bolter and the Buffer, inhabited the dark places of the metropolis. They were described as natives of 'all the flash-houses and patter cribs ... of Great Saffron-Hill'.[155] The same area was described by Reynolds as 'a labyrinth of dwellings whose very aspect appeared to speak of hideous poverty and fearful crime'.[156] The places from which these criminals hailed were areas into which the police seldom ventured. Even if the police made an appearance in the back streets of Saffron Hill, there were places in the labyrinthine alleyways of that district 'in which a man might hide for fifty years and never be smelt out by the police'.[157] Reynolds clearly had little faith in the abilities of the recently-established Metropolitan Police because his criminal characters, clearly unconcerned, view the force as inept:

> "Lord, how much coves as you and me laugh when them chaps in the Common Council and the House of Commons gets on their legs and praises the work of the bluebottles up to the skies as the most acutest police in the world, while they votes away the people's money to maintain 'em!"[158]

When the virtuous hero Richard Markham does approach the police to help him with matters they are not of much use and it is Richard and his friends who have to foil the plots of the notorious criminals. Reynolds's representation of the uselessness of the police at this point reflected the reality of the situation; Clive Emsley notes that in their early years, because the force was relatively small, 'the police were not around when they were needed either to prevent crime or to help victims seize offenders'.[159]

Reynolds's criminal characters form an almost separate society with their own laws and language, or 'thieves' cant', which Reynolds incorporated into his criminal characters' dialogue. For example, 'The Thieves' Alphabet' is a song sung by the Cracksman in one of the 'boozing kens':

> A was an Area-sneak leary and sly;
> B was a Buzgloak, with fingers so fly;
> C was a Cracksman, that forked all the plate;
> D was a Dubsman, who kept the jug-gate.
>> For we are rollicking chaps,
>> All smoking, singing, boosing;
>> We care not for the traps,
>> But pass the night carousing!
>
> E was an Efter that went to the play;
> F was a Fogle he knapped on his way;
> G was a Gag, which he told to the beak;
> H was a Hum-box where parish-prigs speak.
>> CHORUS

I was an Ikey with swag all encumbered;
J was a Jug, in whose cell he was lumbered;
K was a Kye-bosh that paid for his treat;
L was a Leaf that fell under his feet.
        CHORUS.[160]

In footnotes, Reynolds translated this language for his readers: 'ikey' was a Jewish fence, no doubt inspired by the real-life Jewish fence Ikey Solomon. 'Efter' was a thief who frequents theatres. A 'leaf' referred to a hanged criminal.[161]

Thus Reynolds was aware of how crime was evolving in modern capitalist society. In undertaking their criminal activities, for example, the villains were motivated *solely* by the prospect of financial gain. As Tidkins exclaimed: 'I can soon learn any business that's to make money'.[162] Tidkins's gang carried out a variety of illegal activities to make money. As his alias of the Resurrection Man implied, his stock-in-trade is body snatching—the selling of dead cadavers to physicians for dissection. Although it was perhaps a necessary evil, being vital for medical research, Tidkins was uninterested in the advancement of medical knowledge. He and his confederates dig up fresh corpses to earn money.[163]

Tidkins's gang also resorted to extortion, particularly when they were in possession of potentially embarrassing information on someone who was seemingly respectable. When Tidkins visits the crooked stockbroker Mr Tomlinson, for example, the following scene occurs:

> "And what can I do for you, Mr. Tidkins?" asked the stock-broker, In a tremulous tone; for he felt a desperate alarm lest the Resurrection Man should have discovered the one secret which he had taken so much pains to conceal…

> "I have but two wants in the world at any time," answered the Resurrection Man, lighting his pipe: "money most often — vengeance now and then. But it is money that I want of you."[164]

Reynolds's disdain for politicians comes through when he showed Tidkins and his gang collaborating with them. For example, the Cracksman was asked to undertake of a highway robbery by Mr Greenwood, MP for Rottenborough, who plotted to defraud Count Alteroni of his fortune. But first Greenwood must acquire a vital document from Alteroni and for this he employed the services of the Cracksman:

"What's the natur' of the service?" demanded the Cracksman, darting a keen and penetrating glance at Greenwood.

"A highway robbery," coolly answered [Greenwood ...]

"All right!" cried the Cracksman. "Now what's the robbery, and what's the reward?"

"Are you man enough to do it alone?"

"I'm man enow to try it on; but if so be the chap is stronger than me—"

"He is a tall, powerful person, and by no means likely to surrender without a desperate resistance."

"Well, all that can be arranged," said the Cracksman, coolly. "Not knowing what you wanted with me, I brought two of my pals along with me [one of these pals is the Resurrection Man], and they're out in the street, or in the alley leading into the park. If there'd been anything wrong on your part, they would either have rescued me or marked you and your house for future punishment."

"I am glad that you have your companions so near [...] I will now explain to you what I want done. Between eleven and twelve o'clock a gentleman will leave London for Richmond. He will be in his own cabriolet, with a tiger, only twelve years old, behind. The cab is light blue – the wheels streaked with white. This is peculiar, and cannot be mistaken. The horse is a tall bay, with silver- mounted harness. This gentleman must be stopped; and everything his pockets contain - everything, mind – must be brought to me. Whatever money there may be about him shall be yours, and I will add fifty guineas to the amount: - but all that you find about his person, save the money, must be handed over to me."[165]

Note the precision with which the robbery is to be carried out: clear and concise instructions were given. The deed is not a romantic highway robbery of the kind that was told in the novels of Walter Scott. Instead, according to Reynolds, crime in the urban, industrial society is cold and calculated.

Highway robbery is not the only crime which the aristocratic and bourgeois elites ask the Resurrection Man to carry out for them, for occasionally they involve even those of a darker nature—murder! Reynolds despised the aristocracy and his noble characters were in fact not very noble at all. For example, the *Mysteries* introduces Lady Adeline Ravensworth whose life, married to Lord Ravensworth, would seem to be free from hardship. Yet by chance a new Lady's Maid named Lydia is employed by the housekeeper. However, Lady Ravensworth and Lydia have a history: the pair were once friends and the latter knows that Lady Ravensworth had a child out of wedlock and disposed of the baby. Once this happened, the lady cast Lydia aside, after which she fell into dire poverty. When she entered into service at Ravensworth Hall— initially without Lady Ravensworth's knowledge—the pair finally met and Lydia threatened to tell all the other servants and the newspapers if she were dismissed. Lydia then devised mental tortures for her former friend. A flavour of the tortures that Lydia inflicted on the proud and haughty aristocrat is given below:

> "Yes — I am here again," said the vindictive woman. "It is time for you to rise."

> "Oh! spare me, Lydia," exclaimed Adeline; "Let me to repose a little longer. I have passed a wretched — a sleepless night: see — my pillow is still moist with the tears of anguish which I have shed; and it was but an hour ago that I fell into an uneasy slumber! I cannot live thus — I would rather that you should take a dagger and plunge it into my heart at once. Oh! leave me — leave me to rest for only another hour!"

"No: — it is time to rise, I say," cried Lydia. "It has been my destiny to pass many long weary nights in the streets — in the depth of winter — and with the icy wind penetrating through my scanty clothing till it seemed to freeze the very marrow in my bones. I have been so wearied — so cold — so broken down for want of sleep, that I would have given ten years of my life for two hours' repose in a warm and comfortable bed: — but still have I often, in those times, passed a whole week without so resting my sinking frame. Think you, then, that I can now permit *you* the luxury of sleep when your body requires it — of repose when your mind needs it? No, Adeline — no! I cannot turn you forth into the streets to become a houseless wanderer, as I have been: — but I can at least arouse you from the indolent enjoyment of that bed of down."

… Then the revengeful woman seated herself in a chair, and said in a harsh tone, "Light the fire, Adeline — I am cold."

"No — no: I will not be *your* servant!" exclaimed Lady Ravensworth. "You are *mine* — and it is for you to do those menial offices."

"Provoke me not, Adeline," said Lydia Hutchinson, coolly; "or I will repair straight to the servants' hall, and there proclaim the astounding fact that Lord Ravensworth's relapse has been produced by the discovery of his wife's frailty ere their marriage."

"Oh! my God — what will become of me!" murmured Adeline, wringing her hands. "Are you a woman? or are you a fiend!"

"I am a woman — and one who, having suffered much, knows how to revenge deeply," returned Lydia. "You shall obey me — or I will cover you with shame!"

Adeline made no reply; but, with scalding tears trickling down her cheeks, she proceeded — yes, she — the high-born peeress! — to arrange the wood in the grate — to heap up the coals — and to light the fire.

And while she was kneeling in the performance of that menial task, — while her delicate white hands were coming in contact with the black grate, — and while she was shivering in her night gear, and her long dishevelled hair streamed over her naked neck and bosom, — there, within a few feet of her, sate the menial — the servant, comfortably placed in an arm-chair, and calmly surveying the degrading occupation of her mistress.

"I have often — Oh! how often — longed for a stick of wood and a morsel of coal to make myself a fire, if no larger than sufficient to warm the palms of my almost frostbitten hands," said Lydia, after a short pause; "and when I have dragged my weary limbs past the houses of the rich, and have caught sight of the cheerful flames blazing through the area-windows of their kitchens, I have thought to myself, *'Oh! for one hour to sit within the influence of that genial warmth!'* And yet you — *you,* the proud daughter of the aristocracy — recoil in disgust from a task which so many thousands of poor creatures would only be too glad to have an opportunity of performing!"

Adeline sobbed bitterly, but made no reply.[166]

The tables have turned on the haughty aristocrat, and Reynolds must have relished writing this scene. However, Lady Ravensworth sought out someone who will help to put an end to her troubles forever, and Tidkins is just the demon to do the job:

"...Now, ma'am, answer me as frankly as I have spoken to you. You have a bitter enemy?"

"I have indeed," answered Adeline, reassured that she was not known to the Resurrection Man: "and that enemy is a woman."

"Saving your presence, ma'am, a woman is a worse enemy than a man," said Tidkins. "And of course you wish to get your enemy out of the way by some means!"

"I do," replied Adeline, in a low and hoarse tone — as if she only uttered those monosyllables with a great exertion.

"There are two ways, ma'am," said the Resurrection Man, significantly: "confinement in a dungeon, or—"

"I understand you," interrupted Lady Ravensworth, hastily. "Oh! I am at a loss which course to adopt — which plan to decide upon! Heaven knows I shrink from the extreme one — and yet—"

"The dead tell no tales," observed Tidkins, in a low and measured tone.[167]

Tidkins agrees to take on this contract killing and Lydia was soon murdered at his hands. Her body is unceremoniously buried in a shallow grave in the grounds of Ravensworth Hall.

Karl Marx and Friedrich Engels noted in *The Communist Manifesto* in 1848 that the emergence of bourgeois capitalist society had

> Destroyed all feudal, patriarchal, idyllic relations between men. They relentlessly tore asunder the many-sided links of that feudal chain which bound men to their "natural superiors," and they left no bond of union between man and man, save that of bare self-interest, of cash payments.[168]

Whereas in the pre-modern era the aristocracy felt some social obligation to their social inferiors, in the modern capitalist world where people strive for wealth the elites feel as though they have very little responsibility to provide for the less fortunate. Economic and social developments in the underworld mirror those in the upperworld. There may have been, once upon a time, a sense of honour among thieves; Robin Hood and his men, and the highwaymen of the eighteenth century were rarely extravagant in robbing from people, and they mostly took only what they needed for their own subsistence and nothing more. Reynolds kept returning to the message: crime is money. Crime in capitalist societies are a business. Society had become capitalist, so too had its criminals. Crime in *The Mysteries of London* is therefore about making money. For example, before the Cracksman commits the crime against Count Alteroni, he received an 'advance' of twenty guineas, at which the Cracksman exclaimed: 'that's business!'[169] The robbery is carried out, and at Eugène and the Cracksman's second meeting the villains were paid in full for their work. The meeting was concluded with the Cracksman hoping *'that he should have his custom in future'*.[170] To Reynolds's criminal characters, surgeons were their *customers*, or they made themselves available as henchmen-for-hire, willing to do the dirty work of those in from supposedly more respectable stations in life as long as the price is right.

Matters only became complicated for individual gang members when they committed crimes that awere not related to the pursuit of financial gain. For example, in a scene reminiscent of Bill Sikes' murder of Nancy, Bill Bolter kills his wife:

> The woman fell forward, and struck her face violently against the corner of the deal table. Her left eye came in contact with the angle of the board, and was literally crushed in its socket – an awful retribution upon her who only a few hours before was planning how to plunge her innocent and helpless daughter into the eternal night of blindness. She fell upon the floor, and a low moan escaped our lips. She endeavoured to carry her right hand to her now sightless eye; but her strength failed her, and her arm fell lifeless by her side. She was dying.[171]

However, Bolter's wife was not a sympathetic character, such as was Dickens's Nancy: she had plotted to make her four-year-old daughter blind, as she believed that the well-to-do would be more inclined to give a small blind girl charity. But in adherence to the adage, 'murder will out', despite his attempts to hide from the law, Bolter was eventually arrested and hanged for his crime.[172]

While Tidkins and his gang are by no means Robin Hood figures, Reynolds also understood that gangs usually had their own code of honour.

The seeds of Tidkins's downfall are laid at the beginning of Reynolds's novel when it is revealed that he turned evidence against a former associate named Crankey Jem, in return for immunity from prosecution. This was against the gang's code of honour. Tidkins walked free while Jem was sentenced to Transportation.[173] Late in the novel, Jem returned to England to exact his revenge on Tidkins for betraying him, and Jem eventually got Tidkins in his power, imprisoned him in a subterranean dungeon, and left him to die by starvation.[174] Had the Resurrection Man adhered to the gang's unwritten code of honour never to betray one another, he should not have met such a violent end Crankey Jem's hands.

Thus Reynolds, much like Eugène Sue's Rodolphe, did not view the poor as saintly, and he was well aware that some members of the poorer classes could be guilty of heinous criminal acts. But it was the way that society treated the poor which made the upper classes responsible for their criminality, especially when the choice for many poor people was a life in the workhouse or a life of crime.[175]

Although Tidkins was a menacing character, Reynolds humanised him by giving him a lengthy backstory. In his youth, Tidkins's father was arrested for smuggling and, despite the fact that the local worthies all purchased his contraband without compunction, he found his whole family condemned, and

> "This business again set me a-thinking; and I began to comprehend that birth and station made an immense difference in the views that the world adopted of men's actions. My father, who had only higgled and fiddled with smuggling affairs upon a miserably small scale, was set down as the most atrocious monster unhung, because he was one of the common herd; but the baronet, who had carried on a systematic contraband trade to an immense amount, was looked upon as a martyr to tyrannical laws, because he was one of the upper classes and possessed a title. So my disposition was soured by these proofs of human injustice, at my very entrance upon life."[176]

He was soon after imprisoned at the whim of a local baronet, and the Resurrection Man began to realise the inherent nature of the hypocrisy of the upper classes towards their social inferiors. He started to resent the double standards of morality applied to the aristocracy and the working classes. He then related his metamorphosis from a once virtuous adolescent into a hardened criminal in the following manner:

> I could not see any advantage in being good. I could not find out any inducement to be honest. As for a desire to lead an honourable life, that was absurd. I now laughed the idea to scorn; and I swore within myself that whenever I did commence a course of crime, I would be an unsparing demon at my work. Oh! How I then detested the very name of virtue.[177]

Towards the close of his history Tidkins said that 'the rich are prepared to believe any infamy which is imputed to the poor'.[178] By this means, as Reynolds shows, nineteenth-century society got the criminals that it deserved. The Resurrection Man is merely living up to society's expectations of him.

The criminals' biographies in *The Mysteries of London* were Reynolds's way of providing nuance to contemporary beliefs about the existence of a supposed criminal class. Most of the offenders who appeared in the dock at the Old Bailey during the early part of the nineteenth century were drawn from the poorer classes and a great majority of the working poor were increasingly perceived of as a criminal 'Other'.[179] This attitude was reflected in the remarks of William Augustus Miles, who said in 1839, that there are some people whose education and upbringing among the poorer classes 'prevent the possibility of reformation, and whom no punishment can deter' and that they were essentially 'a race *sui generis*, different from the rest of society, not only in thoughts, habits, and manners, but even in appearance, possessing, moreover, a language exclusively of their own'.[180]

But *The Mysteries of London* was not only a tale about the criminal poor and their collaboration with the aristocracy, for in the novel the upper classes were quite capable of committing crimes without the help of underworld figures. The MP Mr Greenwood, for instance, along with several other MPs, a Lord, and the Sheriff of London were seen conspiring together to establish a fraudulent railway company at Greenwood's dinner party:

Algiers, Oran, and Morocco Great Desert Railway.
(Provisionally Registered Pursuant to Act.)
Capital £1,200,000, in 80,000 shares, of £20 each.
Deposit £2 2s. per Share.

Committee of Direction: The Most Honourable Marquis
of Holmesford, G. C. B. Chairman. – George Montague
Greenwood, Esq. M.P. Deputy Chairman.[181]

Greenwood—who turns out to be Richard Markham's 'bad' brother—
assured those assembled at his dinner party that no such railway scheme
existed, and that it had only been devised solely for defrauding investors:

> "And now, my lord and gentlemen, we perfectly understand
> each other. Each takes as many shares as he pleases. When
> they reach a high premium, each may sell as he thinks fit.
> Then, when we have realized our profits, we will inform
> the shareholders that insuperable difficulties prevent the
> carrying out of the project,—that Abd-el-Kadir, for instance,
> has violated his agreement and declared against the scheme,-
> that the Committee of Direction will, therefore, retain a
> sum sufficient to defray the expenses already incurred, and
> that the remaining capital paid up shall be returned to the
> shareholders."[182]

This is an example of what might now be termed 'white collar crime'
and reflects the 'Railway Mania' of 1846-47, which was occurring
when Reynolds was writing the passage above. The wealthier classes
enthusiastically invested in many speculative railway schemes at
this time.[183] But the schemes, many of which sounded too good to be
true, were perfect for fraudsters wishing to embezzle funds from their
investors because investors had very little access to sound financial
advice and accurate financial data.

Sue and Reynolds's portrayals of vice and crime in high and low life
were a sensation and, to Victorian readers, *The Mysteries of London* and
its sister novel by Sue were considered 'classics'.[184] The mysteries genre
was here to stay. *The Mysteries of London* made Reynolds famous in the
United States as well, where several publishers began printing it, although

the titles of these reprints were often amended. *Life in London*, for example, was the title that one New York publisher gave to the *Mysteries*. Due to the lack of international copyright agreements, Reynolds did not earn any money on these reprints. American publishers also had the audacity to attach Reynolds's name to novels that were not written by him. Two American publishers in particular were notorious for this: the New York publisher Hurst and Company, and the Philadelphia-based T.B. Peterson. James Malcolm Rymer's *Mabel* (1846), for example, was republished by Hurst as *The Child of Waterloo* with Reynolds's name on the title page. A total of twenty-seven different titles were spuriously advertised in the United States as having been written by Reynolds and he repeatedly had to disavow them in the *Miscellany*. Given Reynolds's own pirating of other people's work earlier in his career, however, he hardly had the moral high ground on this issue.

The First Series of *The Mysteries of London* ended in 1846. Reynolds brought out a Second Series, which was, like the first, serialised in weekly penny numbers between 1846 and 1848. The *Mysteries* was by no means Reynolds's only project between 1845 and 1846, for Reynolds secured the position of editor for George Stiff and George Vickers's *London Journal*. It was a magazine that lasted until the twentieth century, and it was Reynolds who set it on its path to becoming one of the Victorian era's most widely-read magazines. Sold weekly and costing only one penny, the *London Journal* contained serialised instalments of novels, short fiction, poetry, and essays upon various political and philosophical subjects. It did not contain news, otherwise the proprietors would have had to pay the stamp tax and the journal would have cost much more. Its content and its low cost meant that it was a journal bought mostly by lower middle and working class readers.

It was in the *London Journal* that Reynolds's first supernatural novel appeared titled *Faust: A Romance of the Secret Tribunals*, which was serialised between 1846 and 1847. Based upon a centuries-old German folktale, the title character, Faust, sold his soul to Satan to enjoy luxury and fame on earth for a limited period, at the end of which, demons dragged him to Hell. This was not the first time that the Faust legend had been retold in English; one of Shakespeare's contemporaries, Christopher Marlowe, put his own spin on the tale in his play *Doctor Faustus* (1592). Reynolds's version bears very little resemblance to either the German folk tale, or to Marlowe's play. At nearly 250,000 words, it was a long novel with intricate subplots that were both entertaining and educational.[185] Marlowe's Faust was a fairly sympathetic character, who was led astray by the villain Mephistopheles, but in Reynolds's version of the tale, Faust was evil and took pleasure in causing death and destruction. For example, having been wronged by Count Otto of Vienna—the novel's true hero—Faust asksed the demon to punish the entire city and its inhabitants:

> "These, then, are my Wishes—these are my commands," exclaimed Faust, who was in a state of extraordinary mental excitement:—"by means of thine infernal power thou wilt perform some deed that shall avert the attention of Vienna from the everyday pursuits of life—that shall paralyse public affairs and private arrangements—that shall cause even lovers to forget their hopes of being immediately united at the altar!"[186]

The demon therefore struck the city of Vienna with the Black Death. With scenes reminiscent of modern pandemic movies, Reynolds painted a picture of chaos and hopelessness. However, Victorian readers' favourite characters seemed to be Faust and the demon, rather than the actual hero Count Otto.[187] So when the serialisation of *Faust* ended, Reynolds knew that readers would want to see him again, and indeed he did reappear in a later novel.

Meantime, the Reynolds family had moved house again, and by November 1846, were living at 11 Powell Street West, off Goswell Road.[188] Destroyed during the Blitz, old photographs of the street reveal that it was mainly filled with Georgian townhouses, this residence marked a further improvement in the Reynolds family's finances.[189] However, Reynolds quarrelled with Stiff and Vickers, the publishers of the *Mysteries* and proprietors of the *London Journal*. Although the details of these men's fall out are murky, it was probably over money that they argued. Perhaps they were not paying Reynolds his due? As we shall see later, Stiff and Vickers were unscrupulous in their business transactions. It is not outside of the bounds of possibility that they were not forthcoming with Reynolds's wages. Besides, Reynolds, who was by then a household name because of the success of the *Mysteries*, was capable of striking out on his own. In partnership with the publisher

John Dicks, Reynolds launched a new magazine: *Reynolds's Miscellany of Romance, General Literature, Science and Art* (the first few issues were called *Reynolds's Magazine*). Published from the 'Miscellany Office' at 7 Brydges Street, Covent Garden,[190] the first issue appeared on 7 November 1846 and its opening address declared that,

> The projector of this MISCELLANY has determined to blend Instruction and Amusement; and to allot a fair proportion of each Number of Useful Articles, as well as to Tales and Light Reading ... Appearing in opposition to no existing Cheap Publication,—started without the least idea of rivalry,—and issued in the full belief that there is room for its being, without displacing any other, this MISCELLANY is established to supply a desideratum which has for some time been acknowledged.[191]

In that issue was the first instalment of another famous Reynolds story: *Wagner the Wehr-Wolf*. It takes place in the same universe as *Faust*. The reader first meets Wagner when he was an old shepherd living alone in a hut on the edge of the Black Forest. There was a knock at the door, and a younger, mysterious stranger entered and requested asylum from the tempest outside. The two men struck up a conversation, and the stranger told Wagner that he could make him young again. The man's eyes lit up. But there was one condition: on the last day of every month Wagner would transform into a savage, murderous animal.[192] Wagner accepted this condition. The stranger of course would be familiar to Reynolds's readers: it was Faust who had visited Wagner in his cottage. Having sold his soul to the devil, Faust resolved to create a race of monsters to 'prey upon the human race, whom I hate; because of all the world alone I am so deeply, so terribly accurst'.[193] The usual scenes of violence, intrigue, and sex followed in the novel, and the public lapped it up; *Reynolds's Miscellany* was on its way to becoming a serious rival to the *London Journal*.

After the final instalment of *Wagner the Wehr-Wolf*, Reynolds began another mysteries' tale for the *Miscellany*, titled *The Days of Hogarth; or, The Mysteries of Old London* (1847). This was an adaptation of William Hogarth's *Industry and Idleness* paintings from a century earlier, and follows the life stories of two boys: Tom Goodchild and

Tom Idle. Goodchild, by being an honest hardworking fellow, became a magistrate, and Idle became a highwayman and is eventually hanged. With *Wagner the Wehr-Wolf*, *The Mysteries of London*, and his earliest *Pickwick Abroad*, Reynolds had proved himself an able novelist who could move between genres as diverse as the historical, the gothic, the supernatural, crime, and comedy.

Susannah was not idle at this point, either. She contributed a long-running series of 'Practical Receipts' to *Reynolds's Miscellany*. These were a variety of recipes, fashion tips, and home remedies that might help poorer families eat well and feel good on a limited budget. It was a popular series too, and was later published as a standalone work titled *The Household Book of Practical Receipts*. Both Reynolds, Susannah, as well as other employees, appear to have contributed a series of articles titled 'Letters to the Industrious Classes' which gave readers advice on a variety of issues including, but not limited to, employment rights and politics.

Susannah even started her own short-lived literary magazine titled *The Weekly Magazine*. She served as its editor and it featured, much like *Reynolds's Miscellany*, essays and serial fiction by herself and Edwin F. Roberts, a fellow radical and friend of the Reynolds family.

Just like her husband, Susannah was no stranger to criticism from the press. Her own novel *Gretna Green; or, All for Love* (1847–50) drew the ire of Victorian moralists, and the controversy over the novel began as a dispute between the Reynolds family and their neighbours. At some point in 1847, the Reynolds family had moved to 7 Wellington Street, which served as their home and the office for the *Miscellany*. It seems that Reynolds and Susannah's neighbours at 2 Wellington Street—the legal firm of Roche, Plowman, and Roche—disliked sharing a street with the publishers of 'low' literature. So, these solicitors took it upon themselves to the *Daily News* to complain about the 'impurity' of Susannah's *Gretna Green*. The *Daily News* then published the following remarks:

> The group of publications more immediately under our notice today have a still more insidious and deleterious influence. They act more directly and openly upon the worst passions, stimulating them to precocious and unnatural activity, and exercise an unsettling and disturbing power over the moral consciousness of the reader. [They]

71

deal principally in the criminal ... in the licentious and blasphemous ... We denounce the impurity, but we cannot soil our pages with it—not even as a warning. Those imperil the sanctity of the sentiments which hold men together in society, by investing crime, outrage, violence, disobedience to the laws, with the attributes of heroism ... These poison the very foundations of human life ... The batch of serials under consideration, and the perusal of which has induced the above observations, are—*Reynolds's Miscellany of Romance, General Literature, Science, and Art*; *Gretna Green, or all for Love*, by Mrs George W.M. Reynolds; *The Mysteries of London*.[194]

Reynolds was used to criticism and brushed off any aspersions cast on his own character as a result of negative press. But his wife's work had been criticised. Reynolds leapt to her defence in the pages of the 'Second Series' of *The Mysteries of London* and *Reynolds's Miscellany*. The following was a note which Reynolds inserted into the former:

An obscure threepenny print, called the *Daily News*, published in its impression of November 2nd, an article purporting to be a notice of the leading works belonging to the sphere of Cheap Literature, but in which a vile, cowardly, and ruffian-like attack was made upon Mrs. Reynolds's novel of *Gretna Green*. The article alluded to appeared in the evening of the same date in the *Express*, a paper made up from the contents of the other, but of whose existence we were totally unaware until the occurrence of the matter in question. The attack, though evidently written by some silly boy, was so savage and malignant, and was made up of such a pack of atrocious lies, that it became necessary to take some kind of notice of it, although neither the *Daily News* nor its evening reflex enjoy a circulation or an influence sufficient to effect the amount of mischief which the dastardly scribe sought to accomplish.[195]

Reynolds then implied that perhaps his rival Dickens was behind the attack in the *Daily News*, given that the famous author had had a hand in establishing the paper. But this was not all—in the next week's instalment of *The Mysteries of London* Reynolds had his characters mock the *Daily News* and the *Express*:

"Did you ever happen to read the *Daily News*?"

"I have never seen the paper in my life," answered Mr. Styles: "I had only heard of it."

"And you are not likely to see it," returned the agent, "unless you go into the heart of Wapping or explore the back slums of Whitechapel. No respectable newsman keeps it: not that newsmen are more particular than other shop-keepers—but they only keep what they can sell, Mr. Styles. As for the *Express*, it is a regular cheat of an evening paper—made up entirely of the articles in the *Daily News*, without even having the bad grammar and the typographical errors corrected. But both prints are the most contemptible threepenny things I ever saw in my life; and one would be inclined to fancy that all the real newspaper talent had been absorbed by the pre-existing journals, leaving only the meanest literary scrubs in London to *do* the *News* and the *Express*."

"And yet I thought that the *News* had been started under the auspices of Mr. Charles Dickens—the immortal *Boz*?" said Mr. Styles, interrogatively.

"So it was," replied the advertising agent: "but the name of Charles Dickens was rather damnatory than useful to a newspaper-speculation. Everyone must admit that *Boz* is a great novelist—a very great novelist indeed—the Fielding of his age; but he is totally incapable of writing for a newspaper. The proprietors of the *News* made a tremendous splash with his name; but they only created a quagmire for themselves to flounder in. When their paper was first coming out, every body thought it was to do wonders. The *Times* was to lose half its subscribers; and the *Chronicle* was to be ruined altogether. But, alas! never did so labouring a mountain produce such a contemptible mouse; and people began to fancy that the wags engaged on *Punch* had started the *Daily News* as a grand parody on the newspaper press.[196]

This seemed to be an end to the matter. The *Daily News* did not go after Susannah again. Yet soon Reynolds would draw controversy, not only for his literary work, but also for his political activism and the leading of a 'queer revolution' in Trafalgar Square in 1848.

'Universal suffrage in the hands of the people': Reynolds's Political Activism

> It was well known that, with [Reynolds], politics amounted almost to a mania, so deeply did he feel the wrongs and tyrannies under which the working classes groaned … and he hoped that when they left, they would do so, seriously impressed with the magnitude of the duty which they owed to themselves, their children, their neighbours, and posterity, and endeavour to do their utmost to undermine the foundations of the present iniquitous social system.
>
> *Reynolds's Weekly Newspaper* (1851)

> Where then is British Freedom? Does it consist in the right of the few to revel in luxury, while the millions starve? If so, the privileged orders are free enough, heaven knows!— but no condition of slavery can possibly be more hideous, more scandalous, or more inhuman than the serfdom of the workers and toilers in this country.
>
> *Reynolds's Weekly Newspaper* (1850)

Reynolds may have fallen out with Vickers and Stiff, but he was still under contract to write a Second Series of *The Mysteries of London* until 1848. With characters such as Richard Markham briefly reappearing in it, the Second Series was a direct continuation of the first, although the main focus was upon a different set of people and their lives. There are two heroes in the 'Second Series': the Earl of Ellingham and his long-lost brother Thomas Rainford, a highwaymen.

The character of the Earl of Ellingham actually gives us a glimpse into Reynolds's political ideology. Although a member of the House of

75

Lords, he was a principled democrat who believed that all men should have the right to vote in general elections. With the 'Second Series', then, Reynolds had become a Chartist activist. While his First Series of *The Mysteries of London* was certainly anti-establishment and anti-monarchy, the Second Series was decidedly radical and explicitly pro-Chartist.

Some context is needed: prior to 1832, the only people who had the right to vote in general elections were people who owned property worth over 40s. The number of voters in each constituency, moreover, was not uniform throughout the country. Small towns might return two MPs to parliament, but large towns such as Manchester and Leeds had no parliamentary representation but were represented at the borough or county level. During the late eighteenth and early nineteenth centuries radicals mounted several campaigns for the extension of the franchise, but these fell on deaf ears. Having fought a war against revolutionary and Napoleonic France between 1793 and 1815, the government clamped down on the activities of pro-democracy campaigners at home by restricting freedom of assembly and freedom of the press. Several pro-democracy riots and protests were held in the post-war period in cities throughout the country and these were sometimes brutally suppressed, just like what happened at the Peterloo Massacre at Manchester in August 1819.

The campaign for reform, however, received boost in 1830, when Earl Grey's Whigs won the election. Grey had supported parliamentary reform as early as 1792. Having won the election in 1830, the Whigs tried to pass two reform bills that would have extended the franchise and redrawn the constituency map. But both of these Bills were rejected by Tory peers in the House of Lords, who at this time could veto any law, and when Tory lords did reject the bill, Grey had no choice but to resign.

The king then invited the Tory Duke of Wellington to form the next government, but he could not command the confidence of the house or the country. Campaigners and protesters began calling for tax evasion, a run on the banks, and even the abolition of the monarchy. Wellington soon resigned. The king then invited Grey and the Whigs to form the next government. Wisely, Wellington counselled Tory peers in the Lords not to oppose the passage of the Reform Bill when it was sent up for another reading. The Bill passed and the so-called Great Reform Act received Royal Assent on 7 June 1832.

But the Great Reform Act did not grant universal suffrage. The forty shilling freehold property requirement remained for voters in the towns and boroughs. Copyhold property owners—that is, people who rented land from a manorial lord that could not be passed on to one's descendants—were also given the vote. Another enfranchised group were those who paid £50 per annum in rent. New constituencies were created to represent the manufacturing towns, although some constituencies still had too few voters while others had too many.

The Reform Act divided reformers. Prior to 1832, the middle and working classes both campaigned for the vote. After 1832, the working classes felt abandoned, and there was much bitterness, especially when in 1834, the Poor Law Amendment Act was passed, which extended the workhouse system; its imposition upon the poor seemed to be a sign that the middle classes and aristocracy were conspiring to punish them. It was clear that the working classes had to organise among themselves and put pressure on the government. To this end, a number of associations were founded such as The London Working Men's Association, the National Political Union, and the Manchester Political Union. Then in 1837, six MPs and six educated working men drafted the People's Charter which, in its final form, included six demands: the vote for *all* men over the age of twenty-one; vote by secret ballot; equally-sized electoral districts; the abolition of property qualifications to become an MP; payment of MPs, and annual elections.

Reynolds said little about this 'Chartist' movement in its early years, and what he did say about the movement in 1843 was disparaging:

> The Chartists are the worst enemies in existence to the cause of true freedom. They would claim universal suffrage immediately, when the people are not predisposed by education to exercise the privilege with judgment. As it is, votes are unblushingly sold for money and beer; how much greater would be the amount of bribery if the franchise were extended. Educate the people first—education is their right—their privilege; and then give them universal suffrage, which will, in that case, become their right and privilege also. The Chartists, by their clamorous, intemperate, and absurd conduct, have done much to render the cause of true freedom unpopular with men of even the most liberal minds. God protect this country when such insane men as the Chartists shall become actively interested in its legislation. A true

republican spirit revolts from a mere factious display of prejudice, conceit, and wrong-headedness. Universal suffrage in the hands of the people before they are educated would be as dangerous as a razor in the possession of an infant.[197]

These early remarks were later offered as evidence by one of Reynolds's detractors to suggest that Reynolds was never genuine in his commitment to the democratic cause. It seems rather unfair, however, to assume that these early dismissive remarks about the Chartist cause were representative of his views in later life. It is always best to bear in mind Jonathan Swift's words on this point: 'If a man would register all his opinions on love, politicks, religion, learning and the like; beginning from his youth, and so go on to old age, what a bundle of inconsistencies and contradictions would appear at last?' People change their opinions frequently and it can be stated with much confidence that, by 1847, and in spite of his earlier denigration of the movement, Reynolds had changed his mind and wholeheartedly endorsed the Chartist cause. This was clear when, in the 'Second Series' of the *Mysteries*, Reynolds abruptly broke his narrative in one issue and began talking about politics:

> All men were originally equal; and in no country therefore, could any privilege of birth give one family a right to monopolise the executive power for ever: neither can one generation bind that which is as yet to come. The existing race of human beings has no property in the one unborn: we of the present day have no right to assume the power of enslaving posterity:—and, on the same principle, our ancestors had no right to enslave us. If those ancestors chose to make one set of laws for themselves, we can institute another code for our own government. But of course such a change as this can only be made by the representatives of the People; and in order that the people *may* have a fair representation, the following elements of a constitution become absolutely necessary:—
>
> Universal Suffrage;
> Vote by Ballot;
> No Property Qualification;

Paid Representatives;
Annual Parliaments; and
Equal Electoral Districts.

Give us these principles—accord us these institutions—and
we will vouch for the happiness, prosperity, and tranquillity
of the kingdom. The French now stand at the head of the
civilisation of Europe. They are on the same level as the
fine people of the United States of America; and England
occupies an inferior grade in the scale.

Alas! that we should be compelled to speak thus of our
native land: but the truth must be told!

As yet almost every country in Europe has demanded
and obtained something of its rulers, in consequence of the
French Revolution;—whereas England has as yet obtained
nothing in the shape of Reform!

Oh! shame—shame! what has become of our national
spirit?—are we all willing slaves, and shall we not agitate—
morally, but energetically agitate—for our rights and
liberties?

The aristocracy and the men in power treat the people's
assemblies with ridicule, and denominate the working-
classes, when so assembled, as "a mob." They will not
discriminate between honest politicians and the respectable
working-classes on the one hand, and the ragamuffinry of
society on the other. They confound us all together in the
sweeping appellation of *"the mob!"*

The insensates! Do they not reflect that if ten or fifteen
thousand persons meet for the purpose of discussing
some grand political question, some five or six hundred
pickpockets and mischievous boys are certain to intrude
themselves into the assemblage? Why—black sheep even
find their way into the Houses of Parliament—aye, and into
the very suite of Royalty itself.[198]

No one knows why or exactly when Reynolds converted to the Chartist
cause. But it was clear to all: one of England's most famous novelists,
in one of the most widely-read weekly serials of the age, had endorsed

the movement. The man who had previously sneered at the Chartists as 'uneducated' was gone and in the year 1848 Reynolds would make a large contribution to their cause.

Reynolds became an activist in the truest sense. He not only wrote articles supporting the Chartists' several protests but participated in them. His first appearance at a major rally came on 6 March 1848, when he attended a demonstration in Trafalgar Square. People had gathered here to protest against planned rises in income tax. Taxes on earnings had first been introduced by William Pitt the Younger during the Napoleonic Wars to help fund the war effort. After the wars ended in 1815, the tax was repealed. It was then reintroduced by Robert Peel in 1841. The income tax was a tax which affected the well off. Under Peel, only those who earned more than £150 per annum were subjected to the tax of 7d in every pound. To set this in context: the average annual salary of a working-class labourer in the 1840s was approximately £20 per annum—probably much less when it is remembered that for many working-class people, their employment was seasonal and casual. Furthermore, Peel reduced customs duties on 750 imports, meaning that the working class had access to cheaper goods. In 1846 Peel abolished the Corn Laws, which were tariffs on imports of grain that kept the price of bread artificially high (and which benefitted rural landowners). Peel's repeal of the Corn Laws caused a split in his Tory party—which was dominated by the landowning classes—and his government fell in 1846.

Peel's successor was the Whig, Lord Russell, who barely a year into his premiership was faced with two major crises: famine in Ireland and a financial crisis. The financial crisis in 1847 forced Lord Russell's government to begin exploring new ways to raise money. One measure involved authorising the Bank of England to depart from the gold standard. Another was a rise in income taxes from 3 per cent to 5 per cent. It was in opposition to Lord Russell's proposed tax rise that Charles Cochrane called a 'monster meeting' in Trafalgar Square on 6 March. However, a large a crowd of Chartist activists and working-class people had also signalled their intention to attend Trafalgar Square that day. This spooked Cochrane, who, under pressure from the police, attempted to cancel the meeting. But on the day a great multitude—very few of whom would actually have been liable to pay income tax— had already assembled. Cochrane was nowhere to be seen. This was Reynolds's moment. He decided to 'take the chair' at the meeting and, mounting the hustings, delivered an impromptu speech to the protestors. The *London Telegraph* reported that,

> Mr. Reynolds rose, and, suggesting that the parties present should form a meeting to congratulate the Parisians on their recent triumph, addressed the meeting. He had been voted to preside at this assembly, in the absence of Mr. Cochrane. Where that gentleman was, he could not say. His conduct was, at least, extraordinary, in convening a meeting which he neglected to attend. He (*Mr. Reynolds*) must beg of the meeting to be orderly; it was moral force which would gain their ends for them. Let them, therefore, show that, though met to demand their rights, they knew how to conduct themselves. The French revolution was a glorious triumph of public feeling. The French had recognised the rights of the working-classes. What the people of this country wanted was, that every man who was willing to work and fit for work should have work to do. (*Loud cheers.*) The working-classes only wanted fair wages. They were willing to give the fair value of labour for them. (*Hear.*) The right of labour had been recognised in France; and the rights of labour must be recognised in England. Let them not take the leading articles of aristocratic newspapers as the public voice; but let them listen to the shout which they would now hear from thousands of people met to express their adhesion to the principles of liberty. (*Loud cheers*). This meeting had been called to oppose the income-tax. Let them show by their cheers that they were opposed to all oppressive taxation. But let them be peaceable. Let there be no disturbance. Let them show the police and the Government-spies in plain clothes, that the working-classes of England could conduct themselves in a quiet orderly manner when met to discuss their wrongs. Mr. Reynolds sat down amidst the most vociferous cheering.[199]

Reynolds only paid scant attention to the income tax rises in his speech. Instead he sought to drum up support among the crowd for the Chartist cause and also draw attention to events across the channel, where the

French in February had risen up against their government. Reynolds's up-to-date familiarity with French and European politics at this time came from his role as foreign editor for the *Weekly Dispatch*, a newspaper in which he wrote several articles supporting the revolutionaries and denouncing the French monarchy. An article for that newspaper, published just over a week before Reynolds's appearance in Trafalgar Square, for example, urged the French people to be 'true to themselves— true to their ancient reputation', and if they proved to be so, 'another king must very shortly embark as an exile at Cherbourg!'[200]

His appearance in Trafalgar Square was Reynolds's first appearance as a political activist. Many in the crowd would have known Reynolds's name due of the popularity of his novels, and on reading *The Mysteries of London* they would have had *some* idea of his political leanings. And the crowd loved him, so much so that many of them followed him home to 7 Wellington Street where, from his balcony, he addressed them again.

Back in Trafalgar Square, as the afternoon drew to a close, a separate body of men grew more rowdy and there were some punch ups between the demonstrators and their hecklers. A historian of the Chartist movement stated in 1854 that,

> Some well-fed son of the favoured class, got remarking on the idleness of the persons attending the meeting. This levity exasperated the parties attacked, and excitement ran rather high. This formed a pretext for the police, who attempted violently to disperse the crowds, and in doing so, exercised no little amount of brutality.[201]

Fist fights ensued between the protestors and the police. It was further reported that some of the activists stole food from the shops in the vicinity of Trafalgar Square. In the early evening, meanwhile, another crowd had gathered at Clerkenwell Green. Reynolds went there and addressed the people again. *The London Telegraph* reported that

> Mr. Reynolds, the well-known author, next spoke at some length. He drew attention to the meeting which had taken place that day in Trafalgar-square, and commented on the aggressive conduct of the police. The time, he also contended, was come, when they ought no longer to mince

matters. (*Cheers.*) The people of France had really done their duty, and it now remained with the people of this country to do the same. They were bound to demand their rights by every moral means; and if they were forced to have recourse to bloodshed, their oppressors would have to account for the result, not themselves. (*Cheers.*) He rejoiced at the exhibition of feeling that had taken place in France. (*Cheers.*) The people had raised a man to power, who had turned round and sought, by a large array of armed forces, to crush them. (*Groans.*) They, however, he rejoiced to find, gave him his deserts, and hurled him from his throne. (*Cheers.*) He was now in this country—an exiled villain. (*Cheers.*) Far, indeed, was it for him (the speaker) to wish that the tyrant should be molested or disturbed while suffering in a foreign land the pangs of remorse. No; he wished him to remain harmless and in insignificance. (*Hear, hear.*) But he did not see why the gallant and noble people of France were to be insulted by the feelings of sympathy which Her Majesty and some other personages were exhibiting towards the exiled tyrant (*Hear.*) He complained of this, and particularly that the people of England should be identified with the anti-liberal opinions of those persons. (*Hear, hear.*) What, if the gallant people of France were to be so exasperated as to declare war against this country, would the hard-working people of England, Scotland, and Ireland consent to be war-taxed became of the caprice of a number of individuals— (*no, no*)—who, while wallowing in luxury, had no sympathy whatever with the masses of their fellow-creatures suffering from sickness and starvation? Mr. Reynolds, at some length, very ably and forcibly dwelt on the evils of class-legislation, and showed, from his writings, that he had ever been the friend of the working-men. He concluded, amidst much cheering, by proposing the first resolution.[202]

Reynolds wrote two letters on that evening. The first was to the politician George Grey, the architect of the planned income tax rises, and Reynolds demanded that that Grey scrap his plans immediately; Grey did not respond. The second letter that Reynolds wrote was to Cochrane, admonishing him for not attending a meeting that had him billed as the main speaker; just like Grey, Cochrane did not respond.

Reynolds's actions on this day, and his constant attacks on the government and the monarchy, brought him to the notice of the authorities. Having previously been thought of by the general public as a purveyor of lewd and sensational fiction, the government now thought of him as a potential revolutionary. The Home Office quickly compiled a dossier on him and alleged that Reynolds was a naturalised French citizen and served in the country's National Guard.[203] Where the Home Office obtained this information from is unclear but their informants were wrong: Reynolds was never naturalised and he never served in the National Guard.

This was not the last mass meeting that Reynolds was to attend, however, for in 1848 Reynolds spoke at several rallies held at Kennington Common. The area has been witness to several major events in English radical history. In 1815, it was home to several food riots and prior to the passage of the Reform Act it was a space where radicals could gather and deliver speeches to crowds of thousands, even tens of thousands. Being more than a mile away from Westminster its location rendered it the perfect place to hold a protest for the law required that protests could not be held within a mile of the Houses of Parliament.[204] On 13 March Reynolds was invited to be the chairman of a Chartist meeting on the common. The theme of the meeting was 'SYMPATHY WITH THE FRENCH—UNIVERSAL SUFFRAGE—TOTAL ABOLITION OF THE INCOME TAX'.[205] The cheers with which the crowd greeted Reynolds as soon as he mounted the wagon must have been gratifying to him. On its front page *The Freeman's Journal* reported that,

> Mr G.W.M. Reynolds and some other persons acting with him appeared on the scene at half-past twelve and were loudly cheered. They immediately took up their position in one of the two wagons which had been provided in the middle of the common. Immediately after a van full of people arrived from the direction of the Elephant and Castle. A tricolour flag was borne by one of them and was loudly cheered. The vehicle was driven on the common alongside the others and the tricolour was placed at the back of the speakers. Mr Reynolds having moved into the chair, addressed the crowd. He cautioned those present against

doing anything calculated to create a breach of the peace. The meeting had originated from that held at Trafalgar Square on Monday last, and he had written two letters on the subject—one to Mr Cochrane, and the other to Sir George Grey—both of which he read. To neither of the letters did he receive any answers (*groans*). With respect to Mr Cochrane, he would leave his conduct to the decision of the meeting (*groans*). Mr Reynolds proceeded to say that Sir George Grey's conduct was most uncourteous. The people had a right to meet to express their opinions on public matters. If the rulers had a just cause they would not require any force to put down public meetings; but as their cause was a bad one they were obliged to resort to force. The meeting at Trafalgar Square had been stigmatised as riffraff, and it was most dishonest in the daily and some of the weekly papers to characterise the meeting in such a manner. The press was in advance of the government, but the people were in advance of the press, and he hoped that they would exclude those papers which abused them from the coffee houses. They were met in order to express their sympathy with the brave people of France (*groans, cheers, laughter*). The people of France, if properly governed, were as fine and as righteous a set of people as any on the face of the earth, but the tyrant Louis Phillippe had endeavoured to enslave them; and it would be a disgrace to the royalty of England to countenance the expelled royalty of France. The principles of republicanism were making great progress, and would soon be universally established (laughter and cheers). The income tax, it had been said, did not affect the working classes, but he contended that it did affect the working man, and they ought to use their exertions against it, and he hoped that all parties would join to get all they required. They were told that they were free, but there were laws existing which enslaved them. The aristocracy had all the power, two or three of their number were the owners of almost the whole of London. Let them look at the expense of keeping up royalty and aristocracy. Why should they be paying 400,000*l.* a year to the Queen, when the American President did the work for 5,000*l*. a year? And so it was with all the expenditure of the state. Her Majesty lately had a large sum granted to her to build an addition to her palace, but she paid no consideration to the families of those who were lodging in cellars (*groans*).—Surely Buckingham Palace would have been sufficient but she must have a new palace. Ten they gave one hundred thousand to the Queen Dowager, a foreign woman, who had attempted to persuade William the Fourth not to grant the Reform Bill. Prince Albert had 30,000*l*. a year, besides 12,000*l*. as field-marshall—a young man who had never fired a shot in his life. All the costliness of royalty must therefore be cut down, and he hoped that in future the country would insist on curtailing the royal expenditure (*cheers*). He then addressed the meeting at some length on the French Revolution, universal suffrage, and the rights of labour, and concluded amidst loud cheers.[206]

At this point Reynolds did not hold to a coherent ideology. Most of the complaints in his speech were directed against what he saw as unwarranted and lavish state spending on the royal family and aristocracy, as well as a somewhat simplistic opposition to income tax. Having experienced extreme poverty he was, now that he had become a successful writer, anxious to help ameliorate the condition of the 'white slaves', as he often called the British working classes. In the same speech he asked those assembled: 'Why, in Westminster, there were thousands of families living two or three of them huddled up together in rooms far smaller than those which were declared to be dangerous to the health of infant of royalty?' He also stated that 'there was much talk of sanitary reform, but was there anything substantial done to promote the health of the poor?'[207] It was clear to Reynolds that the government was failing the people and that, in his view, a possible remedy for these social ills was the establishment of universal suffrage, which is why he became a Chartist.

In spite of his endorsement of peaceful protest, however, it was quite brave, or brazen, of Reynolds and his fellow speakers that day to speak in front of a revolutionary tricolour flag and talk about 'cutting down' the monarchy. Reynolds cannot have been naïve: he likely knew that this kind of imagery would, in the minds of most people present—and among those who read the newspaper reports of the day's proceedings later on—recall the French Revolution's Reign of Terror. When Reynolds's speeches earned him comparisons to the English medieval revolutionary leader Jack Cade (d.1450) from the likes of the *Morning Chronicle*, it is little wonder that government agencies compiled a dossier on him.[208]

Already infamous in government circles, after March 1848 he would become one of the most famous radical leaders in Britain and was asked to speak at the planned 'monster meeting' of Chartists that was due to be held at Kennington Common on 10 April. The Chartist meeting on this day has become famous because it was predicted to be the largest protest ever held by the Chartists. After this meeting the Chartists planned to march from Kennington Common to deliver their 'monster petition' to parliament, which called for all six of the Chartist demands to become law.

Only a small number of activists would be allowed to march from Kennington Common and deliver the petition to parliament, and it was Reynolds who, two days before the meeting, arrived at the Home Office to inform the authorities of the route that the Chartists were planning to take, tell them who would be in attendance, and to assure their lordships that the meeting would be unarmed and peaceful. This motion to inform the Home Office was proposed by Reynolds at a meeting of the National Convention, as the *Morning Chronicle* reported on 8 April:

> Mr Reynolds moved that a deputation from the convention immediately be despatched to Sir George Grey in order to report to that minister that the convention discountenance altogether the idea that the procession on Monday should go armed. They would then have the less pretence for attacking the people; and if they did, the horrible sin would lie upon their heads.

The motion was sanctioned by all the leading Chartists who were present, including Ernest Jones, Thomas Clarke, George Julian Harney, and Feargus O'Connor—all of whom will appear later in this history. The convention appointed Clarke and Reynolds to compose the deputation. It was probably this meeting between Reynolds and members of the government that was recalled by Lord Stanley over a decade later who recalled that it was 'one Reynolds, who is believed to have given Govt. information of the plans to which he was privy in Feb and March 1848'.[209] Although Stanley's diary entry implies that there was something of a conspiracy between Reynolds and the government against the Chartists, the truth is rather mundane. The meeting of the National Convention was well-publicised in the mainstream newspaper press where it shows that the Chartists agreed with the idea of meeting with government representatives before the event and Reynolds can at last be exonerated of having conspired against the Chartists.

In spite of Reynolds's assurances to the Home Office, the government was clearly concerned about the impending rally. Queen Victoria fled from the capital to the Isle of Wight. Revolutions were sweeping across Europe with uprisings in France, Germany, Italy, and Belgium, and ministers needed to be prepared for an uprising: the London riots of February had given a foretaste of what might happen. One of the Chartists' well-known slogans—'Peaceably if we may, forcibly if we must'—did nothing to allay the government's fear of impending violence and revolution.

There were in fact two factions of Chartists: the moral force Chartists and the 'physical force' Chartists. The former group were gradualists who wanted to prove themselves worthy of the vote by acting in a respectable manner, and educating the middle-class public and their fellow working men about the need for universal male suffrage. The hope was that, in time, the moral argument for universal suffrage would win the day. The physical force members of the movement wanted, as their name suggests, to impose their demands by force. Before the meeting one prominent physical force activist and Member of Parliament for Nottingham, Feargus O'Connor, declared that if the government rejected the petition as they had done in 1839 and 1842, then the Chartists should organise themselves into a National Assembly. The implication of this threat was clear: it recalled the actions of the representatives of the Third Estate in the French Revolution in 1789 who, dissatisfied with how the Estates-General was proceeding, broke away to form their own legislative assembly. This tactic was highly successful for the French Revolutionaries: the National Constituent Assembly, which was later renamed as the National Assembly, became France's legislative chamber. Perhaps O'Connor thought that the Chartists could copy the revolutionaries' actions. On the question of physical force, Reynolds's statements remained ambiguous. In his articles and speeches, there is a general sense that he would personally prefer to have the principles of the charter established by peaceful means. Yet he often wrote that he could foresee a situation arise where the government would be overturned by force if they did not grant the Chartists' demands. As Reynolds wrote: 'the extremes of poverty and misfortune on the one hand, and wealth and privilege on the other, had combined to create the prospect of a terrific convulsion.'[210] He remained silent, however, on what role he would personally play should any violent Chartist revolution occur.

Unsurprisingly, it was the physical force Chartists that the government was worried about; not only was Europe in the throes of revolution but there had been uprisings of Chartists prior to 1848, such as the Newport Rising in 1839. In 1848, therefore, the Whig Prime Minister, Lord Russell, called for the advice of the Duke of Wellington, to advise the government on making preparations for the defence of the capital from a revolutionary insurrection:

> Great preparations were accordingly made. The inhabitants generally, along the lines of the thoroughfare converging to Kennington Common, kept close houses—doors and windows shut, and in some cases, barricaded for defence. The measures of Government, devised and personally worked by the Duke of Wellington, were on a large and complete scale, though so arranged as not to obtrude themselves needlessly on the view. The Thames' bridges were the main points of concentration; bodies of foot and horse police, and assistant masses of special constables, being posted at their approaches on either side. In the immediate neighbourhood of each of them, within call, a strong force of military was kept ... Two regiments of the line were kept in hand at Millbank Penitentiary; 1200 infantry at Deptford Dockyards, and thirty pieces of heavy field ordnance at the Tower, all ready for transport by hired steamers, to any spot where serious business might threaten. At other places, also, bodies of troops were posted out of sight but within sudden command ... In addition to the regular civil and military force, it is credibly estimated that at least 120,000 special constables were sworn and organised throughout the metropolis.[211]

The Kennington Common demonstration was peaceful and a surviving photograph of the event shows men and women dressed in their Sunday best listening to speeches. In some respects the day was an anti-climax.

In spite of the Chartists' predictions that 150,000 people would be in attendance, between 20,000–30,000 people turned up on the day. It was a sizeable crowd but it was certainly not the 'monster' crowd that the likes of Feargus O'Connor had predicted.

Wellington's military preparations and Queen Victoria's swift removal to the Isle of Wight were clearly an overreaction to the day's events. The Chartists said very little about the monarchy and, with the exception of Reynolds and the proponents of physical force, most of them envisaged a role for the monarchy at the head of a new constitution founded upon Chartist principles.[212] Small groups of Chartists were permitted to march on parliament and deliver the petition. On the way there were some minor scuffles with some of the special constables, but it was clear that the authorities were in control on that day.

When a relatively small group of activists led by Feargus O'Connor reached parliament, the huge petition of five million signatures was presented to the House of Commons. O'Connor had planned to deliver a speech urging lawmakers to approve it but he was stopped in his tracks; the petition had to be first be examined by a committee. In a remarkably short time—a matter of hours, in fact—the committee declared that the petition was invalid because most of the signatures were fake, while other 'signatures' were actually lewd and obscene words. O'Connor had no choice, in view of the committee's findings, but to apologise to the House and inform his activists outside. Far from a violent revolution occurring, the reaction among those gathered outside was one of dismay. An observer of the day's events, recalled seeing the Chartists dejected as they passed by the assembled constables and soldiers on the evening:

> When they came back at night, angry, hungry, footsore, they found the bridges barred and the sullen canon between them and the palaces, public offices, banks, and, what was still more of a hardship ... their miserable homes. They were filtered over in detachments at last and kept on the run till they reached their hovels dead beat.[213]

With the benefit of hindsight, historians have dated the beginning of Chartism's end to the rejection of the petition in 1848, although several activists resolved to fight on. Looking back on the momentous events of 1848 two years later, Reynolds sought to address what he felt were some misconceptions when he said that,

> Nearly half a million of the proletarian race assembled upon
> Kennington Common to hold up their hands in favour of
> the Charter;—and a petition containing quite enough *real*
> signatures to stamp it with a true political value, was rolled
> in upon the floor of the House of Commons.[214]

Whether anyone believed Reynolds when he wrote those words two years later is debatable. But he and several prominent Chartist activists felt that they had unfinished business with the government, and Reynolds soon cultivated warm friendships with those on the far left of the Chartist movement. As a result, Reynolds became a socialist.

One of the men with whom Reynolds struck up a friendship was George Julian Harney, who was the *de facto* leader of the Red Republican movement in Britain. The Red Republicans were socialists, although they did not adopt that name for themselves. Influenced by the teachings of Louis Blanc and Jean Pierre Proudhon—whose *What is Property* Reynolds described as 'thrilling'—the Red Republicans aimed to achieve universal liberty through a complete restructuring of the social and political system.[215] Liberty for humanity could only be achieved, so they believed, once universal suffrage had been instituted along with a social revolution which included the nationalisation of land and factories, and free primary, secondary, and tertiary education, the abolition of primogeniture.[216] In short, as their slogan intimated, the Red Republicans wanted 'The Charter and Something More'.[217]

Harney was born in London to a working-class family and was originally destined for the navy but, being a sickly child, he obtained employment in the printing shop of the radical Henry Hetherington, the publisher of the *Poor Man's Guardian*. While working for Hetherington, Harney met the political activist James Bronterre O'Brien who was a regular contributor to the paper, and who became Harney's political mentor. As a result of working in this environment, by the time of his twentieth birthday Harney had fallen foul of the authorities several times for his radical campaigning, and had been imprisoned several times.[218]

Harney joined the Chartist movement, and in 1845 set up his own organisation, the Fraternal Democrats, to complement Chartism, but also to provide a home for those of a firmly left wing ideology. During the 1840s, Harney also befriended Karl Marx, who Harney entertained at a special 'democrat's banquet' on 13 November 1847. In the immediate aftermath of the events of April 1848, Harney established two newspapers:

the *Red Republican* and the *Democratic Review*. The Red Republican is particularly noteworthy because, in November 1850, it published the first English translation of Marx and Engels's *Communist Manifesto*.[219]

Harney's *Red Republican* and *Democratic Review* were highly intellectual and deeply philosophical, and do not strike the observer as the kind of paper that 'ordinary' working-class people would have read. This is not to insult the intelligence of Victorian working-class readers but, in an era when workers had few pennies to spend on entertainment and reading matter, it was unsurprising that Harney's newspapers, which delved into philosophy of Georg W.F. Hegel and printed dry histories of socialism,[220] lacked a truly popular appeal. It was a boon for the Red Republicans, then, when Reynolds—the most popular author of the age—joined their movement.

Reynolds attended several meetings of the Red Republicans and publicly professed the movement's ideology in 1849. Every year the Red Republicans honoured the memory of 'the Immortal Robespierre' and, in April 1850, Reynolds attended this meeting and gave a speech vindicating the principles of social democracy. The meaning of 'social democracy has changed: in the twenty-first century it generally signifies a capitalist state with extensive welfare provision; in Reynolds's time it signified a *socialist and democratic* state.[221] It is from 1849 onwards that Reynolds's political writings became more ideologically coherent and professedly socialist.

Fired with this new ideology, Reynolds knew that there was work still to be done. He set out on a public speaking tour and delivered lectures on Red Republicanism to working-class people throughout Scotland, Northumbria, Derbyshire, Staffordshire, as well as Bradford, Halifax, and Sheffield.[222] In some areas the provincial conservative press denounced Reynolds when he appeared in their town to deliver lectures. When Reynolds spoke at the London Tavern in Hull on 22 July 1849,[223] the *Hull Packet* did not actually engage with the substance of Reynolds's speech but instead attacked his character and previous writings:

> The tendency of the whole address was warlike ... in the speech subsequently delivered by Mr G.W.M. Reynolds ... who, as we remember, was one of the leaders of the London mobs last year, and who is the author of much political trash, and a writer of obscene tales.[224]

When Reynolds visited Ireland as part of a speaking tour the criticisms followed in the same vein, as the press denounced his *Mysteries* instead of the content of his speech:

> Foremost in the crusade of licentiousness stands Mr G.W.M. Reynolds, the author of numberless printed works, of which we plead guilty of knowing but two, his "Miscellany," and "The Mysteries of London." We give him precedence, not only on his merits, but because he has recently figured among us as a political character, as the accredited ambassador of English democracy, and we desire to sift his claims to that distinction. The most foreign diableries pale before the gross exhalations of the London fens of vice Mr Reynolds chronicles, of the brothels, gin-palaces, gambling hells, "boozing kens," highwaymen's houses of call, and fashionable boudoirs, which he loves to portray as more obscene, hideous, and corrupt than all the other squalid haunts of vice put together … One of our chief aims is to elevate and ennoble the democracy of Ireland. Our hope lies in the purity and virtue of our people. But courage and nobleness can no more live in company with this besotting moral filth, than cleanliness on a dunghill. No English invasion was so appalling to Ireland as the one that would deliver her over to this pollution. We therefore warn off G.W.M. Reynolds. Jack Ketch would be a more respectable and welcome missionary to Ireland.[225]

These commentators were not wrong, of course, for by Victorian standards the *Mysteries* does indeed contain scenes of vice and licentiousness. But it was not only the conservative press which denounced Reynolds; his new-found Red Republicanism drew the ire of moderate Chartist activists like the poet Thomas Cooper who in 1850 'damned Harney and Reynolds as Red Republicans'.[226] Charles Dickens's magazine *Household Words* denounced Reynolds as one of 'the Bastards of the Mountain'.[227] 'The Mountain' was a nickname given to the Red Republicans of France by their detractors. They were so called because, to look at them assembled in the French legislative chamber in 1850, they were so numerous that they looked like a mountain.[228] This nickname was then informally adopted by the French Red Republicans themselves.

As we have seen, Harney had his own periodical, the *Democratic Review*, Reynolds had something that neither Harney nor any of the Red Republicans had: Reynolds had a 'brand' because his novels had already made him famous. Perhaps it was for this reason that, along with the publisher John Dicks, Reynolds founded his own weekly newspaper: *Reynolds's Political Instructor*, the first issue of which appeared on Saturday 10 November 1849 and retailed at a price of 1d.

Each issue of *Reynolds's Political Instructor* featured a brief biographical sketch of a major Chartist activist on its front page, along with an engraving of the person in question. In some cases, the illustrations of activists included in the newspaper, such as William Cuffay, are the only image that historians have of them. Issues also featured signed editorials by Reynolds, articles from Edward Reynolds, as well as the long-running series 'The Rise, Progress, and Phases of Human Slavery' by James Bronterre O'Brien, and 'A New History of England' by Edwin F. Roberts. Bronterre and Roberts's articles were rather colourful interpretations of English history, although at least they were up-front about their biases with readers. Roberts's opening article declared that 'we maintain that the history of kings is the history of tyranny ... we hold that the lives of monarchs form the genealogy of crime'.[229]

There was no animosity between Reynolds and Harney, in spite of the fact that that Reynolds had technically founded a 'rival' newspaper. Each man's newspaper endorsed the other in its advertisement columns. Harney and Reynolds evidently viewed themselves as common travellers on the road to building a better society. However, Reynolds acquired a reputation among some of his middle-class contemporaries for being a charlatan who would attach himself to any cause if it meant that he would be able to sell more novels and earn fame and fortune. It is not necessarily a bad thing, and it does not automatically make one a 'charlatan', to improve one's fame, or even fortune, while promoting progressive causes; it does not make one disingenuous. This is especially the case if, like Reynolds, someone sees themselves as the 'people's champion', which is how he described himself a year later during a dispute with Lord Harrowby. Actions speak louder than words, and Reynolds went to a lot of effort touring the country and speaking out in favour of universal suffrage. This did not count for much with contemporary satirists, however, who lampooned Reynolds's activities in March and April 1848.

The Pre-Raphaelite Dante Gabriel Rossetti, for example, wrote a poem titled 'The English Revolution of 1848' and said this about Reynolds:

> What ho there! Clear the way! Make room for him, the "fly" and wise,
> Who wrote in mystic grammar about London's "Mysteries,"—
> For him who takes a proud delight to wallow in our kennels,—
> For Mr. A. B. C. D. E. F. G. M. W. Reynolds!
>
> Come hoist him up! His pockets will afford convenient hold
> To grab him by; and, if inside there silver is or gold,
> And should it be found sticking to our hands when they're drawn out,
> Why, 'twere a chance not fair to say ill-natured things about.
>
> Silence! Hear, Hear! He says that we're the sovereign people, we!
> And now? And now he states the fact that one and one make three!
> Now he makes casual mention of a certain Miscellany!
> He says that he's the editor! He says it costs a penny![230]

A short-lived comic periodical *The Man in the Moon* devoted a comic sketch to Reynolds titled 'Dips into the Diary of Barabbas Bolt, Esq.' which began with Reynolds going to London to join a rally:

> APRIL 1.—This day I left that cradle of infant freedom, the city of Smokely-on-Sewer, to proceed to London, there to help in the glorious work of overthrowing the tyranny which holds to the grindstone the flattened face of merry England. I was accompanied to the station by a band of patriots who, as I paid the three pewter half – crowns, destined by the local association for my third – class fare, knelt upon the earth and solemnly swore never to wash their faces until the Charter became the law of the land. For my own part, I vowed to return with the glorious tidings, or be brought back pickled in a cask, a corpse to the cause of freedom.

In a moment I was on the platform. There stood train, its three classes, first, second, and third. "Good Heavens!" I exclaimed, and are not men equal? Have not these cursed distinctions of rank been yet levelled by the roar of the speeding steam? But I, for one, will never give in to aristocratic institutions.

So saying, I got into the *coupée* of a first-class carriage. A myrmidon of tyranny—a guard, advanced and asked to see my ticket, and I was forced to submit. Gracious heavens! And is this a land of liberty? Under the vile and insidious pretence of its being a third-class ticket I was dragged—yes dragged, for I refused to walk—from my seat, and forced into a miserable uncushioned sheep pen upon wheels! In a moment I saw a bloated aristocrat take what ought to have been, what was my place. Ha! Ha! Ha! But I forbear. Leaning back in the carriage I muttered "Oh! For one hour of Maximillan Robespierre."[231]

Before joining the rally Mr Bolt decides to spend some time forging signatures for the Chartist petition:

Ere midnight had struck (it is one o'clock now), I had manufactured 3981 signatures for our monster petition. Call this not an unworthy artifice. It is a patriotic contrivance. Under the monstrous system which oppresses us, education is neglected, and many of the people cannot write their own names. Is it not, therefore, the part of a brother to set down their signatures for them?[232]

That Reynolds was the target of this satire was evident from the illustrations that accompanied it showing Reynolds with a big head, a fairly well-fed body, and his distinctive hairstyle. Whether Reynolds ever saw this particular satire is unknown. He never responded to it so even if he did it cannot have bothered him much.

Besides, he was a busy man at this point because he had been elected to the executive body of the National Charter Association. He was the most popular candidate in the running as well, receiving 1,805 votes. His friend George Julian Harney was a close second with 1,774 votes. The pair of them garnered more votes than some of the previous stalwarts of the Chartist movement including Ernest Jones (1,757 votes), and O'Connor (1,314 votes).[233]

The association held several debates, most of which were concerned with discussing the direction that Chartism should take after the government's rejection of the petition. The two years after 1848 are also significant because the executive body of the National Charter Association also began discussing social issues, where previously the mainstream Chartists had been concerned predominantly with ensuring that the six points of the charter were passed into law. Alongside the National Charter Association, a number of different pro-democracy groups were established in the closing years of the 1840s. There was the National Reform League—founded by Reynolds's friend James Bronterre O'Brien—the Social Reform League, the National Regeneration Society, and the National Charter League. Alongside these London-based groups were many more at a local level, and Manchester-based groups exercised just as much influence as those in the south.

It was with a view to uniting all of these disparate groups that the establishment of a new organisation was proposed which would be called the National Charter and Social Reform Union. In theory the idea made a lot of sense, but after 1848, the Chartists were too divided and leading personalities clashed with each other. O'Connor argued with Ernest Jones. Jones and Harney disputed with Thomas Clark of the National Charter League. Reynolds had disputes with seemingly everybody, but Harney. Many of these men's disputes were carried on through the pages of the Chartist newspapers of the day, including in *Reynolds's Political Instructor*.

During Reynolds's political campaigning, however, his monetary troubles came back to haunt him. As well as the impending financial ruin he faced, a new novel would soon draw the ire of critics who, as we shall see in the next chapter, would denounce him for having 'a diseased, corrupt, and sink-like mind'.

'A diseased, corrupt, and sink-like mind': *The Mysteries of the Court of London, Reynolds's Weekly Newspaper,* and the Road to Wealth

> He was well aware that in other quarters there existed towards himself the most malignant spirit: but he thanked God that through his own exertions, succoured by those who were around him, he stood in a position which enabled him to treat with contempt all such despicable animosities.
>
> *Reynolds's Weekly Newspaper,*
> 18 July 1852

As 1848 drew to a close Reynolds finished writing his Second Series of *The Mysteries of London*. The reading public who had followed the adventures of Richard Markham, Thomas Rainford the highwayman, the Earl of Ellingham, and Old Death were no doubt hungry for more of the same. Having quarrelled with his publishers George Vickers and George Stiff, John Dicks contracted Reynolds to begin writing a new novel titled *The Mysteries of the Court of London*, the first instalment of which, priced at 1d, appeared in September 1848.

But Reynolds was still plagued by financial worries. Reynolds was making £500 per year from his writings at which he worked tirelessly. He was not only producing novels, but also editing the *Miscellany,* as well as serving as the foreign editor for the *Weekly Dispatch*.[234] He took £400 per year for the maintenance of his family, and with the extra £100 made payments towards his debts. Reynolds and Susannah tried to pay off their debts by selling part of their extensive book collection, with which they had decorated the library at his home in Wellington Street.

Another method by which the Reynolds family raised funds was by selling the copyrights on some of his works, such as *Wagner the Wehr-Wolf*. The creditor in question, William Spokes, accepted the offer, but made a sneering remark the copyright would do him little good because '[Reynolds] certainly did not rank among the Miltons and Newtons'.[235] Susannah likewise relinquished her copyright to the *Household Book of Practical Receipts*. The creditors' snide remarks of Reynolds's literary abilities aside, this method of paying off his debts seemed to be satisfactory for a time.

Furthermore, *Reynolds's Miscellany* had not yet become the big-selling literary magazine that it was to become in the 1850s.[236] A period of illness—which Reynolds called 'nervousness'—in the summer of 1847 meant that Reynolds had to stop writing completely for the magazine, and as a result, sales of the *Miscellany* plunged. Yet more issues were in store for him, however, as a result of the machinations of Vickers and Stiff, the proprietors of the *London Journal*. As Reynolds had dared to establish a rival to the *London Journal*, Vickers and Stiff founded, in July 1848, a new magazine to draw readers of *Reynolds's Miscellany* back to themselves. They had the audacity to name this new magazine *Reynolds's Magazine*. This was very crafty of Vickers and Stiff: the first few issues of *Reynolds's Miscellany* were titled *Reynolds's Magazine*, so Vickers and Stiff were attempting to snare unsuspecting readers into thinking that their own magazine was endorsed by Reynolds himself. To add insult to injury, in Vickers and Stiff's magazine an instalment of a novel titled *The Corral Island* appeared (with the word 'coral' spelt with two r's). *Corral Island* was an overt plagiarism of Reynolds's *Coral Island; or, The Hereditary Curse* which was then being serialised in *Reynolds's Miscellany*.

Reynolds was understandably furious, and perhaps he by then understood how Dickens felt seeing his creation of Mr Pickwick plagiarised by penny magazine authors back in the 1830s. To counter Vickers and Stiff's new magazine, Reynolds wrote a lengthy article in *Reynolds's Miscellany* denouncing Vickers and Stiff's new magazine and concluded by saying that,

> I now, therefore, throw myself upon the generosity and mercy
> of the British public. I appeal to the millions to support me
> in resisting this diabolical attempt to ruin me. I respectfully

and earnestly solicit all those whose eye this Address may meet, to show it to their friends and acquaintances; and I put it to the honour of and good feeling of BOOKSELLERS and VENDERS OF CHEAP PERIODICALS whether they will assist in injuring me? In fine, I wish it to be as extensively known as possible that I am the Editor of REYNOLDS'S MISCELLANY, and that I have not the slightest connection with *Reynolds's Magazine*.[237]

Reynolds also went on the legal offensive. He took out an injunction against *Reynolds's Magazine* and the court took a dim view of Vickers and Stiff's actions. The pair of them were forced to immediately suspend the publication of *Reynolds's Magazine*.[238]

When sales of the *Miscellany* plunged during the period of Reynolds's illness, the result was that he could not pay as much money towards the debts that had been racked up in connection with the magazine's establishment. His debts, which amounted to £2,109, were largely owed to people who were connected to the publishing trade. For example, among Reynolds creditors were two stereotyping firms, a paper-maker, and engravers' firms. The *Miscellany* featured several images in one issue, so it is easy to see how debts to engravers would add up over a short time. Alongside his business debts were some personal ones, including upholsterers and engravers, as well as booksellers. The high sum, then, was not, as Reynolds's critics charged, solely down to extravagant spending.

But in 1848, seemingly inexplicably, almost all of his creditors started demanding up-front payment. Such an occurrence is anxiety-provoking at the best of times, but earlier in the year the Reynolds family had had another child, a daughter, whom they named Joanna Frances. Reynolds was up to his eyes in debt and with an increasingly large family to provide for. It can easily be guessed how Reynolds felt when, on 22 August, he was once again in court at Basinghall Street, although this time it was him, and not his creditors, who was petitioning for his own bankruptcy.

Reynolds suspected that Vickers and Stiff had privately approached his creditors and convinced some of them to begin making demands for payment.[239] There was probably some truth to this: Reynolds's creditors started to clamour for payment in August 1848. This was the same month that Reynolds secured an injunction against Vickers and Stiff's

Reynolds's Magazine, and the very month in which the final issue of the Vickers-published *Mysteries of London* appeared.[240] While bankruptcy proceedings were ongoing a representative from Vickers's establishment, named Moss, privately approached Reynolds and John Dicks and offered to get rid of all of Reynolds's debts if he would promise never to write again.[241] Vickers and Stiff had lost Reynolds who was a big seller, and to continue *The Mysteries of London,* they had to employ the relatively unknown author Thomas Miller (1807–74). They likely knew that Miller's writing could never compete with Reynolds's new *Mysteries of the Court of London* and they wanted to eliminate the competition.

Reynolds rightly refused to give up writing. Being an author was not simply a job to him: it was his identity and his brand. This is why all of his publications carried his name.[242] One can imagine Reynolds's shock at Vickers and Stiff's request. He would rather go through the court and still carry on writing rather than give it up. Thus Reynolds found himself bogged down in litigation with his creditors.

It is a wonder that Reynolds did not decide to petition the court sooner. On 29 September, his case came before the judge. The judge chided him for being financially irresponsible, especially in view of Reynolds's previous bankruptcies in Paris and London. Reynolds would indeed be subjected to a bankruptcy order, but rather than immediately release him from all financial obligations the judge decided that Reynolds would have to pay *something.* Reynolds was ordered to pay £500 to satisfy his debts, after which he would be completely released from all previous liabilities. As soon as the judgement was made, and in front of the judge, Reynolds apparently made 'insulting expressions' to Moss.[243] John Dicks forwarded £500 in cash to Reynolds so that he could pay off his liabilities. As an astute businessman, Dicks helped Reynolds to sort out his finances. This was the final time that Reynolds was to face bankruptcy.

As for Vickers and Stiff, they continued to produce works in an attempt to rival those which appeared in *Reynolds's Miscellany.* However, a rapprochement may also have occurred between them and Reynolds. From 29 December 1850, *Reynolds's Miscellany* began advertising publications from the Vickers' printing firm in its back pages.[244] At the very least, as the editor, Reynolds had few issues running Vickers's advertisements. After all, Vickers would be paying for advertising space in the *Miscellany.*

It is worthwhile to become better acquainted with John Dicks due to the major part he played in Reynolds's life after 1848.[245] Born on 3 June 1818, in Stepney to a working-class family, he received a minimal education before being articled as an apprentice to the printing firm of Eyre and Spottiswoode. Young Dicks must have been a very good apprentice because, by the age of twenty-three, he was the chief assistant printer in Peter Thoms's publishing firm. Dicks also tried his hand at writing a serial novel in the 1848, titled *Tyburn Tree; or, The Mysteries of the Past,* a title that evoked Reynolds's own novels. Having served as an apprentice, Dicks had struck out on his own and formed his own company, which became the printer for *Reynolds's Miscellany.* Dicks, as the publisher of *Reynolds's Political Instructor*, may also have shared some of Reynolds's political sentiments as well. It seems that both men were dedicated to bringing cheap educational and entertaining literature to the masses: Dicks would later publish the low-cost *Works of Shakespere*, which quickly became one of the century's biggest-selling editions of the famous bard's works.

Dicks also must have repurchased all of the copyrights that Reynolds had sold to his creditors because, from 1848 onwards, reissues of Reynolds's old works began to appear under Dicks's imprint. Although Reynolds's name was still attached to the company's firm, its newspapers and periodicals, it seems that Dicks took charge of most of the tedious financial matters. From now on Reynolds would be paid a regular salary. It was certainly a good salary: by the early 1860s, Reynolds was earning £100 per week from his novels, newspapers, and periodicals.[246]

Dicks now had Reynolds writing exclusively for him and sales of *The Mysteries of the Court of London* soared. Some historians have tended to view *The Mysteries of London* and *The Mysteries of the Court of London* as two separate novels, but they are not, for Reynolds himself stated that they should be viewed as one single novel or 'encyclopaedia of tales'.[247] Its popularity among working-class readers can be gauged from Henry Mayhew's interviews with London's paupers in the 1850s:

> It may appear anomalous to speak of the literature of an uneducated body, but even the costermongers have their tastes for books. They are very fond of hearing any one read aloud to them, and listen very attentively. One man often reads the Sunday paper of the beer-shop to them, and on

a fine summer's evening a costermonger, or any neighbour who has the advantage of being "a schollard," reads aloud to them in the courts they inhabit. What they love best to listen to—and, indeed, what they are most eager for—are Reynolds's periodicals, especially the "Mysteries of the Court." "They've got tired of [Edward] Lloyd's blood-stained stories," said one man, who was in the habit of reading to them, "and I'm satisfied that, of all London, Reynolds is the most popular man among them. They stuck to him in Trafalgar-square, and would again. They all say he's 'a trump,' and Feargus O'Connor's another trump with them."[248]

Of course not everybody loved *The Mysteries of London* and its sequel. James Greenwood decided that the serial was decidedly vulgar:

"What are the assured grounds of safety? Is it because it stands to reason that all such coarse and vulgar trash finds its level amongst the coarse and vulgar, and could gain no footing above its own elevation? It may so stand in reason, but unfortunately it is the unreasonable fact that this same pen poison finds customers at heights above its natural low and foul waterline almost inconceivable. How otherwise is it accountable that at least a *quarter of a million of* these penny numbers are sold weekly? How is it that in quiet suburban neighbourhoods, far removed from the stews of London, and the pernicious atmosphere they engender; in serene and peaceful semi-country towns where genteel boarding schools flourish, there may almost invariably be found some small shopkeeper who accommodatingly receives consignments of "Blue-skin," and the "Mysteries of London," and unobtrusively supplies his well-dressed little customer with these full-flavoured articles? Granted, my dear sir, that your young Jack, or my twelve years old Robert, have minds too pure either to seek out or crave after literature of the sort in question, but not un-frequently it is found without seeking. It is a contagious disease, just as cholera and typhus and the plague are contagious, and, as

103

everybody is aware, it needs not personal contact with a body stricken to convey either of these frightful maladies to the hale and hearty. A tainted scrap of rag has been known to spread plague and death through an entire village, just as a stray leaf of "Panther Bill," or "Tyburn Tree" may sow the seeds of immorality amongst as many boys as a town can produce.[249]

Poorer readers probably enjoyed the highly suggestive scenes and, as Mayhew's costermonger noted, the fact that it 'lashes the aristocracy'. Spanning eight volumes and millions of words, and published over eight years, *The Mysteries of the Court of London* told the story of the vice, depravity, and debauchery that reigned supreme in the English court. The novel's principal protagonist is the Prince Regent whose debaucheries are followed all the way through four of the eight volumes until he becomes George IV. The final two volumes relate the crimes and misdeeds of the nobility during the reigns of William IV and Queen Victoria. Reynolds knew he was writing literature that was decidedly unrespectable, and he had no issue in depicting the Prince Regent and the aristocracy in general as a class of sex-mad voluptuaries. The passage below detailing the extra-marital liaison between the Countess of Desborough and a stranger named Ramsey is just one example of Reynolds's suggestive and steamy writing:

'Twas midnight—and Eleanor was now alone in her chamber.

The lady's-maids had just withdrawn, having assisted their mistress to lay aside her garments and arrange her luxuriant hair for the night.

A loose wrapper enveloped her form—her naked feet were thrust into slippers;—and, half reclining upon a sofa drawn near the fire, the Countess awaited with indescribable feelings the coming of her lover.

The wax-candles upon the mantel had been extinguished; and a small night-lamp, placed on the toilette-table, joined its rays with the light of the fire to shed a soft and subdued lustre through the room. Delicious perfumes exhaled from porcelain vases standing in the window-recesses;—and the warm and fragrant atmosphere seemed to be the voluptuous breath of love itself.

How rapidly beat Eleanor's heart as she lay half-reclined upon the sofa!

A species of timidity—like that which the virgin-bride feels when entering the nuptial couch—was upon her. Her colour changed fifty times in a minute,—now glowing with the richest crimson upon her cheeks—now sinking into a strange paleness; and in her eyes there was an expression of intense anxiety mingling with the fires of burning—scorching—devouring passion.

Was it that she knew she was doing wrong, but that she could not wrestle against the fury of her desires?—did she experience, at the bottom of her soul, a regret that she had gone thus far?—would she have retreated and repented even yet, if it were possible to overcome these sensual longings which consumed and devoured her?

We know not—and we have not leisure now to analyse the feelings of the Countess of Desborough: for, hark—a footstep in the passage reaches her ear—Oh! How audibly her heart beats—how tumultuously her bosom heaves!—the door opens—and Ramsey appears!

Scarcely can he restrain his impatience sufficiently to spare a moment to lock the door: another instant—and he is clasped in the arms of the countess.

"Dearest, dearest Eleanor!" he exclaims as he enfolds that warm, yielding, and lovely form in an embrace rendered almost frantic by the maddening of desire.

"Dearest, dearest Gustavus!" she murmurs, straining him to her heaving bosom.

And if hell's flames were immediately to follow the consummation of her frailty, she would not resign these few moments of Elysium to save herself from that eternity of pain.

Forgotten is her husband—forgotten is every sense of duty—forgotten is the world beyond the four walls of this chamber of love and voluptuousness: she abandons herself to that delirium of bliss in which her enraptured soul now floats—she flings herself headlong into the whirlpool of passion—she yields herself up to the intoxication of a full and overflowing sensuality.

It seemed as if the gates of paradise were opening to her comprehension for the first time; and Ramsey understood, without being told in words, the nature of that secret Eleanor had promised to reveal to him.[250]

Reynolds's approach to the depiction of sex stood in marked contrast to Eugène Sue who, although his characters certainly flirted with each other, only implied it. Indeed, there is some evidence to suggest that Reynolds's appropriation of the urban mysteries genre was detrimental to Sue's reception in England. It is not at all clear whether Sue approved of the fact that English readers viewed him in the same class of authors as Reynolds.[251] In any case, *Mysteries of the Court of London* was not your average Victorian novel. It is unsurprising that the highly respectable Charles Dickens, in his *Household Words* in 1850, called Reynolds's very existence 'a national reproach'.[252] Reynolds was not afraid to hit back at Dickens, however, for he later called him 'that lick-spittle hanger-on to the skirts of Aristocracy's robes'.

Dickens was not the only person to voice his disapproval of *The Mysteries of the Court of London*. The political reformer Thomas Clark declared that the novel sprang from a 'diseased, corrupt, and sink-like mind'.[253] Clark—who had his own reasons for despising Reynolds—did not hold back. At another point he declared that Reynolds,

Has defiled the great fount from whence all enlightenment must descend into the humble and noble industrial walks of life, and has, as far as he is concerned, converted that great engine of civilization, cheap literature, into a curse to the nation. He has insinuated his incestuous trash into those places where Dickens, [James Fenimore] Cooper, [Douglas] Jerrold, [Mary] Howitt, and such others, ought only to be permitted to enter. He has attacked the very foundation of all social happiness and connubial confidence—female virtue! He has scattered abroad the most licentious filth amongst our youthful population, and has made it a matter of boast that from such labours he reaps a large pecuniary reward.[254]

In later life William Makepeace Thackeray castigated Reynolds's novel by saying:

> There was a book which had an immense popularity in England ... in which the Mysteries of the Court of London were said to be unveiled by a gentleman who, I suspect, knows as much about the Court of London as he does of that of Pekin. Years ago I treated myself to a sixpennyworth of this poor performance at a railway station, and found poor dear George IV., our late most religious and gracious king, occupied in the most flagitious designs against a the tradesmen's families in his metropolitan city. A couple of years after I took a sixpennyworth more of the same delectable history: George IV was still at work, still ruining the peace of tradesmen's families; he had been at it for two whole years, and a bookseller at the Brighton station told me that this book was by many, many times the most popular of all periodical tales then published, "because," says he, "it lashes the aristocracy!"[255]

Prints by the likes of James Gillray and George Cruikshank, produced during George IV's reign, did indeed depict him as a fat, womanising voluptuary, so Reynolds was not wide of the mark in his own fictional depiction of Britain's most contemptible monarch. Other sources published shortly after George's reign, such as Olivia Serres's *Secret History of the Court of England* (1832)—which Reynolds had read and gave a glowing review for during his time at the *Monthly Magazine*— also depicts the monarch negatively. Thackeray's comments were also rather hypocritical, given the fact that, in one of his own works titled *The Four Georges* (1861), George IV is spoken of with absolute contempt.

While in *The Mysteries of London* Reynolds often broke the narrative to promote the Chartist cause, *The Mysteries of the Court of London* was less radical. There was some remarks about the squalor in which working-class families lived, but the latter novel was only political insofar as it depicted royalty and aristocracy in a negative light. There was of course no need for Reynolds to make his fiction politically charged anymore: *Reynolds's Political Instructor* had been founded a few months before

The Mysteries of the Court of London began, and every week Reynolds wrote a lead article on the major political issues of the day. He continued writing weekly editorials after *Reynolds's Political Instructor* was wound up, and *Reynolds's Weekly Newspaper* was established in its place.

The first issue of *Reynolds's Weekly Newspaper* appeared on 5 May 1850 and cost 4d. Its establishment marked an exciting step forward in Reynolds's political career, and May of that year was also marked by another happy event for the Reynolds family: the birth of another child, whom Reynolds—evidently wanting to signal his family's revolutionary credentials to the world—named Kossuth Mazzini after the European revolutionary leaders Lajos Kossuth and Giuseppe Mazzini. As Dick Collins notes, the family's finances became 'settled enough' to allow them to move from their home in Wellington Street to the more genteel neighbourhood of Islington, where they occupied a larger house named Clinsby Villa.

John Dicks's sound business management also allowed Reynolds and Susannah to buy a holiday home at Herne Bay in Kent, and the family took a holiday there in September 1850. Yet this was not to be a happy vacation. On 20 September, Reynolds's first-born son George Edward was diagnosed with typhoid fever. Susannah remained by young George's bedside the entire time while treatment was administered by Mr Godfrey, one of Herne Bay's most eminent surgeons. But the treatment was in vain. In the early hours of Monday 23 September George Edward was no more. He was just fifteen years old.[256] George Edward's obituary revealed that,

> He experienced a great interest in that political cause in which his father is engaged, and which receives the best sympathies of his mother, with whom he frequently attended the democratic meetings held in the metropolis. Gifted with extraordinary powers of mind, and possessing a depth of understanding far beyond his years, he was well acquainted with all the leading features of the Chartist agitation, and was personally known to many of its leaders ... He exhibited a taste for literature, and composed many little tales and dramas, which, though of course not polished enough for publication, nevertheless evinced the germinations of brilliant intelligence ... he belonged to a world the brightest

ornaments of which are too often doomed to be snatched prematurely away; and after a short illness, brought on by a cold … he was claimed by the stern hand of death.[257]

The young man was every bit his father's son, it seems, having been a democrat and a budding author. George Edward was shortly afterwards buried in the graveyard of Christ Church, Herne Bay, and the Reynolds family returned to their house in Islington.

As for *Reynolds's Weekly Newspaper*, it quickly became the principal organ of left-wing politics in the post-Chartist era. The tone of the essays that Reynolds wrote for the newspaper's previous incarnation, *Reynolds's Political Instructor*, were serious and intellectual. But in *Reynolds's Weekly Newspaper* the subject matter was still serious but 'light' enough to attract even those with only a passing interest in politics, and the newspaper also contained news of the latest crimes and, later, sport.

Reynolds's editorials included such gems as 'The Crowned Miscreants and Harlots of Europe' which began thus:

> It would appear that Kings and Queens are privileged beings in every sense of the word. They are not only surrounded by all the enjoyments, the luxuries, and the blandishments of this world: but they may indulge in murder, plunder, perjury, adultery, debauchery, and every other hideous crime or loathsome vice without losing the respect of their courtiers or the love of their admirers. They may perpetrate, or cause to be perpetrated (which is precisely the same thing) the most damnable deeds that ever disgraced humanity; and they still find sycophants to kneel at their feet and journalists to applaud their actions. Kings may become such monsters that even Satan himself must grow pale at their tremendous iniquities,—and Queens may outvie Messalina herself ion the flagrant dissoluteness of their lives; but they proceed with impunity—being *above* the law, and *above* public opinion likewise.[258]

The article in question then proceeded to highlight all the personal flaws of European monarchs before enjoining his working class readers to ensure that they were not beguiled by the pomp and 'craft' of monarchy in Britain.

The newspaper was staunchly opposed to the British Empire. Reynolds—the man, who in the 1830s, had positively endorsed European imperialism in North Africa—had well and truly changed his mind by the 1850s. As the historian Antony Taylor remarks: 'for Reynolds the empire was an emblem of the corruptions of crown and aristocracy'.[259] To criticise the empire was to criticise the British social system. The blame for the world's ills could be placed squarely at the feet of these moneyocrats and aristocrats. As Reynolds stated in 'The Selfish and Rapacious Oligarchy':

> The British Empire is ruled ... by an Oligarchy. And now let us see what amount of power, prerogative, and authority, is vested in the hands of this tyrant Oligarchy. In the first place ... the Crown is in their hands: it is the talisman of all their honours, wealth, and privileges. Secondly, they leave their own House of Lords; and the House of Commons is likewise theirs's [sic] by means of their sons, their relatives, their nominees, and the innumerable place-hunters who find their way into Parliament. Thirdly, the Church is entirely their own, its patronage being in their hands, and the Bishops sitting as legislators in the House of Lords. Fourthly, the Army is the plaything for the scions of the Aristocracy, and is almost exclusively officered by persons on whom they can rely in any emergency. Fifthly, the Navy is in the same condition; and promotion in both services is awarded for political purposes and as a recompense for the avowal of particular opinions. Sixthly, the Judicial Bench and all the Law Departments are filled with the nominees and favourites of the Aristocracy; and the highest honours have invariably been heaped upon those Attorneys- General who have been most active and virulent in prosecuting and persecuting democratic reformers. Seventhly, the Colonies are under the control of the Aristocracy, for whose poor members they furnish places with rich emoluments, and for whose blood-thirsty instincts they afford ample opportunities of gratification and practice in the form of hangings, shootings, and other diabolical atrocities.[260]

Right: George W.M.
Reynolds. (1814–79)

Below: The former Norton
Knatchbull Grammar School
which Reynolds attended.
(used with permission,
courtesy of Dave Skinner)

Above: The earliest photographical image (a daguerreotype) of the Boulevard du Temple, captured by Louis Daguerre in 1838—only a few years after Reynolds left Paris. (Wikimedia Commons)

Below: A reproduction of Eugene Delacroix's *Liberty Leading the People* (1831) which celebrated the events of the French Revolution of 1830.

Reynolds's *Ellen Percy: Memoirs of an Actress*.

Reynolds's *The Soldier's Wife*.

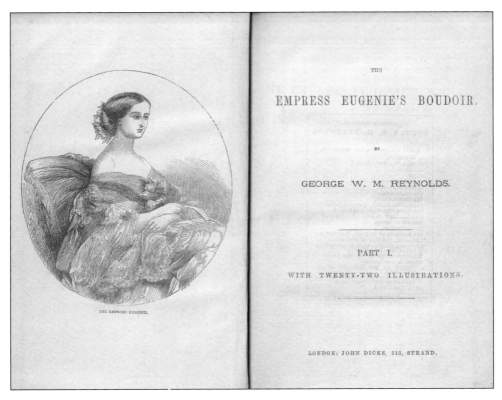

THE

EMPRESS EUGENIE'S BOUDOIR,

BY

GEORGE W. M. REYNOLDS.

PART I.

WITH TWENTY-TWO ILLUSTRATIONS.

LONDON: JOHN DICKS, 313, STRAND.

THE EMPRESS EUGENIE.

Reynolds's *Empress Eugenie's Boudoir*, a story which incorporated several of Reynolds's previous novels.

Yet Reynolds did more than just complain: he also set forth a vision of a future society, founded upon universal suffrage and aligned on Red Republican principles, and urged the working classes to fight for it. He was clearly trying to inspire his readers when he declared:

> I tell the unrepresented millions that they have only to demand representation—and they will obtain it. But they must demand it loudly, continuously, and unanimously: they must agitate for Universal Suffrage. So long as they remain apathetic, they will remain unrepresented, they will remain serfs, slaves, and bondsmen. Let the demand for Reform, then, resound throughout the land: and the millions raise one united voice that shall shake the nation with the cry of UNIVERSAL SUFFRAGE.[261]

It would be a mistake, however, to call *Reynolds's Weekly Newspaper* a Red Republican newspaper. The message which Reynolds imparted to readers through his own weekly editorials did indeed spread a Red Republican message but the newspaper as a whole contained a diverse range of radical thought. Alongside Reynolds's writings were articles from Samuel Kydd. Kydd was born in Arbroath, Forfarshire in 1815 and moved to London in 1839 in search of work. During the 1840s, Kydd first met Harney and other Chartist leaders, such as Feargus O'Connor and William Lovett, and became associated with their movement.[262] Yet after 1848, Kydd aligned himself with the Tory radicals and became a close ally to its leading campaigner Richard Oastler (1789–1861), who had spent a lifetime campaigning for 'gradualist' social causes. By 1850, when Kydd began writing articles for *Reynolds's Weekly Newspaper*,[263] he was serving as Oastler's private secretary.[264] Yet Kydd's new-found Toryism did not disqualify him appearing in the newspaper, so overall it was truly dedicated to diversity of radical political thought.

Reynolds was also elected to the newly-established National Parliamentary and Financial Reform Association (NPFRA). Founded on 19 June 1849 at Sadler's Wells Theatre in the Borough of Finsbury. The NPRFA was dedicated to procuring universal suffrage and, while it included middle-class radicals, the bulk of its membership was comprised of people from the working classes and the representatives on the executive body.[265] The elected representatives included several people whose names have featured previously in this history: Feargus O'Connor, Thomas Clark, as well as the MP Joshua Walmsley. Reynolds joined the association because

> Of all such movements which have taken place within the present century, that of the National Parliamentary and Financial Reform Association appears to offer the best guarantees for sincerity of purposes, unflinching determination, and breadth of fundamental principle; and in my opinion it deserves the strenuous support of all true patriots and honest Reformers.[266]

The NPFRA was therefore conceived of as a broad church that would accommodate a variety of ideological positions. Although all of the members were wholeheartedly in favour of gaining universal suffrage, for example, Walmsley was firmly against the 'forcibly if we must' ethos.[267] Middle-class Manchester School reformers, such as Richard Cobden, who were proponents of the doctrine of free trade, were also welcomed at the NPFRA's meetings in London, and Cobden set up a similar organisation in Manchester.

As for the London association, when it was first founded in 1849, everything appeared to be harmonious between its ideologically diverse members. But issues came to a head when Clark and Walmsley proposed a formal alliance with the middle classes: under their proposals the working classes would have to first prove themselves 'worthy' of the franchise and the 'Red' Chartists among the NPFRA's members would have to commit to a gradualist programme of reform. This was too much for Reynolds and O'Connor, and they both rejected this measure. In 1849 Reynolds had foreseen the dangers of surrendering to the wishes of middle-class activists when he wrote that,

> The history of nearly every moral agitation and of every movement accomplished by means of physical force, shows that after the immediate object has been either partially or wholly gained, the middle classes have reaped the greater advantage, and the toiling millions have seen their own material interests neglected—their wrongs unredressed—their rights unrecognized—and their claims disregarded.

In a word, they have been cheated with the shadow, while the middle classes have grasped the substance. Then, too, the middle classes have proclaimed the necessity of desisting from any further agitation, on the plea that absolute tranquility becomes necessary for the revival of trade; and if the working classes have persisted in continuing the agitation, they have been denounced as disturbers of the peace-inveterate malcontents-and incorrigible foes to order,-while middle-class juries have been called upon to become the *media* of dealing forth the vengeance of sanguinary and barbarian laws. It is indeed a painful fact that the middle classes have too often proved themselves as hostile and as oppressive as the Aristocracy towards the industrious millions;-and therefore the sons and daughters of toil must at least be upon their guard, if not actually animated with suspicion, whenever they are called upon to give their adhesion to a political movement which originates with the middle classes.[268]

A split inevitably emerged between the members of the body. Yet the issue of an alliance with the middle classes could have been surmounted. What seems to have irked Reynolds and Harney more was Clark's suggestion, at a meeting in May 1850, that the NPFRA should formally distance itself from socialism and Red Republicanism.[269] After the measure had been proposed Reynolds stood up and declared that

Mr Clark had lost the confidence of the Chartist body; and that the Reform Association was committing a suicidal act by engaging him, inasmuch as the working classes would never allow the association, after such conduct, to hold another meeting. It was nothing more nor less than a defiance flung down, and a flagrant insult levelled at the whole Chartist body. There was nothing to allege against Mr Clark's private character: he (Mr Reynolds) was merely speaking of him in a public capacity.[270]

The debate became very heated as Joshua Walmsley stood up to remind all present that he had personally invited Clark to serve on the NPFRA's

113

executive body. Reynolds answer to this was then to turn his ire on Walmsley, whom he had previously praised a few months before in *Reynolds's Political Instructor* for having been 'an honest reformer'.[271] 'Then I boldly and empathically accuse you, Sir Joshua Walmsley', Reynolds thundered, 'of bargaining for the betrayal of the Chartist cause, and the sale of the interests of the middle classes'.[272] All of those present at the meeting requested Reynolds's immediate resignation from the NPFRA.

Clark maintained that he was unfazed by Reynolds's outburst against him. He was so *unbothered* by the spat with Reynolds, in fact, that he wrote and published a forty-page pamphlet castigating Reynolds, titled *A Letter Addressed to G.W.M. Reynolds reviewing his Conduct as a Professed Chartist* (1850). Clark opened by stating Reynolds was scarcely 'worth one moment's notice'. Clark then went on to pride himself over having lost the confidence of Reynolds and his associates 'because it was impossible that I could longer cooperate with the violent idiot knaves'.[273] The 'violent idiot knaves' were the Red Republicans or, as Clark termed them, 'Red Chartists'. Clark referred to Reynolds's Red Republican friend George Julian Harney by name and evidently listed him among the number of these 'violent knaves'. Harney had sided with Reynolds, while Feargus O'Connor—a physical force Chartist who did not subscribe to Walmsley's moral force argument—surprisingly came out to support Clark. When Harney attempted to publish a response to Clark in the Leeds-based Chartist newspaper *Northern Star*—edited by O'Connor and to which Harney had previously contributed—O'Connor would not let him.

In the June 1850 issue of the *Democratic Review* Harney published his own response in which he formally resigned from all association with the *Northern Star* and berated Clark for his treatment of Reynolds and for betraying the Chartist movement.[274] The matter had progressed beyond a simple disagreement between Reynolds and Clark. This was now a formal schism between the Red Republicans and the NPFRA.

One of Clark's motives in publishing his pamphlet was to destroy Reynolds's election hopes. In May 1850 Reynolds had announced his intention to stand as MP for the Borough of Finsbury at the election due to be held in 1852. At the end of his open letter Clark signed off by advising the electors of Finsbury not to elect 'the purveyor and retailer of infamy and debauchery'.[275] Reynolds was serious about standing for election and he published his Chartist-inspired manifesto in his editorial for *Reynolds's Weekly Newspaper* on 26 May:

> [I] am an advocate for Universal Suffrage, the Vote by Ballot, Short Parliaments, the Abolition of the Property Qualification, the Equalization of the Electoral Districts (basing the representation upon population), and the Payment of Members. I am also an advocate for the Separation of Church and State, an enemy to the existing Poor Law, and a friend to Free Trade in the most comprehensive meaning of the term. I am likewise convinced that the most rigorous economy must be introduced into the management of the National Finances, by the diminution of the cost of all the Government institutions, the total abolition of all sinecures, and a thorough revision of the Pension-List.[276]

Reynolds withdrew from his intention to stand for parliament later in the year, although whether Clark's words made Reynolds think twice remains unknown. It is doubtful that he ever had a serious chance of getting elected, and the borough was in fact already represented by the radical liberal MP Thomas Slingsby Duncombe, who had been the constituency's MP since the 1830s.

There is no doubt that Reynolds could often rub people up the wrong way, a fact that is illustrated in his altercation with Lord Harrowby, and which is one of the more amusing incidents in Reynolds's political career. On 6 June 1850, Reynolds attended the Sixth Annual Meeting of the Society for Improving the Condition of the Labouring Classes, held at St. Martin's Hall (now the Sondheim Theatre, London). There were several dignitaries present such as Lord Harrowby as well as Prime Minister Lord John Russell, but there seemed to be more people on the platform than in the audience, as Reynolds recalled,

> The Hall was however thinly attended, and at no part of the proceedings was it more than half filled. The larger portion of the audience consisted of ladies; two-thirds of the male portion were ... sanctified gentry; and the remaining third consisted of persons belonging to the working-class. But upon the platform, amongst the eighty or ninety individuals

sprinkled about an amphitheatrical array of benches capable of accommodating at least five hundred. There were half-a-dozen Lords, three or four parsons, and the usual number of sleek and oily maw-worms who fatten upon every so-called religious or philanthropic society.[277]

The usual speeches and resolutions commenced, all of which were mocked by Reynolds. 'The prayers being ended', Reynolds sneered, 'Lord John Russell made the usual appropriate speech for a chairman; and the Secretary droned through a windy and somniferous report, stuffed with statistics'.[278] It was after this that Dudley Ryder, 3rd Earl of Harrowby, stood up and began to deliver a speech. Ryder was a former military officer who was trying to carve out for himself a career in politics.[279] Harrowby was no friend of the working class, in Reynolds's view, and the lord's speech was was filled with,

> The characteristic display of aristocratic ignorance, arrogance, narrow-mindedness, and incompetency; he could not give utterance to ten consecutive words without hem'ing and haw'ing in a most exemplary manner—and yet he was by no means abashed at his own stupendous stolidity, nor did he sit down and give up the thing as a bad job when he found himself foundering amidst all kinds of ungrammatical twaddle, inconsequent verbiage, and vain attempts to connect ideas which would persist in remaining disjointed.[280]

The remarks over Harrowby's speaking abilities aside, Reynolds's main point of contention with Harrowby's speech was when he advised the working classes to be,

> Obedient, docile, submissive, and follow [the aristocracy's] advice in all things without venturing to have an opinion of your own. But above all, don't dream of becoming landowners: leave the land where it is—in the hands of the Aristocracy—because no good could possibly arise from your having anything to do with it, You see how deep an interest I take in your welfare, and what excellent counsel

I am gratuitously bestowing upon you; and the only reward
I ask, is that you shall continue to put faith in the honest,
disinterested, humane, and intelligent class to which I, the
Earl of Harrowby, belong.[281]

If Harrowby's talk truly contained those sentiments, one can imagine
that Reynolds's jaw probably hit the floor on this occasion, and no
doubt he was gasping and guffawing through the entire speech. He
despised the aristocracy, and to hear such a patronising speech by a
member of that august class delivered to the working classes present,
made Reynolds want to add his own tuppence to the debate. Despite
only being an audience member and not on the billed list of speakers,
Reynolds mounted the stage and requested permission to speak, in order
that he might defend the working classes from Harrowby's calumnies.
As he approached the Prime Minister to ask permission, Lord Harrowby
jumped upon him in a rage and thumped Reynolds in the face. This
was a lord silencing the people's representative—another instance of
aristocratic tyranny! At least, that is how Reynolds, masterfully playing
the victim in his newspaper, portrayed the event when he wrote about
it the following week. Had Reynolds been a lord, so he reasoned, Lord
Harrowby would never have dared to assault him. But Reynolds insisted
that he was completely unfazed by Harrowby's actions:

> Lord Harrowby and his conduct would be beneath
> contempt, were not the former a type of a domineering
> class, and the latter a sample of aristocratic arrogance. In
> fact, the Privileged Orders think that they can ride rough-
> shod over the working-classes and their champions ... Lord
> Harrowby knew that I should not hesitate to expose cant
> and treachery, humbug and tyranny; and [he was] therefore
> equally interested in silencing me at St. Martin's Hall.[282]

Reynolds did later apply to the police to have Lord Harrowby arrested
but the police refused to follow up on the matter. This was another
instance of class injustice, in Reynolds's view, for had Reynolds been a
lord, he reasoned, then the police would have investigated straight away.
Nevertheless, for Reynolds to confront not only the Prime Minister and
others assembled, was bold, to say the least; on this occasion his boldness

made others intensely dislike him. His detractors probably thought that he deserved the assault. One commentator took pleasure in the fact that Reynolds had got his comeuppance, and remarked that 'of all the dolts that were ever pooh-poohed, probably the greatest is Mr George William MacArthur Reynolds'.[283]

After 1852, Reynolds thought no more of standing for elections. He continued to engage in politics at a local level and remained a member of various reform societies. He would also write a weekly column on political matters until 1856, and began writing further novels. In fact, his literary career went from strength-to-strength, and he became a very wealthy man.

Seamstresses, Soldiers, and Statues: Reynolds's 'Memoirs' and Historical Novels Series

> The eagle that dwells upon Glencoe's height
> Guards the MacDonalds by day and by night.
> By day when his pinions sweep up to the sun,
> He marks the wild scenes where battles were won.
>
> George W.M. Reynolds,
> *The Massacre of Glencoe* (1851–52)

The fourth volume of *The Mysteries of London* sees a villain named Martha Slingsby accost a young maiden named Agnes as she was reading in her garden. The book in Agnes's hand was *Ivanhoe* (1819) by Sir Walter Scott. 'You are engaged in the perusal of one of the finest tales in the English language',[284] Martha remarked, and she went on to extol the brilliance of Scott's novel. Scott was an historical novelist whose novels were extremely popular with the Regency and Victorian reading public, and Reynolds clearly admired him; his admiration for Scott may be the reason why Reynolds began writing a number of thrilling romances set in the days of old, while another portion of his fiction took a decidedly socialist turn.

In 1849, a friend challenged Reynolds to write 'a mystery so well veiled and maintained that I should be unable to see through it'.[285] Rising to the challenge, Reynolds set to work and produced the mammoth *Coral Island; or, The Hereditary Curse* which was serialised in *Reynolds's Miscellany* between 1849 and 1850—the same novel that Vickers and Stiff attempted to plagiarise with the publication of their *Corral*

Island. The entire novel takes place in Naples and this is perhaps why American publishers renamed it *The Mysteries of the Court of Naples*.[286] Supernatural curses, damsels-in-distress, and intricate subplots were the order of the day, which sees a young hero from medieval Italy attempt to escape his family's hereditary curse of leprosy.

Reynolds went on to write other novels in a similar vein. After *The Coral Island* appeared, there was *The Bronze Statue; or, The Virgin's Kiss* (1849–50), set in early modern Germany and Austria. The novel has thrilling gothic scenes of dark castles, dimly-lit churches, and the fearsome Inquisition. 'The Virgin's Kiss' is actually an elaborate torture device: it is a statue of the Virgin Mary, the front of which opens up to reveal a large mangling machine studded with sharp blades. Into this machine unsuspecting young maids are thrown to their deaths, and the illustrators that Reynolds employed always made sure to depict the most shocking incidents of this narrative.

Other gothic tales written by Reynolds included *The Necromancer* (1851–52), subtitled by American publishers as *The Mysteries of the Court of Henry the Eighth*. It tells the story of the mysterious Lord Danvers who, like Faust, having sold his soul to the devil for eternal life and the power of shapeshifting, can only be released from his curse if he sacrifices the lives of six young virgins who fell in love with him. He sets his sights on Musidora, and impersonated Henry VIII to make her fall in love with him, in the hope that she would be dazzled by the prospect of a royal marriage. But Musidora saw through Danver's schemes and called off the engagement, after which Danvers disappeared for years. At the end of the novel, Musidora came to the rescue of another girl who had also fallen victim to Danvers—the girl who turns out to be Musidora's own child—and Danvers, shamed, finally pays the penalty of his Faustian bargain and descends into hell.

The four Reynolds's novels most clearly inspired by Walter Scott, however, were *Pope Joan* (1850); *Kenneth: A Romance of the Highlands* (1851), *The Massacre of Glencoe* (1852–53), and *Margaret: The Discarded Queen* (1856). These tales were firmly historical and there were few, if any, supernatural elements in them. *Kenneth* was the tale of a feud between two noble Scottish families during the 1500s. *The Massacre of Glencoe* told the tale of William of Orange who, before the Glorious Revolution of 1688, arrived in Scotland in disguise to undermine people's support for the Catholic James II. Once William became king, he plotted with members of the Campbell clan to wipe out the MacDonalds, who were loyal to James II. Imagining himself always as the champion of the underdog, Reynolds also retold the story of Mary, Queen of Scots in *Mary Stuart* (1859). In terms of its plot, it is much simpler than Reynolds's previous novels: an Italian messenger arrived in Scotland carrying a papal bull, which would allow Mary to marry the somewhat effeminate and devious Lord Darnley. Along the way, the Italian hero foiled various plots against the beautiful young queen. Mary represented all that was good, while the men around her were scheming and treacherous. The portrayal of Mary as the embodiment of queenly virtue in this story stands in marked contrast to Reynolds's depiction of Queen Elizabeth I in *Canonbury House; or, The Queen's Prophecy* (1857–58). In the latter the Virgin Queen is, in fact, not a virgin at all, having secretly given birth to a child named Ada Arundel, who was subsequently adopted by the kindly Spencer family. Elizabeth's scheming and callous behaviour in the novel—much different to Victorian historians' opinions of her—mark her out as 'a cold-blooded, calculating, yet capricious tyrant'.[287]

Reynolds was a busy man. While writing his Scottish novels between 1853 and 1854, he and Susannah welcomed two more children into the family: Ledru-Rollin, named after two continental revolutionaries, and Louise Clarice, the eighth child in the Reynolds family. To celebrate the latter's birth, Reynolds reprinted one of his earliest poems titled 'To a Newborn Child' in *Reynolds's Miscellany*:

> Frail plant, condemn'd to crouch beneath the storm
> Of earthly ills, and shiver to the blast
>   That rules in this cold world
>   Th'ungenial atmosphere:
> May thy diminutive and fragile frame
> Survive the shocks of ev'ry latent pang,
>   And live to smile at that
>   Which once had startled thee!
> Sweet babe! were all as innocent as thou,
> Then might we deem the glorious times call'd back
>   When our first parents rov'd
>   Sinless in Eden's realms,
> Alas! the tainted elements of earth,

That form the compact being which we call
   Man, is a living mass
   Of sorrow and of sin!
Yet live thou on, sweet child!—and like the brave
And dauntless sailor toss'd on lawless seas,
   May'st thou thus meet the ills
   That wait thy future day.[288]

However, it must have been a difficult birth for Susannah, whose health was failing at this time. It was for this reason that the family left the smoky, polluted city of London and moved permanently to the house at Herne Bay in Kent. With Reynolds no longer in London, it can be assumed that Edward Reynolds had become *de facto* editor-in-chief for *Reynolds's Weekly Newspaper*, even though Reynolds's name still adorned the newspaper's masthead.[289] Reynolds continued to write a weekly editorial for the newspaper until 1856, but he concentrated much more upon the *Miscellany*, as well as local politics in the town of Herne Bay where he became active in the affairs of the local corporation.

All the while, sales of *Reynolds's Miscellany* and *Reynolds's Weekly Newspaper* kept increasing. During the Annual Dinner of the Reynolds Establishment in 1853 Reynolds boasted that

> The Newspaper, as the machinists present could testify, rose steadily and continuously every week … Moreover, it occupied the proud position of being the organ of British democracy—the organ of the working classes—the champion of their interests, the asserter of their rights, and the proclaimer of their wrongs.[290]

Reynolds was not being vain when he uttered those sentiments: they were also echoed by Karl Marx, who declared that *Reynolds's Weekly Newspaper* was the main organ of the democratic cause in Britain during the post-Chartist era.[291]

The annual dinners became a regular feature for the employees of Reynolds's publishing house. Every year all of Reynolds's employees—editors, journalists, artists, engravers, and printing office workers—travelled for a weekend away in the country. The staff enjoyed an all-expenses paid four day summer holiday, and good food and drink.

Reynolds's firm spared no expense at these events. As the report of the Annual Dinner of 1854 revealed: 'all the delicacies of the season, in the form of fish, flesh, and fowl, *entrées*, pastry, dainties, and sweets of all description constituted the several courses; and the wines were of the finest quality'.[292] It was certainly unusual for any Victorian business to give its employees paid leave, especially a big firm such as Reynolds's, which employed eighty people across its departments by 1857.[293] For the vast majority of workers paid holidays would not come into force until the Bank Holiday Act (1871).[294] Reynolds was clearly living by his principles of fairly rewarding the valuable work conducted by those under his charge.

As was customary, Reynolds made a speech at each of these events which usually began with him toasting the efforts of John Dicks and Edward Reynolds, and finishing by thanking all of his employees for their hard work. The speeches that Reynolds gave often had political undertones to them as well. One year, for instance, he delivered a lengthy speech on the meaning of democracy and patriotism, and he asked all those present: 'Can true democracy ever mean anything else than true patriotism? I love my country and I cannot bear to see masses of its population suffering from causes of which they themselves are innocent'.[295] He was probably preaching to the converted, however, and it is difficult to imagine that the people working for Reynolds's firm did not share his radical sentiments.

It was usual for Reynolds to boast about the ever-increasing circulation of the *Miscellany* at the annual dinners. There was a demand for cheap light fiction, and Reynolds's magazine fulfilled that demand. But it is little wonder that sales of the *Miscellany* soared in the 1850s, for in 1857, another celebrity joined the ranks of Reynolds's establishment: Pierce Egan the Younger (1814–80).[296] One of the most popular novelists of the age, Egan's penny novels such as *Robin Hood* (1838–39) and *Wat Tyler* (1840–41), in the words of one correspondent, 'sold by the half million'.[297]

Egan had served as the editor of the *Home Circle*, which was one of the more respectable penny publications, between 1849 and 1851. He then became a regular contributor to the *London Journal*, which it will be recalled, was first edited by Reynolds when it was set up in 1845. When Reynolds left the *London Journal*, John Wilson Ross took the reins and it was Ross who employed Egan. However, the *London*

Journal was bought out by the owners of *Punch* magazine in 1857, and a new editor, Mark Lemon (1809–70), who replaced John Wilson Ross.

Despite Egan being one of the big names in the world of Victorian popular fiction, Lemon unceremoniously dispensed with his services. In place of Egan's stories Lemon began printing the old novels of Walter Scott. Reynolds must have recognised that having Egan's name alongside his own would have been a big draw, and serialised novels and short stories from Egan began to appear in *Reynolds's Miscellany* from 1856 onwards. In the meantime sales of the *London Journal* plummeted. As brilliant as Scott's novels were, readers wanted new content and evidently voted with their feet.

The *London Journal* was soon re-purchased by George Stiff, the man who had financed the magazine's establishment back in 1845. Stiff immediately appointed a new editor, Percy B. St John. St John quickly re-employed Egan and the *London Journal*'s fortunes improved. Egan then became the editor of the *London Journal* in 1861, at which time St John then joined Reynolds's establishment. Authors and editors' constant switching between various establishments was normal in the world of Victorian 'penny publishers' as many of its famous stars, much as Reynolds had done earlier in his career, had served as the editor of several magazines.

Reynolds had however relinquished all managerial control of the newspaper to his brother Edward. Reynolds still took an active role in the running of *Reynolds's Miscellany* and several of his new novels were serialised in it. In addition to his Scottish novels, Reynolds embarked upon writing a series of novels that focused upon telling the stories of social outcasts struggling to make their way in a heartless and alienating industrial capitalist world.

Reynolds began this series when he published *The Seamstress; or, The White Slave of England* (1850–51). The figure of the young and poor seamstress was used by a variety of Victorian novelists to expose social ills and tug at their readers' heartstrings because, although real-life seamstresses were usually poor, they were viewed as morally pure. They were not prostitutes and did not sell their bodies for money, and unlike factory women seamstresses carried out their work at home, so they had not abandoned the domestic sphere.[298] Of course, Reynolds went further than many of the reform-minded novelists of his day, and in *The Seamstress* presented a strong socialist critique of capitalist society by telling a tale of a young dressmaker who worked all hours in her miserable garret, to produce opulent dresses for aristocratic women, yet was never able to make ends meet herself.

In the *Seamstress*, Reynolds sought to explain to his readers why poor people remained poor despite doing everything that Victorian moralists said they should: living by strict moral principles and dedicating themselves to a life of hard work. The reasons why the seamstress, Virginia, was poor was explained to her when she visited Julia, who lived in the apartment directly beneath her own. To acquire any work, Virginia must approach an agent of a high-class haberdasher named Madame DuPlessey, who acted as an intermediary between the customer (the Duchess of Belmont) and the labourer (Virginia). Julia told Virginia that, while in an ideal world she would get a fair price for her labour time, once the garment she was to make had been completed, Virginia's labour would not be valued very highly. When the various agents in the process had also taken commission out of the price paid by the Duchess of Belmont, the amount that Virginia finally received in wages was far lower than what it should be.[299]

The 1850s were a period in which many socialists began analysing the market in commodities and seeking to explain why workers came out with lower wages than they should. Ledru-Rollin discussed this in *The Decline of England* (1849), as did Helen Macfarlane in the *Red Republican*. Harney's magazine did, in fact, print several articles discussing this question. A more complex scientific critique of the value of the labour process and commodities, once they had entered the marketplace, when the value of a person's labour had been 'hidden' from the final product, would later be explained in much further detail by Karl Marx in *Capital*.[300]

With attempted suicides, clandestine aristocratic love affairs, and the tragic death of the heroine at the end, *The Seamstress* paved the way for Reynolds's other stories about poverty-stricken figures. After *The Seamstress*, there appeared several novels written in the first person, which the literary critic Graham Law has dubbed the 'Memoirs' series: *Mary Price; or the Memoirs of a Servant Girl* (1851–52); *Joseph Wilmot; or, the Memoirs of a Manservant* (1853–55); *Rosa Lambert; or, the Memoirs of an Unfortunate Woman* (1853–54); *May Middleton; or, The History of a Fortune* (1854–55); *Ellen Percy; or, The Memoirs of an Actress* (1855–57); and *Agnes; or, Beauty and Pleasure* (1855–57).

All of these were published as standalone penny issues and not in the *Miscellany* and, with the exception of *Joseph Wilmot*, the focus was upon poor and friendless women's adversities.

Reynolds also adopted a new method of telling a story in *Mary Price*: the 'memoirs' were written in the first person. As this new manner of writing was a departure from the style of fiction that Reynolds's devoted readers were used to, he decided that he would offer a lengthy justification for it. The novel's aim was,

> To dissect the social body in the minutest manner—to penetrate beneath the surface of everyday life—to draw aside the veil from the domestic hearth, and look deep into the modes of existence practised by families of all grades— and thus to lay bare the mysteries of English society,—such is a faint shadowing forth of the author's design in his New Tale. In carrying out this aim he has adopted a machinery which has appeared to him the best suited for the purpose— namely, the autobiography of a Servant-Maid, whose experiences, observations, and adventures in the various families which she successively enters, form the basis of the work.[301]

Mary Price was still a 'Mysteries' novel, then, but unlike the *Mysteries*— which were set not only in Britain, but also in places as far afield as Australia, India, Italy, France, and featured recognisable political figures — the focus of the new 'memoirs' was to be centred on England and its 'unknown' people.

Whereas in *The Seamstress* the heroine died at a young age and remained innocent (which is to say, Virginia does not become a prostitute), the women of the memoirs series did not always remain pure in character. Oftentimes they had to do *whatever* it took to survive in a cold, unfeeling world. Thus, in *Rosa Lambert*, readers were introduced to the title character who, with a drunken father in debt to a local landowner and good-for-nothing brother who refused to work for a living, settled her father's debt by sleeping with the lecherous landowner for money. Ashamed of herself, Rosa escaped to London and became the mistress to over sixteen men.

Meanwhile in *Ellen Percy*, readers met the title character living in a dingy flat in Leeds, but who eventually became an actress, and charmed her way through all stratas of society. At the end of the novel Ellen, as happens in many a Victorian novel, married a viscount and formally entered high society. One of the characters in *Ellen Percy*, named Mary Glentworth, proved to be so popular with readers, that Reynolds brought out a new tale with her as the protagonist: *The Young Duchess.* American readers likewise warmed to the story of Mary Glentworth, and the New York publishers Pollard and Moss released *Mary Glentworth; or, The Forbidden Marriage.* This last one was a completely new tale, written by an anonymous American author, who was trying to capitalise on Reynolds's success.

Just as controversy had attended the publication of Reynolds's previous novels, more was to follow as Reynolds drew the ire of the British Army's bureaucracy. This occurred when Reynolds published one of his finest novels: *The Soldier's Wife* (1852–53), which was published in weekly penny numbers. It told the story of two young lovers, Frederick and Lucy, living in the village of Oakley. The former was a poor farm labourer, and the latter was from a middle-class background. Lucy's father would not allow her to marry Frederick because he was too poor. A recruiting officer then visited the village and convinced the young lads assembled in the village square to enlist, by beguiling them with tales of exciting adventures overseas:

> "Talk of the hardships of a soldier's life ... why it's the most beautiful state of existence that can possibly be conceived. Here you have great lords and wealthy gentlemen paying large sums of money out of their own pockets to travel on the continent and see the fine things there; but the soldier travels to the most distant parts of the earth at no expense of his own. His sovereign pays for him. Think of that, gentlemen—only think of that, I say! What an honour to have your sovereign take such an interest as to pay your travelling expenses."[302]

Frederick devised what seemed like a simple plan to counter the objections of Lucy's father: he would join the army, gain respectability, and make some money so he could finally marry Lucy. Yet Frederick was not treated well in the army: he has the ill luck to make the enmity of an aristocratic officer who orders Frederick's flogging. Realising that his life would be made a misery in the army under the command of the aristocrat, he deserted and returned to Lucy in Oakley. The pair of them then fled to the continent where they got married. After some years and the birth of a son, Lucy and Frederick were called back to England on the pretence of visiting Lucy's dying father. Unfortunately for the young couple, it was a scheme hatched by the original recruiting officer, in concert with Lucy's estranged father, to arrest Frederick and make him serve out the rest of his time in the army. When he was back in the army, Frederick suffered further floggings and made several attempts to desert. In the meantime, Lucy was forced to take lodgings in a miserable one-room apartment, and to work as a lowly-paid seamstress to support the whole family, for Frederick's wages did not cover their expenses, especially as he became an alcoholic. As a result of a misdemeanour, Frederick is court-martialled and executed by firing squad.

Melodramatic but well-executed, *The Soldier's Wife* caused a sensation in public life and particularly among the army's top brass. The writing of the novel was part of Reynolds's personal crusade against the punishment of flogging, a cause he had supported since 1844. In *The Mysteries of London* he broke the narrative—which he often did—to deliver to readers a thundering excoriation of flogging. The rant was occasioned by the recent flogging to death of a poor private soldier, upon the orders of the Duke of York. The event also allowed Reynolds to go on one of his usual rants against the aristocracy:

> We shall here interrupt the thread of our narrative for a brief space, in order to make a few observations upon the condition of the private soldier. And, in the first instance, let us record our conviction that there is not a more generous-hearted, a nobler-minded, or a more humane set of men breathing than those who constitute the ranks of the British Army; while there is not a more tyrannical, overbearing, illiberal, and self-sufficient class than that composed of the officers of this army. But how is the latter fact to be accounted for? Because the Army is the mere plaything of the Aristocracy—a means of providing for the younger sons of noblemen, and enabling titled mammas to show off their striplings in red coats. What opinion can we have of the constitution of the army, so far as the officers are concerned,

when we find Prince Albert suddenly created a Field-Marshal! Such a spectacle is nauseating in the extreme; and the German must have execrably bad taste, or else be endowed with inordinate conceit, to hold the *baton* of a Marshal when he has not even the military knowledge of a drummer-boy. Since the Army is thus made a mere tool in the hands of a rascally Aristocracy, what sympathy can possibly exist between the officers and the men? The former look upon the latter as the scum of the earth—mere slaves on a level with shoe-blacks; and hence the barbarous cry of "Flog! flog! flog!" But there is no love lost between the classes: for the soldiers hate and abhor their officers, whom they naturally and most justly look upon as their tyrants and oppressors. It is enough to make the blood boil with indignation to think that those fine, stalwart, gallant fellows should be kicked about at the caprice of a wretched ensign or contemptible cornet just loosened from his mamma's apron-strings,—or bullied by older officers whose only "excellence" is their relationship to nobility, and their power to obtain promotion *by purchase*. The generality of the officers in the British Army are nothing more nor less than a set of purse-proud bloodhounds, whose greatest delight is to behold the blood streaming down the backs of those men who alone win their country's battles. When the Duke of York (who was a humane man, though as great a scamp as ever had a COLUMN OF INFAMY erected to his memory) limited corporal punishment to 300 lashes, the full amount was invariably inflicted in nineteen out of twenty cases: but even this would not satisfy the bloodhounds, who annoyed and pestered the Duke on the subject to such an extent that he was literally bullied into empowering them to hold General Regimental Courts-Martial, by whose decision 500 lashes might be administered to the unhappy victim. For years and years was the torture of military flogging in England a shame and a scandal to all Europe; and it was absolutely necessary that a fine fellow should be *murdered* at Hounslow by the accursed lash, before the barbarous Government would interfere. All the world

129

knows that a BRITISH SOLDIER *was murdered* in this revolting manner, and in the presence of his horror-stricken comrades: for be it remembered that when these appalling spectacles take place, the eyes that weep and the hearts that grow faint are those of the soldiers—never of the officers![303]

In view of Reynolds's repeated denunciations of flogging and the publication of *The Solider's Wife*, the army banned soldiers from reading Reynolds's novels.

The army's banning of Reynolds's novels simply made him more determined to speak out, and soon army newspapers began attacking him. In September 1853, the *United Service Gazette* published an editorial attacking Reynolds and the publication of his correspondence with a pseudonymous Private Robert Lithgow, who had leaked the details of several instances of army brutality to *Reynolds's Weekly Newspaper*.

Rather than engage with the substance of Reynolds's criticisms, the article in the *United Services Gazette* decided instead to draw attention to the immorality of *The Mysteries of London* and mocked Reynolds for having 'got up that queer revolution in 1848'. The *Gazette* also sneered at Reynolds's working-class readership by saying that 'his newspaper is in the hands of deluded thousands who can just manage to spell and absorb discontent over their pipes and pots'.[304] Of course, the actions of the *Gazette* just made Reynolds more popular with the army's rank-and-file, and soon more soldiers began writing to Reynolds with accounts of army brutality. One correspondent assured Reynolds that, in spite of the *United Service Gazette*'s condemnation of Reynolds's work, 'the perusal of [Reynolds's] paper, [was] a luxury, not only to me but to all my acquaintance because it abounds with a commodity in which too many others are bankrupt; viz., *truth*'.[305] Over a decade later, some in the army were still bitter towards Reynolds and attempted to place the blame for soldiers' drunkenness on his allegedly 'seditious' writings.[306]

It was not until 1868, however, that the British Army abolished flogging as a punishment for soldiers serving in peacetime. Perhaps the decision was, in part, a result of the country's biggest-selling radical newspaper drawing attention to the issue? In 1888 flogging was completely abolished. However, for some time after this, soldiers were on occasion subjected to corporal punishment. Between 1902 and 1903, several cases of flogging came to public notice and there was justifiable outrage. As late as 1946, it was clear that, in some corners of the army's ranks, floggings were occasionally meted out as punishment for minor offences.

Alongside his historical novels, Reynolds also turned his attention to a major contemporary event, the Crimean War, and he made this war the focus of three novels: *Omar: A Tale of the War* (1855–56); *The Loves of the Harem: A Romance of Constantinople* (1855–57); and *Leila; or, The Star of Mingrelia* (1856). All of these were published in weekly penny numbers and collectively they might be given the name of 'the Mysteries of Eastern Court Life' because they tell of the plots and intrigues of sultans, pashas, and women in harems. The last of these, *Leila*, proved, like many of Reynolds's works before it, to be immensely popular in India. One of the nineteenth century's biggest-selling books in India was *London Rashaya*, a translation of *Mysteries of the Court* by Rabindrath Tagore.[307] The literary critic Suchetta Bhattacharya points out that a number of educated Indian academics followed Tagore's lead by translating several of Reynolds's other works: *Loves of the Harem* appeared as *Abarodh Prem* (1885); *The Young Duchess* as *Rani Krishnakamini* (1889); *Mary Price* was published as *Mary Prais* (1893); and *The Soldier's Wife* appeared as *Sainik Badhu* (1895). With these novels often containing lengthy digressions which railed against the British establishment and imperialism, it is unsurprising that his stories found a ready audience among the increasingly nationalist Indian middle classes. It was this same class of Indians who led the campaign for Indian home rule and, finally, for independence in the twentieth century. *Leila* was even adapted as a silent movie by R.S. Prakash in 1931. It was reportedly the most expensive film made in India at the time.[308]

Aside from drawing the ire of the army chiefs, Reynolds's life at Herne Bay—where he wrote most of these novels—was pretty good. He was now a man of property and active in local politics. Further happiness came to the family when Reynolds and Susannah's next daughter Emily was born in 1856. Reynolds and Susannah's older boys were carving out respectable careers for themselves in law and their daughters were making 'good' marriages. The now twenty-year-old Blanche Reynolds secured a respectable marriage for herself in the spring of 1858 when she wed a solicitor named William Wright Eadon.[309] Theresa Isabella married a solicitor named Archibald Douglas Lamb. Frederick Reynolds had also married a woman named Florence around this time.

Although he was older, Reynolds was presumably no wiser because he found himself in court yet again, but at least it was not for a bankruptcy case this time. Still an active campaigner for universal suffrage, Reynolds felt no affinity with men like the former Chartist activist Ernest Jones who still advocated for moral force Chartism and proposed alliances with the middle classes.

In 1852 Jones had founded a newspaper that was intended to rival *Reynolds's Weekly Newspaper* and promote moral force Chartism. Jones's *People's Paper*, as it was called, was never a serious rival to Reynolds's own newspaper as Jones never had the far-reaching 'brand' that Reynolds did. In the meantime, the first history book of the Chartist movement was published in 1854 titled *The History of the Chartist Movement*.[310] Written by Robert Gammage, the book alleged that Jones was guilty of a number of shady business practices including embezzling funds from the *People's Paper*. Gammage also alleged that, when Jones was elected to the executive committee of a Chartist association in 1852, he had rigged the vote in his favour. The allegations were completely false. But when the book was first published Jones appears to have brushed them off. After all, few people would read Gammage's book as it was quite expensive and Jones had the support of his employees at the *People's Paper* who knew the accusations were untrue.

However, Gammage's allegations received further amplification when they were repeated on several occasions in *Reynolds's Weekly Newspaper* between 1858 and 1859, to an audience of hundreds of thousands. Jones sued Reynolds for libel and won. Yet the damages were not extensive for Reynolds, who was ordered to pay only £2, as well as Jones's legal costs. Reynolds was also required to apologise and cease his smear campaign against Jones.

Jones had claimed that Reynolds's accusations had caused the *People's Paper* to founder and that he had had to close the newspaper down as a result. This of course would be difficult to prove: the libel law as it then stood required someone to *prove* that they had suffered a financial loss. Perhaps, then, the judge had reasoned that, as Reynolds was merely repeating information that was already available in the public domain (from Gammage's book), then Reynolds was not in fact guilty of creating a new libel, but was instead guilty of giving further amplification to it. The only remaining information on this trial comes from a pamphlet that was published by Jones, and heavily edited by him, so the judge's exact reasons are unknown. In January 1859, as the case was brought to a close, the Lord Chief Justice summarised the case as follows:

> All of us may disagree with Mr Ernest Jones's political sentiments—all of us may hold him to be a political enthusiast; but I think the proceedings of this day show that there has been nothing sordid in his conduct, and that, after this proceeding, not a shadow of imputation can rest upon him, nor a shadow of pretence for the imputations made.[311]

The proceedings of the case drew the attention of Karl Marx and Friedrich Engels, who were then resident in London. Marx had written several articles for the *People's Paper* between 1852 and 1856 and knew Jones well. It is not clear if Marx knew Reynolds personally, but for a variety of reasons Marx distrusted Reynolds, although the two men were both agreed that Jones was the 'dupe' of the middle classes,[312] and Jones's proposed alliances with the middle classes were the reason that Marx stopped writing for his paper.[313] The entire spat between Jones and Reynolds, and the proceedings of the subsequent court case, appears to have amused Marx. The private correspondence between him and Engels reveals what the father of communism thought of the whole affair, and of Reynolds in particular:

> I enclose extracts from Reynolds about Jones. You will see for yourself where R gives facts and a judgment based on facts, and where he is airing his venom. R is a much bigger rascal than Jones, but he is a rich and able speculator. The mere fact that he has turned into an out-and-out Chartist shows that his position must still be a 'bearable' one.[314]

Reynolds was a Red Republican and closer in spirit to Marx's outlook than the gradualist and reformist Jones, but Marx must have known that Reynolds could sometimes be unpleasant when he set out to attack someone; hence, the remark about Reynolds 'airing his venom'. Marx and Engels were not the only contemporary observers to pass comment on the case for public opinion seemed to be firmly on Jones's side. The *Saturday Review* accused Reynolds of 'dirt throwing', while a commentator in the *Leeds Mercury* was firmly on the side of Ernest Jones, and wished that the damages awarded had been higher. Then, as became customary for Victorian journalists commenting on Reynolds, the writer went on to attack *The Mysteries of London* for its immorality.[315]

While the court case with Jones was proceeding, tragedy struck. Susannah had been ill for some time and on 4 October 1858, she collapsed and died at their home in Herne Bay. The cause given by the doctor who attended was 'disease of the heart'.[316] This was a catch-all term which could signify anything from angina, arrhythmia, atherosclerosis, and even congential heart defects.[317] Few details are known of the funeral, and it is when episodes such as these cross the historian's path that we regret having no letters or diaries that might give us a glimpse into how we imagine Reynolds might have felt at the time. Susannah, sadly, did not live to see the birth of her first grandchild, Kate Eadon, born in 1859. From publicly available writings, we might assume that Reynolds and Susannah's marriage was a happy one; she shared his literary ambitions and his politics. We might surmise that her death was very painful for Reynolds. Very soon after Susannah died, Reynolds moved back to London and settled at 41 Woburn Square. Maybe the house at Herne Bay, where the couple shared many happy memories, was not the same without her.

Perhaps Reynolds had lost his muse. This might certainly be inferred from his publication record after Susannah's death. He had already stopped writing weekly editorials for *Reynolds's Weekly Newspaper* in 1856, and he finished the serialisation of *Empress Eugenie's Boudoir* in 1858, and *Mary Stuart* ended in 1859. *Empress Eugenie's Boudoir* was a rehash of his earlier *Drunkard's Progress* combined with a condensed version of his 1840 translation of Paul de Kock's *Sister Anne*. Reynolds was clearly putting minimal effort into his storytelling at this point. The novel did, however, contain some original material featuring scenes at the court of Napoleon III's wife, Eugénie, hence the American title: *The Mysteries of the Court of France*.[318]

After his final full length novel, *Mary Stuart* Reynolds only published two short stories: *Two Christmas Days* and *The Young Fisherman; or, The Spirits of the Lake*, printed in *Reynolds's Miscellany* in 1860 and 1861 respectively. Although Reynolds still served as editor of *Reynolds's Miscellany* he ceased to write new tales for it. Besides, a new writer had joined the ranks of the *Miscellany* in 1857 and became its star attraction:

James Malcolm Rymer, author of the original *Sweeney Todd* tale. The *Miscellany* was by this point so well-established that it was no longer reliant on Reynolds's fiction as it had been in the 1840s.

Reynolds's gradual retirement from publishing should not be surprising, of course; Susannah had passed away and he probably decided to focus on raising his own children. Ledru-Rollin was but six years old when his mother died, and lived with his father at the family home in Woburn Square in 1861, as did the young Louise Clarisse. The four female servants doubtless took a large role in raising the children. And Reynolds was of course a grandfather now. Blanche and her husband William went on to have a large family. The aforementioned Kate Eadon was born in 1859 and in quick succession Blanche gave birth to Charles (b. 1861), Ellen (b. 1862), Gertrude (b. 1864), Frank (b. 1865), and Hilda (b. 1866).

Reynolds's other daughter, Joanna Frances, married Arthur Henry Woodham Lamb on 1 August 1865.[319] They too would introduce yet more grandchildren to Reynolds: Frances E Lamb (1866–1950); Edith Lamb (1866–1950); and Florence Lamb (1868–1952). With nine grandchildren and two children of his own to attend to, any grandparent's literary endeavours would have to take a back seat, which is what must have happened with Reynolds, as there were no new novels during the 1860s.

However, Reynolds returned to political activism in 1865 when the government seriously began discussing extending the franchise. In 1832, the Whigs had extended the right to vote to include £10 copyholders, £50 renters, £2 freeholders, and had created a number of new constituencies but, as we have seen, this excluded the working classes. However, when the American Civil War broke out in 1863, several factory workers' organisations signalled their public support for Abraham Lincoln's Union army and his Emancipation Declaration. This support came in spite of the fact that the Union had blockaded the Confederacy's ports, meaning that British factories' imports of cotton from America dried up, as did many jobs in Britain's textile industry.

The working classes' support of a noble cause abroad, even when it negatively affected their income, impressed the Liberal statesman William Ewart Gladstone (1809–89). He declared it 'a shame and a scandal that bodies of men such as these should be excluded from the parliamentary franchise'.[320] Gladstone's opinion mattered, and he was ready to publicly support an extension of the franchise. Soon Edward Baines—a veteran of the Peterloo Massacre in 1819—brought a private members bill to parliament in 1864 which proposed lowering the financial qualifications attached to the franchise. Baines's bill, however, failed to gather enough support in parliament and it was rejected.

Now that the question of reform was back on the political agenda, the old guard of Chartists, Red Chartists, and middle-class reformers sprang back into action. Associations were formed and tracts were printed. John Bright, a major figure in the Anti-Corn League and now M.P. for Birmingham wrote an essay titled 'Speech on Reform', which was widely circulated, arguing that that it would be better for the authorities to extend the franchise in some way, rather than do nothing and risk violent class conflict, the likes of which were feared during the heyday of the Chartist era.[321] One of Bright's associates from his Anti-Corn Law League days founded the National Reform Union in 1864 whose aims were to:

1. obtain such an extension of the Franchise as shall confer the Parliamentary Suffrage, in Counties and Boroughs, on every male person, householder or lodger, rated or liable to be rated, for the relief of the poor.
2. secure the free exercise of the Franchise, by affording to the voter the protection of the Ballot.
3. procure an equal distribution of Members of Parliament, in proportion to population and property.
4. establish more frequent opportunities for the expression of national opinion, by shortening the duration of Parliament to three years.[322]

The middle classes dominated the Reform Union, and it was left up to the motley crew of old Chartists to establish the National Reform League in 1865. Its founding members included Reynolds and Ernest Jones— who must presumably have forgiven Reynolds for the libel against him a decade earlier—as well as the Red Republican, George Julian Harney, and Edmond Beales, who served as the League's president. As John Belchem notes, with such titans of the Chartist movement at its head, the League was Chartism's true heir. And it was the League which was instrumental in securing the support of the London Trades Council (a forerunner of the Trades Union Congress), and the International

Working Men's Association, even when the eventual measures fell short of full universal suffrage.

Unlike some of the internecine squabbles that occurred between the Chartists and associated movements in the 1840s and 1850s, there was very little animosity between the National Reform Union and the National Reform League. Both groups in fact were aiming at a different demographic: the Union campaigned among the lower middle classes and the League targeted the working classes. The League was also willing to make trade-offs: although universal suffrage was their overall goal, its members initially agreed to support both household suffrage measures, as well as more limited extensions to the franchise, if these were the only feasible options. This perhaps is a result of the fact that the likes of Harney, Reynolds, and Jones had matured and become seasoned political campaigners, being willing to modify their goals with what was politically possible. It is likely that Reynolds returned to writing weekly editorials for *Reynolds's Weekly Newspaper* during this time, for many of the articles are similar in tone to those he wrote during the 1850s. However, none of them are signed by him so this cannot be stated with certainty.

Liberal stalwarts such as Gladstone were in favour of reform, but even Lord Derby's Conservatives came out in favour of extending the franchise. By this point the Conservatives had been in opposition for so long that they had to support *something* to stand a chance of getting re-elected. Yet a major obstacle remained: in 1865 Lord Palmerston, a Liberal, was Prime Minister. As far as he was concerned the issue of parliamentary reform was settled for eternity back in 1832. Luckily for pro-democracy campaigners—although most unluckily for the Prime Minister—Palmerston died in October 1865, which left the door wide open for a pro-reform minister to step in.

Lord Russell succeeded Palmerston, and, counting on support from some liberally-minded Conservatives, brought forward a bill which would have extended the franchise. The bill aimed to enfranchise the 'respectable' working classes: under its terms, if over £7 per year was paid in rent, or a lodger paid out over £10 per year in rent, or had savings of over £50, then there would be an entitlement to vote. But the bill failed. Benjamin Disraeli, the leader of the Conservatives in the House of Commons, convinced enough back-bench Tories and even some Liberals to oppose the bill. The public was with the Liberals, however, and large protests against those who opposed the bill were held outside Houses of Parliament. Nevertheless, Lord Russell felt that he had no other choice but to resign and the Liberal government collapsed.

Disraeli's actions were, unsurprisingly, purely political. Reynolds once described him as 'the most trumpery shuffler that ever displayed the chameleon hues of a political turn-coat',[323] and Disraeli's actions in 1867 lent credence to Reynolds's remarks; Disraeli did indeed support an extension of the franchise, although for him it was never an urgent issue. Disraeli simply wanted the Conservatives back in power. He knew that if Russell's reform bill failed then his government would as well. When the Liberal government did resign the Conservatives stepped up to lead a minority administration. Lord Derby served as Prime Minister from the House of Lords and Disraeli, in the Commons, became Chancellor of the Exchequer.

Campaigners feared that, with the Conservatives now in power, all hope of parliamentary reform would be lost. As a result, both the Reform Union and the Reform League intensified their campaigning. John Bright began a nationwide speaking tour. The Reform League organised several rallies throughout the country. At one of the Reform League's major rallies, held in Trafalgar Square and attended by old-school militant radicals—perhaps Reynolds was among them—the speakers began calling on working men to organise a general strike. It was beginning to feel like 1848 again. The Conservatives now *had* to address the issue of parliamentary reform.

In the Commons, Disraeli decided that he would support the extension of the franchise after all. If the franchise were extended, so Disraeli reasoned, the new voters would be exceedingly grateful to the Conservatives and vote them into power again—hopefully with a majority. Thus, Disraeli introduced a reform bill into the Commons in 1867. Not having a majority in the lower house, the Conservatives had to accept *all* amendments tabled to the bill (but due to his personal animosity against Gladstone, Disraeli would not accept any that had been personally forwarded by him). There now arose the bizarre situation (bizarre by Victorian standards at least) in which each party tried to outdo the other by going farther with their amendments. If the Liberals proposed extending the vote to people in receipt of a £20 pension, then the Tories went further and tabled what John Bright mockingly dubbed 'fancy franchises': the amendments enfranchised students, lawyers, medical doctors, and clergymen regardless of whether they met the proposed financial qualifications.

In the end, because of the several amendments proposed by people on all sides, the second Representation of the People Act that was passed in August 1867 was more far-reaching than what the Liberals had proposed in 1864. The vote was accorded not only to 40 shilling freeholders and £10 copyholders, but it was extended to all men living in borough constituencies who paid over £10 per year in rent, and also to those who were paying £12 in rent per annum in county constituencies; this was in addition to those enfranchised under the 'fancy franchises'. Some towns containing fewer than 10,000 inhabitants were disenfranchised, while major cities such as Manchester and Leeds, were given extra seats in parliament.[324] It was such a messy and complex bill, that the government had to revisit it in 1884 and pass the third Representation of the People Act.

In spite of the fact that it was Disraeli's Conservatives who had introduced the Second Reform Act, it was seen by the public as a 'Liberal' victory. But reformers quickly began pointing out the bill's flaws, as the *Beehive* reported in their coverage of a banquet organised by the London Working Men's Association in October:

> What has the Bill done? Has it given manhood suffrage? No. It has given household suffrage, but it has coupled with that the condition that the enfranchised householders are to pay their own rates ... What has it done for the working men of London? Do you think that such of you as pay 4s a week for your lodgings will get votes? No. You will not get votes unless you pay 5s a week ... It only affects the boroughs ... leaving out altogether more than half the whole country.[325]

Disraeli's prediction that new voters would remain grateful to the Conservative Party remained unfulfilled. In the 1868 General Election, the Liberals, now led by Gladstone, won a landslide over Disraeli's party, gaining a majority of 100 seats.

Reynolds, Jones, Harney, and Beales's National Reform League was disbanded in 1868. This is not to say that these men gave up their ideals of eventually securing universal suffrage. Jones continued practising as a solicitor, and conducted a high profile defence of Fenian prisoners who had been charged with the murder of a police officer alongside writing plays, poetry, and novels. Although he was never prosperous, he was well-liked in radical circles and when he died in January 1869 in Manchester, a large number of well-wishers who turned out to pay their respects.[326]

Harney almost sank into obscurity but continued to write articles on the theme of, among other things, universal suffrage for the *Newcastle Weekly Chronicle* until his death in the 1890s. *Reynolds's Weekly Newspaper* likewise continued to campaign for universal suffrage. But the task of campaigning for further extensions to the franchise would be left to the Labour Representation League, which was founded with the aim of getting greater numbers of working men into parliament to promote working-class interests. The Labour Representation League was replaced by the Labour Electoral Association. Both of these organisations, along with the Independent Labour Party founded in 1893, prepared the way for the modern UK Labour Party.

'Kind Reader, who have borne with me so long': Reynolds's Later Life and Death

> Kind reader, who have borne with me so long ... have we not taught, in fine, how the example and the philanthropy of one good man can 'save more souls and redeem and redeem more sinners than all the bishops that ever wore lawn-sleeves?' If then, the preceding pages be calculated to engender one useful thought—awaken one beneficial sentiment—the work is not without its value.
>
> George W.M. Reynolds,
> *Mysteries of London* (1844–48)

> Should this little volume meet with the approbation and favour of those thinking few ... I shall remain grateful and satisfied.
>
> George W.M. Reynolds, *Errors of the Christian Religion Exposed* (1832)

By 1869, changes were coming to the Reynolds publishing firm. The newspaper continued but was reduced in price from 4d to 2 1/2d, owing to the abolition of the stamp duty.[327] *Reynolds's Miscellany* was discontinued and all of its staff were transferred to John Dicks's *Bow Bells: A Magazine for General Literature and Art for Family Reading*, which had been in print since 1862. Reynolds served as the editor *Bow Bells* for a while but he was not credited.

The timing of the change is interesting: Reynolds had largely ceased to write any new novels, and so the magazine was no longer 'Reynolds's miscellany' in any meaningful sense. Additionally, his political activism over the past few years might have had something to do with the decision to wind the miscellany up. He had been active during the campaign for the Reform Act of 1867, and he was famous for being a radical. Victorian readers knew, furthermore, that *Reynolds's Newspaper* (having by now dropped the word 'weekly' from its title) was a radical organ, and if they bought it, they knew what kind of politics to expect from it. But readers who enjoyed light fiction might have been put off by the fact that a famous radical's name was attached to the *Miscellany*. It certainly would have been good business sense to separate the radical Reynolds brand from a light fiction magazine to attract more readers.

As for Reynolds's later life, very little is known. There is a rather romantic story that he apparently found God in later life and became the warder for St Andrew's Church in Well's Street.[328] Reynolds's previous biographer, Dick Collins, doubts this however: the job of warder is an appointed post, and the person is chosen from among the local congregation. Yet Reynolds was never a churchgoer and his only association with the church occurred when his children were married. Instead it must have been a different George Reynolds—someone who actually went to church.[329]

Besides, more grandchildren arrived and they doubtlessly occupied Reynolds's time. His daughter, Joanna Frances, had married a solicitor named Arthur Lamb on 1 August 1865 and the couple had several children: Frances E. Lamb (1866–1950); Edith Lamb (1866–1950); Florence Lamb (1868–1952); Eva Blanche Lamb (1871–1961); Isabella J Lamb (1873); and George E. Lamb (1876–1957).[330]

Frederick Reynolds and his wife also had a child in 1877, named Dudley. Louise Clarisse had married a solicitor named Adolphus Bell on 5 August 1873.[331] Louise gave birth to three children named George, Jessie, and Dora between 1875 and 1878.

Reynolds's sons, Kossuth-Mazzini and Ledru-Rollin, were by this time grown up. The former married a lady named Harriet, and the couple had two boys; the latter married a woman named Marian Rees in December 1875. The Reynolds family was indeed a large one, even by Victorian standards.

Reynolds appears to have done some editorial work for *Chambers' London Journal* in the final months of his life, but the extent of the work he undertook for this journal is unclear.[332] After all, Reynolds was certainly not a well man during the 1870s. As Collins remarks: Reynolds was quite overweight at this period of his life and was likely diabetic: pictures of him in later life do indeed suggest that he had grown quite fat. He also had high blood pressure and kidney failure. In 1877, he suffered a stroke that left him paralysed down one side and dependent upon carers. It is likely that he suffered another stroke two years later when, on Thursday 19 June 1879, Reynolds collapsed and died in his home.[333] His brother Edward, and his son Frederick, attended to the funeral, and Reynolds was buried in the catacombs of Kensal Green Cemetery.

The conservative press decided to ignore Reynolds's death: despite his immense contribution to national life in the form of his best-selling novels and the biggest-selling radical newspaper, the *Times* did not print an obituary for him. Reynolds died a wealthy man. His estate was valued at 'under £35,000', as the brief details recorded in the probate index reveals:

> *4 July 1879.* Personal Estate £3,000; Resworn August 1880 under £35,000. The Will with two Codicils of George William Macarthur Reynolds late of 41 Woburn-square in the County of Middlesex Esquire who died on 19 June 1879 at 41 Woburn Square was proved at the Principal Registry by Edward Dowers Reynolds of Wellington-Chambers Lancaster-place Wellington-street in the City of Westminster Newspaper Editor the Brother and Frederick Reynolds of 26 Rothbury Villas in Stroud-Green-road in the said County Surgeon the Son the Executors.[334]

Reynolds's friend John Dicks passed away two years later.[335] Edward Reynolds lived a good while longer until he passed away in 1894. As editor of the biggest-selling radical journal Edward was famous in the world of newspapers and his obituary was reprinted in a number of newspapers. The following is typical of those which appeared:

> DEATH OF A LONDON JOURNALIST—Mr Edward Reynolds, who for the past 13 years has been the responsible editor of *Reynolds's Newspaper* has just died. Edward Reynolds was a peculiar man, and it was not everybody who understood him; but to those who knew him well he

was a kindly, genial gentleman, who enjoyed life in his own peculiar way. He lived an almost hermit life in his secluded chambers at Lancaster Place, just off the Strand, and those who imagined that the editor of *Reynolds's Newspaper* was a man of fierce, truculent, and unyielding character would have been wonderfully disappointed could they have seen that same editor playing with pet monkeys and instructing favourite parrots in the proper and distinct use of the English language. The late Mr Edward Reynolds succeeded as editor of the paper his brother, G.W.M. Reynolds, a somewhat prolific writer who fell under the displeasure of Royalty for a publication which had a large sale entitled *The Mysteries of the Court of London*. The late Edward Reynolds was too kindly a man to hurt anyone and it is well known that he was strongly opposed to the publication.[336]

This obituary reveals the extent of historians' knowledge of Edward's life. After Edward passed away, W.M. Thompson took over the editorial chair at *Reynolds's Newspaper* and steered the paper into a respectable liberal newspaper.

As for Reynolds's children, their families increased. In the same month that Reynolds passed away Ledru-Rollin and Marian had a daughter, whom they named Hilda. The couple had another girl whom they named Vera, born in 1881. In 1886, two more children were born: a boy, named Cyril, and a girl, whom they named Gladys. Louise and Adolphus had another two daughters, who they named Winifred and Marie. Frederick Reynolds and his wife Florence had four children: Jane, Harcourt, Frederick, and Ada. Quite soon after her father's death, in 1881, Theresa Isabella and her family emigrated to New York,[337] and she passed away on 21 January 1920. Joanna Frances Reynolds must likewise have emigrated to the USA, for she died in the early 1900s in Virginia. As for Reynolds's daughter Emily, little is known of her marriage or family. And poor Alfred Dowers Reynolds should not be forgotten: he seems never to have figured in his father's life, and he died, seemingly alone and bankrupt, in New Zealand in 1881.

None of Reynolds's novels ever earned him lasting fame, however, and he remains a figure of interest to a limited group of Victorian literature scholars. Although he was a writer who was as popular as Charles

Dickens, in our modern era only three of his novels have been reprinted: *Wagner the Wehr-Wolf* (1846–47), *The Necromancer* (1851–52), and an abridged version of his *Mysteries of London* (1844–48). No publisher has as yet decided to launch a large-scale, multi-volume critical edition of his other works. One of the reasons for him having been neglected is the fact that, although Reynolds's novels remained popular throughout the Victorian era, the only reprints of his novels after his death in 1879 were in John Dicks's 'Standard English Novels' series, and a limited edition reprint of *The Mysteries of the Court of London* by an obscure Oxford Society based in New York c. 1900. In contrast, after Dickens's death, publishers flooded the literary marketplace with cheap reprints of that famous author's works.

In 1886, perhaps owing to the recently-released John Dicks paperback editions of his novels, in the 'Peelite Conservative' *Saturday Review*'s issue on 6 February, there was a glowing account of Reynolds's literary career. The article credited Reynolds with having inspired working-class people to join the democratic cause and there was even a hint of admiration for his radicalism:

> The late G.W.M. Reynolds was a person with a mission ... and that mission was the exposure of a bloated and criminal aristocracy. Fearless was he—fearless in enterprise, indomitable in offence. While he lived, the upper classes had in him a critic of the most merciless habit ... He is (so to speak) the Titus Oates of fiction; and, like his illustrious prototype, he has rejoiced in the faith of multitudes. From his glowing page does that great creature, the Radical Working Man, imbibe his hatred of Dukes, his contempt for social distinctions, his noble longing to possess the property of his betters—in a word, all the beautiful democratic virtues which have made him a nuisance in the present and a terror in the future.

The same article went on to extol the brilliance of two of Reynolds's novels: *The Seamstress* (1850) and *The Soldier's Wife* (1852–53), 'in which our author's genius is at its brightest and best'. Yet by 1893, it seems, one writer in *The Quarterly Review* remarked that he had 'inquired in vain for the catchpenny romances that were popular in his

youth' such as '*The Mysteries of the Court, The Mysteries of London.*'
That same year, the Irish writer Kathryn Tynan recalled her youth in
Dublin and remembered how she and the other girls used to visit a small
village outside the city and go to an elderly book lover's house. While
there, the old man would read a variety of by then forgotten shocking
tales to them such as Eugène Sue's *Mysteries of Paris* and Reynolds's
Coral Island. Tynan remembered these books vividly; *The Coral Island*
was filled with horrors while Sue's book was particularly noteworthy for
its illustrations, 'with a picture to every two inches of letterpress'.[338] By
1898, a journalist for *The Pall Mall Magazine* had to explain to readers
who Reynolds was, and remarked that only readers whose memories
went back to 1848 would remember him.[339]

Time, then, is the only critic which counts, if we might misquote
George Orwell—and time has not been kind to Reynolds or his legacy.
Just as Reynolds's novels were soon forgotten, so too was his contribution
to the Chartist movement and radical politics. In Gammage's *History of
the Chartist Movement* in 1854, Reynolds emerges as a major figure in
the latter years of the movement. Yet when W.M. Thompson published
Democratic Readings (1896), which was a series of essays reprinted
from *Reynolds's Weekly Newspaper*— the very newspaper that Reynolds
founded—there was nothing from Reynolds in it. There were, however,
summaries of Marx and Engels's teachings,[340] excerpts of some writings
by Giuseppe Mazzini and other Chartist thinkers. Thompson's book
was not an isolated case: the journalist and historian Joseph Clayton
(1867–1943) wrote several works on working-class history and the
rise of democracy. *Leaders of the People* (1910) and *The Rise of the
Democracy* (1911) were Clayton's two most notable works and, while
he listed many of Reynolds's contemporaries and fellow Chartists as
being important in the history of the growth of democracy in England,
Reynolds was nowhere to be found. Furthermore, in Mark Hovell's *The
Chartist Movement*, which appeared in 1918, Reynolds's contribution to
the movement was significantly diminished and he was mentioned just
three times in the entire book. By the 1940s Reynolds had almost been
entirely erased from the history of Chartism; G.D.H. Cole's *Chartist
Portraits* (1943), for example, listed Reynolds's name just once.[341] The
only exception to this was the fact that Reynolds secured an entry in the
Dictionary of National Biography. The entry for Reynolds was written by
none other than the first Labour Prime Minister Ramsay MacDonald.[342]

But it took the publication of Louis James's *Fiction for the Working Man* (1963)—the first work which presented an authoritative history Victorian popular literature—to restore Reynolds to historians' notice.

There are a number of possible reasons for the neglect of Reynolds by early twentieth-century literary and social historians. One of these might have been the fact that, while Reynolds wrote good and highly entertaining fiction, he was never 'original'. As the foregoing account of his life and works has revealed, his most famous works piggybacked on the success of other people's ideas: Reynolds's *Pickwick Abroad* took a Dickens character, and *The Mysteries of London* was inspired by Eugène Sue's *Mysteries of Paris*. Sue's *Mysteries of Paris* has at least had the honour to enter into Penguin Books' 'Classics' series, while Reynolds's *Mysteries of London* is reprinted only by the small, independent Valancourt Books. A similar fate has befallen many an author of so-called penny bloods, although that term was rarely used by the Victorians themselves. The lack of originality can also be said of Reynolds's political ideology. He was a Red Republican, but he did not formulate any theories of his own, but instead took the theories of other radical and socialist thinkers and distilled them for popular consumption in his newspaper.

The final reason for Reynolds's having been forgotten may be the fact that, unlike some of the other major authors of his day like Dickens, Reynolds did not bequeath to posterity any great collection of letters or diaries, which prevents scholars from knowing more about his life. In my own time collecting various editions of Reynolds's novels, I have only ever come across two of his letters for sale. Furthermore, due to the lack of reprints of both his novels and his newspaper articles by the early 1900s, to truly know Reynolds, a researcher would have had to travel across the country to get hold of his works. This situation appears to be changing, thankfully, for the British Library's digitisation of their newspapers and penny dreadfuls. Thanks to Louis James's work, and those scholars who have followed him, Reynolds is now fairly well-known among Victorian history and literature scholars. Jessica Elizabeth Thomas has recently embarked on a quest to rediscover Susannah Frances Reynolds's writings and reprint them. Nevertheless, what is available to researchers today is but a *partial* glimpse of his life. The sources which historians have to draw upon to write about Reynolds's life is the very public image he cultivated through his writings, as well as the writings of his rivals and detractors.

Reynolds never lived to see his dream of universal suffrage implemented—that would not happen until 1918 when all men and *some* women received the right to vote. He and Susannah would likely have wholeheartedly approved of the women's suffrage movement of the late-Victorian and Edwardian periods. Indeed, the fact that he attached himself to the National Reform League late in life suggests that, had he lived longer, he would have supported many more progressive and democratic causes. His contemporary critics who questioned his motives and portrayed him as a charlatan, and some of those modern historians who have uncritically regurgitated those accusations, have clearly been unacquainted with the facts of Reynolds's life. His fundamental belief, that only universal suffrage could ameliorate the condition of the poor, was the motivation behind his support for several progressive causes. Despising the power of the hereditary and financial aristocracies— an issue which plagues the political systems of several nations in our own day,—Reynolds's message can inspire all those today who wish to improve society. For as Reynolds said:

> No system of society can be good, under which some men revel in every luxury and others starve. No government can be just, which abstains from the enactment of measures calculated to take away the surplus wealth from the enriched few and distributes it amongst the necessitous many. No individual should be allowed the enjoyment of luxuries, until all men in the community have been assured necessaries. In fact, no one should be permitted to have butter upon his bread, so long as a single person remains without bread at all. When the rich man dines sumptuously and the poor man has no dinner whatsoever, the latter's share of the earth's produce has been plundered from him to place upon the table of the former.[343]

Reynolds's Political Instructor (1849–50)

Transcribed and Edited by Mya Driver

*

A NEW PERIODICAL.

[...]

REYNOLDS'S POLITICAL INSTRUCTOR
Edited by
George W.M. Reynolds

This publication, which will be issued weekly, is established to advocate the *political rights* of the masses in the most liberal sense of the term, and to inculcate sound political knowledge which will teach the proper and worthy exercise of those rights when once they shall have been obtained. For this purpose, Mr Reynolds has ensured the assistance of first-rate talent in the several departments of the "INSTRUCTOR;" and he trusts that his own sentiments upon the leading topics of the day are too well-known to render it necessary to make any specific pledges or enter into elaborate details concerning the spirit in which the publication is to be conducted.

Advertisement for *Reynolds's Political Instructor* printed in *Reynolds's Miscellany* (1849)
*

The following section contains all of G.W.M. Reynolds's weekly editorials that he wrote for *Reynolds's Political Instructor*. This penny newspaper's first issue appeared on 10 November 1849 and the final issue appeared on 11 May 1850 (the first issue of its successor, *Reynolds's Weekly Newspaper*, appeared on 5 May, shortly before the *Political Instructor*'s final issue).

On the front page of each issue there was usually an engraving of a prominent political figure. The famous Chartist campaigner Feargus O'Connor and the MP Sir Joshua Walmsley were the first men to appear in *Reynolds's Political Instructor*. Advertisements for the newspaper reveal that the images, in fact, were one of its main selling points.[344] These figures' engravings were accompanied with a short biographical sketch outlining their importance in the pro-democracy movement. Although they were written anonymously, Reynolds probably wrote them, judging by their tone and style.

Historians have *Reynolds's Political Instructor* to thank, in fact, for bequeathing to posterity the only surviving images of some of these activists. A notable example is the image of William Cuffay, whose image was featured on the issue for 13 April 1850.[345] The descendant of African slaves, he was elected as a delegate to the Chartist National Convention but was subsequently convicted and transported under the Treason Felony Act for trying to start an insurrection in 1848.

Several other people were employed by *Reynolds's Political Instructor*. Edwin F. Roberts wrote a long-running 'New History of England' under his initials E.F.R. Other authors named themselves simply as 'A Chartist', or 'A National Reformer'. Lengthy letters from working-class people were also printed in the *Political Instructor*'s columns. It is highly likely that Reynolds wrote most of the miscellaneous back matter in the newspaper as well, although attribution of these shorter anonymous pieces cannot be stated with certainty.

However, Reynolds's authorship of the weekly editorials in *Reynolds's Political Instructor* is beyond doubt because he signed these with his name, appearing either as 'G.W.M. Reynolds' or 'George W.M. Reynolds'. These articles usually appeared on the second page, inserted directly after the biographical sketch. In them Reynolds commented upon a variety of issues including Chartism, the wrongs and crimes of the aristocracy, European politics, and working-class men and women's strikes. In the final months of the newspaper's run Reynolds moves from talking about Chartism and begins to speak more specifically about Red Republicanism and socialism—'The Good Cause' that was 'making immense strides upon the Continent of Europe'.

The text of Reynolds's articles has been reproduced with few alterations and retains the spelling, grammar, and punctuation that Reynolds used, although obvious printing errors have been corrected.

The Revival of a Working-Class Agitation

Saturday, November 10, 1849

The history of nearly every moral agitation and of every movement accomplished by means of physical force, shows that after the immediate object has been either partially or wholly gained, the middle classes have reaped the greater advantage, and the toiling millions have seen their own material interests neglected—their wrongs unredressed—their rights unrecognized—and their claims disregarded. In a word, they have been cheated with the shadow, while the middle classes have grasped the substance. Then, too, the middle classes have proclaimed the necessity of desisting from any further agitation, on the plea that absolute tranquility becomes necessary for the revival of trade; and if the working classes have persisted in continuing the agitation, they have been denounced as disturbers of the peace—inveterate malcontents—and incorrigible foes to order,—while middle-class juries have been called upon to become the *media* of dealing forth the vengeance of sanguinary and barbarian laws. It is indeed a painful fact that the middle classes have too often proved themselves as hostile and as oppressive as the Aristocracy towards the industrious millions;—and therefore the sons and daughters of toil must at least be upon their guard, if not actually animated with suspicion, whenever they are called upon to give their adhesion to a political movement which originates with the middle classes.

Of all such movements which have taken place within the present century, that of the National Parliamentary and Financial Reform Association appears to offer the best guarantees for sincerity of purposes, unflinching determination, and breadth of fundamental principle; and in my opinion it deserves the strenuous support of all true patriots and honest Reformers. But as the subjects of that Association are defined and

152

limited, it must necessarily expire when its mission is accomplished; and as the working classes demand *more* than it undertakes to procure for them, a well-organized agitation should at least be in embryo, if not in actual existence, to perpetuate the moral struggle of democracy against class-legislation and of right against wrong, until the full measure of reform be obtained and the regeneration of society be accomplished.

Moreover, for the reasons alleged at the outset, the working classes must be careful how they compromise their claims by throwing themselves heart and soul into a movement which is professedly instituted to obtain for them *less* than the amount of those claims. They should support that movement to the utmost of their power: but they should not, by abandoning a legitimate agitation within their own sphere, lead the world to suppose that they have entered into any compromise to take *less* than all they were wont to claim. They should assume that imposing attitude which seems to say to the National Parliamentary and Financial Reform Associate, "We go with you hand-in-hand as far as you are travelling, because our journey lies along the same road: but we tell you honestly and frankly beforehand that we do not intend to stop at the same mile-stone where you propose to halt, inasmuch as we are bound to travel on to the end." For it cannot be for a moment admitted nor tolerated that any Association organized by the middle classes shall settle the privileges and define the rights of the working classes. Indeed, if any one section of the community ought to have the power of establishing the nature and equilibrium of the governmental and administrative institutions, that section assuredly consists of the industrious millions, who are not only the numerical majority, but are likewise the origin of all wealth and the producers of everything necessary for the support and enjoyment of life.

Again, the working classes have much to agitate for, in which they do *not* receive any sympathy from the middle classes. I especially allude to the rights of labour, the evils of competition, the measures regulating the periods of labour in factories, and all the varied grievances of coal-miners, stockingers, cutlery-manufacturers, potters, weavers, agricultural labourers, &c. &c. But I need not enter into any detail of all those points on which there now exists a war to the knife between those who work and those who give work—between those whose capital is *money* and those whose capital is *labour*—between those who revel in luxury and those who starve. It is sufficient for the present purpose to know and to feel that inasmuch as a vast proportion of the wrongs and sufferings of the working classes emanates directly from the avarice, injustice, neglect, and ignorance of the middle classes, it is useless to look for total redress to this latter section of society. No middle-class movement, therefore, can ever lead to results calculated to give entire satisfaction to the working classes; and this fact constitutes perhaps the strongest argument that can be advanced to show the necessity of the working classes maintaining an incessant but peaceful and constitutional agitation of their own, *despite of* and *in addition to* any other agitation which may be concurrently instituted by the middle classes.

That an union between the two classes is most desirable, no one will attempt to deny: but an union cannot possibly be otherwise than transitory so long as the one class is resolute on stopping at a certain defined point and the other is equally determined to push the work of progress on to the extent indicated alike by reason and justice. Thus, an union between the two classes may now take place, under the auspices of SIR JOSHUA WALMSLEY, a view to wrest from a reluctant Ministry certain measures of reform: but when once that point shall have been gained, the coalition must inevitably cease—one party relapsing into quiescence, and the other still magnanimously toiling on in the case of progress.

A trite smile will not be here out of place. The millions are starving and exclaim, "We have no bread!" Forth come certain individuals of the middle class, saying "We will agitate in order to obtain you half a loaf." To this the working-classes should reply, "We will certainly join you in the endeavor to obtain that half-loaf, because it is better than none: but inasmuch as the whole loaf is our just right and what we have always claimed, we shall perpetuate the agitation, *with or without* you, until we have obtained it."

To my mind the various arguments which I have thus ventured to throw together, are conclusive in showing the necessity of a revival of that working-man's agitation which under the good old Saxon name of CHARTISM has already more than once convinced a tyrannical oligarchy that the millions feel their wrongs and have become impatient under them. And that the demands of the working classes may be fully understood,—and that they may stand forth in juxta-position with any petty concessions which a frightened Ministry may within a short time be disposed to grant,—I think that these demands should be recorded as follow:—

1. Universal Suffrage.
2. Vote by Ballot.

3. Annual Parliaments.
4. Equal Electoral Districts.
5. Paid Representatives.
6. No Property-Qualification.
7. The Recognition of the Rights of Labour.
8. The Abolition of the Law of Primogeniture.

It will be seen that two principles are here added to those contained in the noble document called the PEOPLE'S CHARTER; and I thus annex them because the events of 1848 brought one of them so prominently before the eyes of the world, and because the other is so intimately connected with the causes of the wide-spread pauperism existing in this country. For the Rights of Labour may be summed up in the axiom that "there should be a fair day's wage for a fair day's work; and that every man able and willing to work, should have work found for him." As for the Law of Primogeniture, it is abhorrent to those principles of common justice and common sense which proclaim that "the earth belongs first of all to those who are upon it; and that every one is entitled to receive a subsistence from the earth, before any one individual has a right to *more*." But the laws of entail, of mortmain, and primogeniture, instituted for the purpose of retaining wealth in particular channels, have been ably defined as measures that "prevent the natural circulation of property—obstruct the coming together of land and useful labour—and by thus hindering the production of food from advancing at the same rate as the production of people, spread pauperism and misery over the face of the country."

I have now stated my opinion in behalf of a revival of a working-man's agitation; and I have recorded the principles on which I think that agitation should be based. But I must emphatically declare that I contemplate only a legal and constitutional agitation,—adopting those means and having recourse to those expedients which are comprised within the meaning of the term—"MORAL FORCE."

Sir Joshua Walmsley, the Member for Bolton, must now be considered the Leader of the Middle Class Movement. This gentleman is thoroughly honest and an undoubted Liberal: indeed, he himself has admitted in the public meetings, that he goes beyond the principles set forth in the "profession of faith" promulgated by the National Parliamentary and Financial Reform Association. Sir Joshua is a man of business-habits, shrewdness, tact, and indomitable perseverance: he is straightforward in his character and his speeches; and his acquaintance with the real wants and interests of the masses is apparent in the mode in which he addresses them from the platform. His votes in Parliament have always been on the right side; and it should be recorded that he was one of the *fifteen* who supported Mr. O'Connor's motion for the People's Charter last session.

Mr Feargus O'Connor, the Member for Nottingham, is the Leader of the Working Class Movement. To the cause of the sons of toil he has devoted the best years of his life: day and night has he served them with energy, fidelity, and intelligence;—and the best proof of his patriotism is to be found in the fact that he has been weariedly, shamefully, and atrociously maligned by the illiberal portion of the public press and by the upholders of existing abuses. Him whom the people love, the Aristocracy are certain to hate;—and therefore the hated of the Aristocracy and of that large portion of the press which the Aristocracy can command, is sure to be a man whose talent, integrity, and influence are an object of dread on the part of despots.

Chartism

Saturday, November 17, 1849

What is Chartism?—why is it made a bugbear by the Government and the press to frighten the richer and middle classes?—and why are its apostles denounced as factious demagogues, and its votaries as a turbulent rabble? Let us ask in order to find a reply to those questions, why every man, and every class of men that have over promulgated new doctrines of real utility to the world in general, have been similarly maligned by the selfish prejudiced and ignorant portion of society? And this has not been the case with regard to politicians only; but likewise in respect to innumerable of pioneers of progress in science and art. The truth is that there always has been and still is, a favoured class of mortals, whose wealth, honours, positions and influence depend upon the corruption of society and the existence of governmental tyranny. These men are therefore wedded to established systems; and the idea of *progress* is loathsome to them, because it implies a necessary change in all those institutions the rottenness of which is fraught with a rich fecundity of gain for them. The priests saw, or fancied they saw, the destruction of their colossal sway in the discoveries of Galileo and they persecuted him. The inquisition fastened its fangs and its claws upon all men whose teachings were calculated to enlighten the world,—because the enlightening of the world is in itself a war to the death against political despotism and ecclesiastical domination. Therefore has the scientific explorer been persecuted as well as the apostle of the rights of man—and therefore too, was it held as great a crime to proclaim that the earth moved round the sun, as to assert that the millions had privileges to be rescued from the group of oligarchical usurpation.

Chartism is a principle and not a mere proposition. It contains within itself the evidence of its own truth. Its programme consists of six axioms admitting of no dispute. To those who have studied Chartism with an unbiased mind, there is no merit to becoming proselytes—because such proselytism is only a natural adhesion which men of common sense give to principles of common sense. It requires no large draught upon a man's faith to believe that the sun at noon-day is bright, because he sees that it is; neither does it require any straining of the imagination. To recognize the excellence of those principles which are summed up in the work Chartism. Because *universal suffrage* is an unquestionable right for all communities, whether great or small; inasmuch as the laws of all communities are supposed to be made for the benefit of the whole mass of the population and not a mere section of that population; and therefore every member of such population is clearly entitled to a voice of choosing agents or representatives who are to make those laws. Secondly, these agents or representatives should return frequently to their constituents to give an account of their stewardship, and receive new powers, or else make way for other and more trust-worthy men; and hence the necessity for annual elections. Thirdly, care must be taken to preserve the poor but independent voter from the influence of the rich and intolerant one; and this aim can only be accomplished by the *ballot.* Fourthly, the agents or delegates chosen to defend the rights and represent the interest of their constituents, must be remunerated for their services, not only to render them independent of Government patronage and proof against the bribes which a corrupt Ministry may hold forth, but likewise because many able, excellent and valuable men could not afford to abandon their own profession or calling, and give their time to the public, unless furnished with the means subsistence: hence the principles of paid representatives. Fifthly, the agents elected upon the above principles must be men chosen with a view to their fitness only, and not with regard to their pecuniary position in life; and therefore it is requisite that the qualification should be of intelligence and integrity and *not the qualification of property.* Sixthly, as there can only be a certain number of agents chosen to represent the entire nation, each agent must be allotted to so many persons; in a word, if there be five hundred agents representing five millions of male adults the country must be divided into equal districts, each containing ten thousand voters; because if one district contains a thousand and another ten thousand, each having only one delegated agent, then the larger one is unfairly represented. This is the principle of *equal electoral districts;* although it is evident, as a matter of course, that in order to prevent a very minute subdivision of districts, three or four representatives may be accorded to each one.

And this is Chartism. Now, reader, where is the element of disorder in this system?—how does it merit to be held up as a bugbear?—why do the Government and the press denounce it? Because the six principles whereon Chartism is based—or rather, which constitute Chartism— are the sublime effluence of Truth; and Truth is dreaded by those who fatten upon the rottenness of political institutions and the corruption of a vitiated society. The Government denounces Chartism, because that Government belongs to the Aristocracy and not to the people— because it springs from oligarchy and not from the nation;—and the press denounces Chartism, because the newspapers, with a few glorious exceptions, are either subsidized by the Government or are the property of men belonging to those classes which have usurped all rights, all privileges, and all powers.

Thus the world has been viewing Chartism through a false medium; and the consequence is that many persons who are naturally well-disposed and even of liberal tendencies, have been taught to look upon Chartism with abhorrence. It has been the study, because it has been the interest, of the Government to throw all possible odium upon Chartism; and the newspaper organs have artfully contrived, while seconding that view, to associate all infamy, all horror, and all ideas of spoliation, with the *names* of CHARTISM and CHARTISTS, carefully avoiding all calm and dispassionate discussion of the *principles*. A scented, kid-gloved, and white-waistcoated aristocratic Member of Parliament would as soon be accused of having brought the pestilence with him from Cairo, as of being a Chartist—and yet this man might possibly hold the very doctrines enunciated by Chartism, if he were intelligent enough to think for himself and honest enough to avow the results of his thinking. A millocrat will say to his over-looker, "We will have no Chartist in our factory;"—and a rich West-End tailor or linen draper, who keeps his carriage, would discharge his groom or his footman, if he were to overhear either one whispering to his fellow-servants a confession that he was a Chartist. Thus my dear readers, you perceive that the slur is thrown upon the *name*, and not upon the *principles* of Chartism. For the latter are beyond all possibility of attack: no argument can destroy them—no sophistry refute them;— and thus those who dread Chartism because it is a system of Truth,

159

have recourse to the dirty, mean, and despicable expedient of dragging its name in the mire.

Were the name of Chartism altered to some other *ism,* still preserving however the principles whole and entire, how many thousands of persons would exclaim, "Ah! This is indeed a glorious system! I shall give my instantaneous adhesion to it. All honest and right-minded men ought to support it." Such would be the exclamation; and those who have been taught by influential friends, by habit, by the press, and by the constant outpourings of aristocratic and middle class virulence, to look upon Chartism as a monstrosity, and its adherents as brigands, would rush to array themselves under the standard of the same doctrines with another name.

But those doctrines shall retain the name of Chartism, – because it is more glorious for the votaries of Truth to conquer prejudices than to concede any point to the ignorance and illiberality of classes. Yes— the name of Chartism shall be preserved, because many good and great men have already embarked on the cause—suffered on its behalf—and valiantly fought the battle of common sense against despotism and intolerance. It shall be preserved, because the working-classes love it and are proud of it:—and, *inasmuch as the real intelligence of the country resides in the masses,* those who were the *first* to appreciate the sublime truths of Chartism shall not be called upon to abandon one tittle of all they have learnt to admire, to uphold, and to demand—no, not even the name!

And let us not despair. The cause of Chartism shall triumph—and that speedily. False systems and corrupt institutions may last for a time: but in the end they must yield to the increasing pressure of truth. The day must come when those who are now terrified at Chartism, will bless it as a means of political and social salvation, and will look with loathing and disgust upon those men and those newspapers who dared to misrepresent it.

The lonely traveler who has lost his way, is terrified when he imagines that he sees a gigantic phantom appearing through the mist of twilight: but if he be brave, he walks up to it—and, to his joy, he discovers that it is a finger-post indicating the path which he is anxious to pursue. He then blames himself for his folly in yielding to so undergrounded a fear; and he blesses the object which at first startled him. But why was he thus startled when that object gradually began to develop itself to his view

160

and stand out in hideous unshapeliness from the obscurity of evening? Because his mind was accessible to those superstitious terrors which nursery-tales and old women's stories had been wont to create in earlier years, and the influence of which remained dormant in his imagination, to be easily aroused again. Well, then, let the man who is wandering in the fog of his own thoughts upon political and social questions—let *him* walk straight up to the bugbear which has been made an object of terror and alarm to his imagination—let him look Chartism in the face, and he will learn to love and bless it as the finger-post pointing towards the goal of freedom which he so ardently longs to reach.

What is the mission of Chartism? A peaceful, legal, and constitutional change in those systems which are invested with too much of ancient feudalism to suit modern civilisation. Chartism does not contemplate a bloody revolution—does not want it: its very votaries would be the first to suffer by such an insane course. Chartism does not intend spoliation and general plunder: its leaders and its adherents are too honest and too humane, too just and too generous to entertain such a barbarous idea. Chartism does not seek to upset society; its apostles and disciples are intelligent philanthropists whose object is to remodel and not to destroy. Those who live by industry, are not desirous to paralyse industry: they will not burn the dwellings which shelter their own heads, nor the Corn-fields which feed their mouths. Away, then, with all calumny relative to the Chartists and Chartism: be ye honest, O Aristocracy, if ye can—and ye too, O Middle-class, if you will—and confess at length that Chartism is truth, not falsehood—philanthropy, not atrocity—order, not chaos!

Great, then, is the mission of Chartism; and never were men called upon to work out greater consequences than the Chartists. Aye—and never were men less authors of the causes which render such consequences necessary. For all the evils and abuses which have led to the establishment of the Chartist doctrines and the promulgation of Chartist principles, have been created and propagated by the very classes who denounce Chartism with such spiteful malignity and such bitter virulence. And now the millions must assert the aristocracy of mind in juxtaposition with the aristocracy of birth—the aristocracy of virtue in contrast with the aristocracy of wealth. The task is difficult, but glorious; and, as Truth is at its basis, none need despair. For already have all reforms been wrung from Governments and Legislatures by the *mind* and *will* of the masses; and the same bloodless victory shall be won over again. The small amount of freedom which Englishmen do now enjoy, is the hard-earned booty which the intelligence of the past and present millions have carried off from Time—the prize of a long wrestle with ages of barbarism, ages of oppression, of fanaticism, and of blood,— the amount of health which difficult precautions and tedious cures have rescued from old and still unsubdued disease. Look at England from her Heptarchy to her conquest—from that to her Revolution—from that to the present time. Mark her long and weary efforts to pile up her freedom—how often was it the toil of Sisyphus! Consider the stubborn and closely guarded quarries from which she was forced to hew out her greatness. Trace the course of her civilization,—at first like a little silver stream in a rocky wilderness—then widening and deepening—always flowing and fretting onward, though not always seen: now diverted from its way by some rugged obstacle- and now dammed up until the weight of its waters break down the impediment: thus, sometimes free and sometimes checked, until its channel becomes broad and deep, and its waters expand into a glorious flood.

Sights of Pomp and Sights of Horror

Saturday, November 24, 1849

Within the last four weeks no less than *three* "Sights" have put forth their claims upon public attention. Two had nothing to recommend them beyond the average amount of interest which belongs to such exhibitions as Punch and Judy and Itinerant Mountebanks; while the third was fraught with a far different and awfully harrowing interest. The trumpery and pageantry of the Lord Mayor's Show attracted its thousands and thousands of gaping beholders: the ostentatious progress of a Prince in a gold-bedizened barge to open a Coal Exchange, congregated a still larger multitude. The trashy rubbish and tinsel finery of those absurd displays weaved a vast proportion of the metropolitan community from its propriety and animated the breasts of many individuals of even mature years with a childish delight utterly inconsistent with their claims to be looked upon as intelligent persons. Then came the appalling tragedy enacted last Tuesday week, at Horsemonger Lane Gaol—the execution of the Mannnings; and at that barbarian, atrocious, demoralizing exhibition upwards of fifty thousand persons were assembled. Within four weeks, then, the sight-seers of the metropolis must have been surfeited with shows of pomp and shows of horror: the mingled impressions left upon their minds must ben of a somewhat extraordinary character; and they at least have food for the reflections that while society chooses to make demigods of some of its members, without receiving the slightest proof of any superior merit on their part, it also delights to hang up others like dogs, without giving them the slightest opportunity to reform or even allowing them an adequate leisure to repent of their enormities.

However arduously and unweariedly the peoples instructors may strive to elevate them in the political and social sphere, these endeavours will be essentially impeded if not absolutely neutralized altogether, unless individuals will at the same time exert all their powers to elevate themselves. When a youth is just verging upon the important era of manhood, his parents, if they be enlightened persons, will endeavour to inspire him with manly notions, and inculcate the necessity of throwing off those puerilities which were all very suitable to his school-days. For when he lays aside the round jacket and assumes the coat, his amusements must no longer consist of hoops and marbles: books and intellectual pursuits should engage his attention. If his father treats him as a "young man," he must divest himself of his "boyish habits;" and instead of indulging in childish recreations, he must learn to appreciate the proper dignity becoming his entrance into the world. So it is with the masses of the population generally. If they claim to be treated as men, they must not act as children: if they wish to thought worthy of serious things, they must not give their minds to trifles. No: they should assume that dignified demeanor and adopt that becoming gravity of conduct which will not allow any party or class to suspect their intelligence. I do not mean to say that they must never laugh-never laugh indulge in amusement, but I *do* mean that there should be reason in their mirth and purpose in their recreations. I have been led to chronical these observations because there is a large proportion of the community who really seem to require the advice contained within them. For when we see thousands and thousands collecting to behold the ginger-bread pageantry of Lord Mayor's Day, and the feudal splendor of a young German Prince who has been fortunate enough to become the Queen's husband, and to whom the people are unfortunate enough to pay about 47,000*L* a year, independently of his royal wife's immense revenue,—when we remember that these traditionary specimens of barbaric mummery would not be persisted in at all, were it not for the species of enthusiasm that appears to welcome their appearance,—and when we recollect that they would sink into utter insignificance and perish of pure inaction were the people to display a rational spirit by remaining away from them,—we really think that it is the fault of the millions themselves if common sense be thus insulted by the donkeyism of Lord Mayor's Day and flunkeyism of princely processions. But so long as such spectacles shall have the power of inspiring the multitudes with a childish delight, how could we surprised if the youth of nineteen or twenty should suddenly leave his father's table to indulge in a game of marbles? And were such a thing known to happen, everyone would exclaim in mingled disgust and pity. "You will never make a man of one whose mind is so thoroughly childish!" Yet those persons of mature years who flock to feast their eyes upon the despicable nonsense of a Lord Mayor's Show or, the gaud and glitter of a Prince's Procession are equally liable to have the strength of their minds and the solidity of their intelligence very grievously suspected.

Let it however be observed that the middle-classes are even more childish and puerile in these respects than many of the working-classes. Your middle-class-man will run a mile to see a lord—a real, living lord:—and if the said lord should only enter his shop, he will talk of the incident for a year afterwards. The men who are the heroes of the tom-foolery of Lord Mayor's Day and who don their Sunday's best to give a Prince what they call "a fitting welcome," likewise belong to the middle-class. The Lord Mayor is a member of that class: the individuals forming the committee for the opening of the Coal Exchange were members of that class;—and at all such exhibitions the wealth merchants and chiefs of the shopocracy are sure to have a finger in the management and arrangements then, what of the aristocracy? Why, at the public strangulation of the Mannings, there were present numerous scions of that oligarchical class. One "noble lord" paid ten guineas for a seat and drove down in his cab at six o'clock on the fatal morning, alighting in Great Suffolk Street, and repairing on foot to the house where "a window" was reserved for his special behoof. Another "noble lord" entertained seven or eight "honorables" at a champagne breakfast in a public house commanding a view of the hideous scene:—and "gentlemen of fashion" were as plentiful on the occasion as "gentlemen of the swell-mob." Thus did the representatives and scions of the immaculate aristocracy mingle with the multitudes whom, on their return to their Clubs, they denounced as "the rebel," the "riff-raff," "the unwashed," &c. &c.

Now, what is the lesson that these facts should teach the working-classes? That they would in future do well to abstain from visiting either sights of pomp or sights of horror. By acting in this manner, they will show their intelligence in the one sense and their humanity in the other. Do the people wish to put an end to trumpery raree-shows and the false, hollow, and barbarian splendor which only stands out in more tremendous contrasts with the rags, squalor, and destitution of the sons and daughters of toil? Do the people wish to put an end to the punishment of death and all its demoralising influences upon society? I am certain that the response to both queries is in the affirmative. Then, let the people abstain from gathering in crowds to gaze open-mouthed upon the tinsel shows which ought to be despised, and the barbarian scenes which ought to execrated. By adopting this course, they will prove that their intelligence and humanity are in advance of the upper and middle-classes.

A correspondent of the *Times* newspaper addressed a letter the other day to that journal, complaining of the annoyance and nuisance caused by barricading the principal streets and bridges of the metropolis on Lord Mayor's Day. The complaint was most just—most rational: for it is intolerable that business should be impeded for the behoof of the civic asses who play off their inane pranks on that occasion. But the same kind of remonstrance might be made against Prince Albert's water-procession to the Coal Exchange, on which occasion the river was blockaded in many parts and the utmost inconvenience produced. Talk of the liberty of the subject, when a decree bearing the signature of "Duke, Mayor," or "Farncomb, Mayor," can suddenly paralyse locomotion through all the great thoroughfares of the metropolis—suddenly check circulation through all the leading arteries of this mighty city! *Such* liberty is all of a piece with the amount of freedom which Britons do really possess: and heaven knows that this is little enough!

But did it strike anyone, while perusing the disgustingly fulsome trash that was penned relative to the Prince's procession to the Coal Exchange,—did it strike anyone, we ask, that the Queen's husband was actually countenancing upon that occasion a monopoly of the very worst and most oppressive description? Upon every ton of coals that enters the port of London, a certain tax is levied: and the metage duties flow likewise into the treasury of the bloated Corporation of the City. This monopoly is a curse upon the port: it is a monopoly of the basest, cruelest, most flagrant, and most scandalous character. The greater portion of the City revenues is expended on beastly guzzling and filthy gormandizing: and the poor are plundered and robbed in the shape of a tax on fuel, in order to afford the means of swelling the enormous revenues of those precious devourers of turtle and venison. Those who have the least acquaintance with the habits of the poor, are well aware that amongst innumerable families, a quarter of a hundred weight of coal is all they can purchase at one time: some of them even buy seven pounds, this amount being all that they can afford. Is it not cruel, then—is it not infamous to a degree to allow monopoly to raise the price of the most necessary article? The wealthy aldermen and common council men do not feel the influence of that monopoly: a few shillings a-year more or less to them are nothing. But the striving, wretched, famished poor *do* feel it-and feel it most acutely too.

And now let us look for a moment at the effects of this monopoly. At the beginning of October coals were selling at 22*s*. per ton during a few cold days; and then they rose to 26*s*, 27*s*, and 28*s*.—*not because there was any scarcity, but from monopoly alone!* From October the 26th to November the 5th, there were 1855 colliers "at market," of which the contents of 514 only were sold, the remaining 1341 remaining unsold. Thus there was no deficiency of supply to produce the above-mentioned increase of price. The London market alone requires a supply of about 2,500,000 tons a-year, for the conveyance of which 8,000 ships (making repeated voyages) are used. The City dues and metage impose a duty of 1*s*.4*d* per ton; and thus upon 2,500,000 tons an annual tax of 166,666*l*. is levied. At the moment when I pen this article, Wednesday, Nov. 14th, coals are selling in the pool at 14*s*. 6*d*. per ton, and retail at 1*l*. 8*s*. 4*d*.; or 1*s*, 5*d*, per cwt. The winter is approaching; and the price of coals will be run up considerably. Thus adding to the wretchedness which the poor already suffer at the hands of the rich.

But my readers will perhaps ask what on earth all this has to do with the title, object, and aim of the present article. Surely the facts just laid bare will teach sightseers in future to pause and reflect upon the nature and meaning of the royal procession which they may be disposed to turn out and contemplate. Surely they will stop to ask themselves whether the object of these princely visits be to confer a benefit upon the masses, or to give a kind of sanction to a cruel engine of oppression. At all events, before they begin to cheer, and applaud, and raise their voices in loud acclamations, they ought to take the trouble to look below the surface of the gilded pageantry, and penetrate into its purport, its aim, and the influence its proceedings may have upon their own interests.

And now to proceed a step farther with my argument. In the same way that sights of horror tend to brutalize the mind, so do sights of pomp and ostentation tend to debase it. Nothing can be more servile, more groveling, more spaniel-like, than to go and cheer great folks simply because they are great folks. First ascertain if their conduct be deserving of your applause; and in deliberating upon this point, do not be misled by any negative virtues which they possess. It is not sufficient that they are merely harmless and inoffensive people; they should actually display the positive qualities of doing good. When Prince Albert went to the Coal Exchange, had it been for the purpose of remonstrating against the monopoly of which that place is the head-quarters, he should have been loudly cheered: but as he went with no such philanthropic object in view, I cannot for the life of me conjecture wherefore he was enthusiastically applauded. If it were simply because he is a Prince, I do not envy the intelligence of those who made themselves hoarse in yelping after him.

I can very well understand and appreciate a desire to behold such a patriot as Kossuth – and such a great man as Mazzini – or so undaunted a champion of Republicanism as Ledru-Rollin: but I cannot comprehend why thousands and thousands should congregate to feast their eyes upon a fat citizen who is chosen to a transitory office. If the attraction lie in the gingerbread coach, the sword-bearer's fur-cap, the Recorder's wig or the "Ancient Knights" who are obliged to be held upon their horses. I envy the intelligence of the spectators still less than in the former instance.

But it is positively awful to contemplate the avidity with which the multitudes rush to gaze upon the hideous paraphernalia of the scaffold—the proceedings of Jack Ketch—and the death-writhings of our fellow-creatures. The hangman's holiday demoralises thousands. The public houses thrive royally upon gibbet-days: thieves and rascals of all kinds reap a rich harvest;—and heaven only knows where contamination ceases. Government advocates the *solitary system* in gaols, for the alleged purpose of preventing the old and hardened criminal from utterly destroying all remnants of good feeling in the minds of those who are as yet young in the ways of iniquity;—and yet the very men who adopt that maddening, torturing, atrocious, and cold-blooded *regime,* are likewise the cause of assembling all the rogues and miscreants of the metropolis together and affording them an opportunity of making proselytes amongst the harmless and unsuspicious with whom they scrape acquaintance on the loathsome occasion.

Again, therefore, do I declare that the well-disposed, the intelligent, and the reflective man should keep away from scenes of pomp as well as from spectacles of horror. He should not by his presence give his adhesion to the wanton extravagance which supports the former, nor countenance the sanguinary laws which create the latter. By his absence he virtually protests against them all;—and he likewise avoids the chance of mental abasement and moral contamination. So long as the rich, the titled, and the great are run after and applauded, they will not believe that the whole system whence originates their exceptional social position, can possibly be unpopular. If a lord be treated as a demigod, he will naturally believe that lords are not only necessary but are absolutely loved. And so long as vast multitudes throng around the gibbet, Governments will perpetuate the punishment of death on the plea that a wholesome example is held out to those who thus have an opportunity of beholding with their own eyes the terrors of the gallows. Were there no spectators, the gibbet would soon disappear: the hideous drama would not be put upon the stage to be performed to an empty house.

A Glance at Continental Europe

Saturday, December 1, 1849

The revolutions, insurrections, and various political ferments which characterised the year 1848, must not be viewed superficially nor disposed of as matters already belonging to *the past*. On the contrary, they should be studied with the most earnest attention; inasmuch as they positively affect *the present* and are ominously significant for *the future*. It is all very well for the newspapers to proclaim that "tranquility is restored upon the Continent," – that "order prevails in Europe,"—and that "the revolutionary spirit is crushed." It is likewise easy for such a man as Lord John Russell to declare that certain countries are infested by a number of professional agitators and notorious fomenters of disturbance,—thus sneeringly attributing the various great movements of the past year, *not* to and impatience under the infernal yoke of despotism, but to the machinations and intrigues of men who trade in revolution. But let the newspapers be well assured that although the crowned miscreants of Continental Europe have succeeded in crushing freedom for a time by means of the bayonets of standing armies, yet that the spirit which burst forth in 1848 is only temporarily subdued and not extinguished altogether;—and let Lord John Russell, on his part, study the causes of revolutions with a more profound philosophy than he has hitherto brought to bear upon the subject, so that he may learn to attribute them to their real source, and not be reduced to the pitiful necessity or else the dishonest expedient of fabricating for them an origin and a motive from the fertile warehouse of his own brain.

Now it is quite clear that when the newspapers speak in such a flippant, off hand, complaisant manner of "order and tranquility being restored," they are laboring under the same ignorance or else acting with the same duplicity as Lord John Russell when this nobleman attributes insurrectionary movements to the exciting influences of

170

certain inveterate and professional perturbators. No—such *never was* and *never will be* the origin of the uprising of whole nations. Will any one save a madman believe that a few restless and disconnected spirits could stir up the millions to rebellion, if these millions had no cause of complaint against their rulers? – will anyone save a Bedlamite or else a thorough-paced hypocrite venture to affirm that it would be possible to arouse the inhabitants of the United States of North America to take up arms against their government? No: for where the people are free, prosperous, and happy, they have neither need nor inducement for violence; and when the Government has been raised up by themselves— when, in a word, it springs from the nation at large, and not from an oligarchy,—it is absurd to talk of even the possibility of arms being taken up against it. Believe me, then, that there is no instinctive love for anarchy, turbulence, violence, and constant change, implanted in the bosom of any nation. It is the nature of man to fear death, to avoid unnecessary danger, to prefer a tranquil existence to a stormy one, and to make many sacrifices for the sake of those who are dependent upon him. Hence it is clear that he will put up with a great deal of oppression and wrong ere he can be goaded to the state of desperation when he springs up and flies in the face of his oppressor. Because in doing this, he incurs a fearful risk: the gibbet looms in the distance— exile may become his fate—or a prison wall may separate him from his wife and little ones for years and years to come. Think you, then, that nations, which are made up of individuals of this cast of mind, can possibly have a natural hankering for revolution, anarchy, and strife? It is ridiculous. Make them free—let them be well governed—let no favoured class consisting of a few, self-appropriate all the luxuries and elegance of life while the millions starve—let labour as well as property have its rights,—and in a country with such institutions as these, the bare idea of the possibility of revolution would be laughed at—standing armies would be utterly useless so far as "the preservation of order" was concerned—and even the very policemen and constables would have to throw down their truncheons and grasp the spade or the hoe.

Well, then,—if there be no instinctive love of disorder in the breasts of nations, and if entire communities as well as individuals prefer tranquility and safety to anarchy and danger,—what is the cause of revolutions? The answer is easy. For it is the tyranny of the few that goads the millions to desperation: it is the arrogance, the usurpation, the greediness, and the selfishness of Kings and Aristocracies that drive the nations into insurrection. So long, then, as the reign of tyranny shall continue on Continental Europe, will the spirit of revolution be in existence,—now subdued and smouldering, it is true, but only to flame forth again at the first opportunity with a more translucent glory than ever.

When, therefore, the newspapers observe, with so much insolent coolness and presumptuous self-sufficiency that "order is completely restored in Europe," and that "the spirit of rebellion is crushed," they ought to add—"but only for a time:"—and if they were wise or honest they would avail themselves of the interval to read Kings, Princes, Presidents, and Aristocracies, a lesson how to avert those menacing popular attitudes in future. They would say, "Do not trust to brute force. It may succeed for a moment: but in the long run it will redound upon your own heads. Besides, by employing violence to put down the popular voice, you only prompt the nations to call into requisition the same weapons wherewith to back their own demands. Be wise while there is yet time: the people are stronger than you—and, although you have succeeded in purchasing the support of hundreds of thousands of bayonets for the present, yet modern history is fecund in proofs of how those bayonets sometimes remain sheathed when the tyrants have the greatest need of them, or else are turned upon the very tyrants themselves. Take warning, then, from these facts and signs: the people have already shaken the nations from the banks of the Seine to the waters of the Danube; and though the earthquake has subsided, the convulsion may return again."

In such language of mingled remonstrance and warning would the press speak to the rulers of Continental Europe, if it were wise and honest. For, inasmuch as the pandemonium of tyranny has been rebuilt by the treachery of Louis Bonaparte, the villainy of the King of Prussia, the cowardice of the German princes, the accursed hypocrisy of the Pope, and the hellish barbarism of the Emperors of Austria and Russia,—inasmuch, I say, as the Temple of Freedom has been once more converted into a loathsome Golgotha, and Humanity shrinks aghast from the human holocausts which the miscreant Haynau has offered up to the bloody maw of the Kaiser of Vienna and the Czar of St. Petersburgh,— on account of all this, I repeat, is it inscribed in the Book of Fate that the nations of Europe shall rise again,—from the green banks of the Seine to the fastness of the Transylvanian provinces shall they rise—and, the banners of Freedom once more flung forth the winds of heaven, the names of Kossuth and Mazzini. Ledru-Rollin and Unruh, Manin and other patriots of all nations, will become gathering cries in the mouths of the democrats of Continental Europe.

Twenty months have now elapsed since the tremendous series of commotions which succeeded each other as rapidly as if the spirit of insurrection had been propelled from Paris by means of electric wires reaching to the souls of all the patriots throughout Europe. At that time nearly all the great capitals of Europe suddenly fell into the power of the people. Monarchs either fled or were paralyzed—the ordinary governments were either upset or rendered powerless—and nine-tenths of all Europe were positively, literally, and actually in the hands of the PEOPLE. What was the consequence? Did anarchy prevail?—did rapine ensue? Did spoliation take place? Were any cruelties committed? Did vengeance stalk abroad, striking at the rich and the great?—did the poor and the oppressed seek liquidation of old scores from the wealthy oppressor? No: "mob-law" did *not* prevail—the "riff-raff" did *not* take to pillage—the "unwashed" did *not* deal forth retribution upon their tyrants. In all those countries where the commotion took place, every man became a special constable on the spot to preserve order: and the intelligence of the masses shone to as great an advantage as their humanity. They might have pillaged, plundered, sacked and destroyed at will,—they might have gratified personal animosity and private pique with as much ferocity as impunity,—they might have set to work against kings and aristocracies all those hideous engines of tyranny and persecution which kings and aristocracies had so often brought to bear upon them,—they might, in a word, have given full employment to the hangman the gaoler, and the captain of transport-ship,—they might also have confiscated here, fined there—pillaged the houses of some and handed over to conflagration the property of others,—all this might the masses have done had they chosen:—and in thus acting they would only have taken a leaf out of the book of "their betters." But they did nothing of the sort. Never was forbearance more noble—never did the spirit of conciliation appear more generous. In the same way never was intelligence more sublime—never was the attitude of men more godlike!

And it was precisely because the masses were *too* forbearing— *too* merciful—*too* confiding, that the tyrants whom they spared have since been enabled to enslave them again. And now mark the contrast! No sooner did those tyrants recover themselves, when, aided by their aristocratic or middle-class Ministers, and backed by their soldiery, they began to put into prompt requisition all those engines of atrocity and cruelty which the masses had disdained to use. The hangman was set to work—murderous platoons were constantly practicing at living human targets—gaols were inundated with victims—and transport-ships plowed the waves of the ocean. Nevertheless, the men whom the resuscitation of tyranny thus recalled to power, are eulogised as "the party of order," while the patriots of 1848 are stigmatized as the "enemies of tranquility!"

The party of order! Eternal God, what a party of order! It is this party, and the principles which it upholds, that originally goaded the nations to despair, and consequently caused the revolutions and insurrections which have swept over Continental Europe: it is this party which has destroyed the French Republic in all save its name, and which has banished from the soil of France the bravest and best of her sons: it is this party which caused the massacre of the people in the streets of Berlin, when the King looked gloatingly upon the same from his palace window: it is this party which murdered the brave Roman patriots who so gallantly defended their city against the Algerine cut-throats led by Oudinot: it is this party whose principals are apparent in the bloody massacres which made the streets of Naples flow with human gore, and which turned the fairest towns of Sicily into a charnel-house: it was this party who decreed that Hungary—glorious gallant, admirable Hungary—should be yielded up, unaided and friendless, to the blood-stained tyrants of Russia and Austria: it was this same party whose savage instincts and ferocious vengeance have been impersonated with such hellish truthfulness by that incarnate demon Haynou;—and, lastly, it is this same party whose iniquity, selfishness, ambition, and treason, our now so actively at work to restore the affairs of Continental Europe to even a more appalling condition than they were in when the revolutions of 1848 commenced. Such is "the party of order," gentle reader,—that party which dares to denounce the masses as inveterate disturbers of the peace, and which tells those same masses that they are not fit to exercise the franchise nor any other privilege of civilisation! And yet all the infamy—all the cruelty—all the blood-thirstiness—and all the real origin of anarchy, are on the side of this "party of order" whereas all the forbearance—all the leniency—all the intelligence—all the honesty—and all the patriotism, were on the side of the People!

I said just now, it was written in the Book of Fate that the nations will rise again; and on this point there cannot be the slightest doubt. One year—two years—even three years, may possibly pass over in comparative quietude: but, sooner or later, as assuredly as there is a god in heaven, will the people of Continental Europe be up in arms again. And on this occasion it will be no child's play. The masses have already been cheated too often, to be deluded again; and no one possessing a grain of sense, can suppose for a moment that they will do their work by halves when next they get the upper-hand of their oppressors.

Nothing but physical-force revolutions can obtain justice and freedom for the masses of certain States upon the Continent of Europe. The moral influence of public opinion in those countries, is scarcely perceptible; and, however deeply violence is too be deplored and bloodshed to be abhorred, yet if the denizens of the States alluded to, were to trust their cause to moral means only, centuries must elapse ere the object could be attained. And it is in this point of view that England presents so striking a contrast to most of the countries of Continental Europe. For in the British Isles public opinion *does* possess an influence; and the history of our land shows us how abuses and errors in out governmental systems, gradually but irresistibly yield to the continuous though silent pressure of truth. Moreover, small as is the amount of real freedom which the millions possess, we nevertheless *do* enjoy the right of public assembly— of discussing out grievances and suggesting the remedies—of printing our opinions, and disseminating them for the general advantage, as in the case of the "INSTRUCTOR." We are likewise well assured that, selfish and unprincipled as the aristocracy is, and servile to the aristocracy as the Government is known to be, yet no flagrant violation of individual rights and no direct attack upon personal property can be safely attempted by the oligarchy or its myrmidons. Therefore, the people of England stand in quite a different position from the nations of the Continent. *Here*, we can achieve all we require by moral means: *there*, oceans of blood must be waded through by the sons of Freedom. In England, the man who deliberately and systematically promulgates doctrines of physical-force, is a traitor to the popular cause—a foe to real progress—and on enemy to civilisation: because we have, in our institutions themselves, the means of obtaining all those reforms which we demand, if our voices be only raised loudly enough and if our agitation be conducted in a proper manner. Corrupt as the legislature is, it cannot long withstand the moral pressure from without;—and if the leaders of the people be honest and sincere, and the people themselves peaceably firm and passively resolute, no great length of time can elapse ere the principals of the Charter shall be promulgated as the law of the land.

The day has gone by when "wisdom of our ancestors" could be deemed a sufficient vindication for those institutions which that "wisdom" raised. In politics, as in literature, in science as in art, there was for many an age the same superstitious reverence for the past – the same reverted and adoring glance. But the intellect of the masses has become agitated with new desires: the present business of mankind has become the proper object of their knowledge;—the craving of their interests summons science to its aid and science, being practical, finds itself in communication with every man, stimulating every man, and teaching him that the *present* should be his study, as the *future* will be scene of his triumph. Thus is he weaned from his veneration for antiquity; and he smiles in pity or contempt when "the wisdom of our ancestors" is alluded to, by some besotted or benighted individual, in his presence.

Society was for a long while, in its intellectual progress, like a traveller, who,—fixing his eye on the point of his departure,—keeps steadily in view all its features while he can- reproduces in his imagination such as he can no longer see—and has neither concern nor attention for the objects which surround him, save as by some accidental resemblance recall the objects he has left. The pure, clear landscape of the present, with its broad masses of fertility, its virgin soil that asked but the slightest tillage, was contemned as an unfruitful waste while the future seemed but as the prolongation of the desert which the exile must pass in his eternal pilgrimage from home. But the scene has changed: our long vigil at the tomb of antiquity is broken—and forever! The spirit song of the past may still float melodiously around some few: but to the many it is a music fraught with barbarism and breathing the notes of slavery,—so that they joyously welcome to their ears a louder, a nearer, and a dearer strain—the paean of an enfranchised intellect!

Political Victims

Saturday, December 15, 1849

The mere fact of the existence of Political Victims in any country, is a proof of bad government, vitiated institutions, and tyrannical rulers. For it is only because there is something to amend or something to eradicate, that political agitators spring up;—and when the Government becomes frightened, it pounces upon half-a-dozen of those plain-speakers and thrusts them into gaol. The laws of treason and sedition have all been framed for the purpose of surrounding vicious and oppressive institutions with as many defences as possible: they are the necessary and invariable means by which tyranny, monopoly, and injustice protect themselves. The matter lies in a nut-shell, so far as the facility of explanation goes. In the beginning, each community of individuals—each separate society, in a word—needed laws for its government. These laws were made by the votes of all the members of the community; and certain officers were appointed to carry out those statutes. Thus, in the origin, did universal suffrage frame the laws and raise up the Executive. But in process of time the persons forming the Executive seized upon power as a right and not as a delegation; and, their arrogance and selfishness increasing, they proclaimed this right of power to be hereditary in their own families. Thus arose Monarchies and Aristocracies. But then, in order to fortify their usurpations with as many defences and outworks as possible, these persons pushed their insolence and their tyranny to such and extent as to exclude a large portion of the community from that right of suffrage which had existed from the beginning: and the franchise was narrowed until it became confined to the wealthy class, which was interested in sustaining the usurpations of hereditary rulers and privileged orders. In many countries the right of suffrage was crushed altogether; and absolutism was established in its stead. Thus those monarchical and aristocratical institutions, which must clearly have originated in usurpation, have become sanctioned as it were by the lapse of ages; and the nations, having either accepted or endured them, they have become established governments against which it is no doubt improper for a minority to take up arms.

But if physical force be an alternative not to receive our countenance save under exceptional circumstances, the strength of moral persuasion and oral or written argument may fairly, properly, and righteously be brought to bear upon our institutions. Every man, as a member of the community, has rights to defend and interests to proclaim; and it is as atrocious tyranny to deprive him of the power of expressing his wants and opinions by means of a representative in Parliament,—a foul wrong also to attempt to gag him when he speaks out for himself on account of not being suffered to have such a representative,—but a more diabolical outrage still, to tear that man away from his family and plunge him into a gaol because he will not allow himself to be so gagged when proclaiming his wrongs and demanding redress. Granting that his language is violent and that he even fulminates menaces,—granting, too, that his conduct as well as his speech is calculated to excite the inflammable mind and terrify the weak one,—still, before this man is punished, the question should be asked—Whether he had any provocation? His reply would be couched in these terms:—"I am naturally a peaceable man. I have a wife and children whom I love, and for whom I will cheerfully work from morning till night. But I can obtain no work: and they, the loved ones are perishing with hunger, cold and misery before my very eyes! Even *this* I could endure with proper resignation and Christian fortitude, were it a calamity sent by God and common to the human race. But when I know, or at least believe, that there are in this country a sufficient resources to afford honest labour to all and enough food to supply all with an abundance,—when I find that I am deprived of work and deprived of food on account of the false, vitiated and barbarous condition of our social and political institutions,—when I implore the Parliament by means of *humble* petitions to grant me and the millions of my starving fellow countrymen some little redress and receive a cold, stern, and arrogant refusal to that earnest and respectful prayer,—then, when I am called upon to obey laws in the making of which I have no share, to pay taxes in the levying of which I am permitted to have no voice, and to venerate institutions which are clearly established for the benefit of the few to the enormous prejudice of the many,—when I think of all this,

I am goaded to desperation—I feel that I have nothing to bind me to a servile tranquility, but everything to urge me on to rebellion—I know that my position cannot possibly be made worse, but may become a great deal better—and I will fly in the face alike of Man or God, if I am told that my destiny on earth is misery for myself—misery for my wife—and misery for my little ones!"

Now in this strain would political victims of the working class speak, if they were closely, frankly, and lucidly questioned by some Judge who was honestly determined to sift the men and their motives to the very bottom. This judge too, were such an one to be found, would draw many distinctions and trace many lines of demarcation, all bearing upon the subject under his notice. He would see that whereas the man who is in comfortable circumstances, who has received a good education, and who enjoys the franchise by virtue of his property,—that whereas, I say, such a man could offer but little apology for recommending violence and preaching civil war as the stepping-stones towards reform,—yet that, on the other hand, the poor starving, houseless wretch, who beholds his wife and children perishing before his eyes, cannot be held equally responsible for any intemperance of language or of deeds into which the frightful keenness of misery and the barrowing poignancy of distress may hurry him.

What is it, then, that makes Political Victims? *A vitiated condition of society?* And what makes a vitiated condition of society? *Unjust, oppressive, and partial institutions.* And what makes these inappropriate and pernicious institutions? *Bad government.* Ah! Now then, we are tracing things back to their real sources and giving them their proper names: and therefore we will at once leap to a climax by asking once more—*What makes Political Victims?* And the response is—*Bad Government!*

Then this Bad Government makes its own victims and punishes them: its influence turns men into certain channels where pit-falls are already digged to receive them. A most merciful—humane—and paternal government is this! 'Tis the case of a man setting up for a school-master, but refusing to teach his pupils anything, and then scourging them murderously because they are ignorant. 'Tis the case of a parent who sternly refuses his children all the rights and kindnesses to which they are entitled, but nevertheless exacts from them a blind obedience, and cruelly maltreats them when they do not pay it cheerfully.

'Tis the case of an employer who agrees to supply his apprentice with food only in proportion to the amount of work done—but who will not give that apprentice the slightest work to do, and then treats him brutally because he complains that he is starved, kept in ignorance of his trade, and reduced to the condition of a beggarly outcast. For if in all the cases which I have just named, there is a special compact made or understood,—as between the schoolmaster and his pupil, the father and his child, the employer and his apprentice,—so likewise is there a compact, either made or understood, between the governing and the governed,—a compact which binds the former to administer the laws with impartiality and distribute the fruits of the national industry with fairness—to avoid all favouritism and treat one member of the community as well as another,—so that in return the governed may have reason to express their gratitude, their confidence, and their approval in respect to the governing.

For, after all, the favoured few who are now the *masters*, should in reality be only the *servants*, of the people. How is it that the millions look upon the Government as an enemy, and not as a friend?—how is it that the Government is a source of terror, and not an object of love?—how is it that the nation is always agitating to obtain something from the Government which the Government is invariably indisposed to grant? It is because the nation's servants have thus become its masters: it is because the Sovereignty of the People has dwindled down into despicable farce, and those who dare assert that Sovereignty are made Political Victims!

And speaking of Victims, who that reads this article will not be reminded of the awful fate of Joseph Williams and Alexander Sharp? Sentenced by the Judge to two years' imprisonment, they were doomed by our gaol discipline to death! The tribunal dared not sentence them to the scaffold: but the prison-system was allowed to make the penalty capital. The Government was not venturous enough to employ Jack Ketch: but the Cholera—another agent of the Destroying Angel—was permitted to do the work that might not be entrusted to Calcraft.

And those two men—those *victims* in more senses than one,—were they rather to be blamed or pitied? Alas! Poverty—destitution—the spectacle of a famine-stricken wife and starving children, drove them mad;—and in their madness they spoke and acted intemperately. But mark this well, reader! Though thus goaded to desperation, they used not a word more violent nor adopted an attitude more menacing that the Whigs themselves did in the year 1831. Turn to No. 2 of the *Instructor*— read the first column of the sixth page thereof the language enunciated by Mr. Edmonds and approved of by Lord John Russell. I declare solemnly that neither Williams nor Sharp said anything more threatening to the public peace that the language thus alluded to. As for those poor victims marching through the streets with a few hundreds of unarmed men—why, what was this peaceable demonstration in comparison with Mr. Atwood's assemblage of 150,000 men at Birmingham,—an assemblage sanctioned by Lord John Russell, and gathered with the avowed intention of marching to London if necessary? What, too, was the conduct of Williams and Sharp in comparison with the Whig letter written to a certain General-officer directing him to be in readiness to head a rebellion in case of need?

But Mr. Edmonds was not prosecuted: Lord John Russell did not have proceedings instituted against *himself*;—nor was the Treasury-hack who wrote the above-mentioned letter ever put upon his trial. Yet the most milk-and-water language of such men as those ought to be held more blameable than the hardest words which a starving, crushed, unenfranchised serf of a working-man could possibly utter.

When Lord John Russell was asked the other day for reform, he replied, "The people are too ignorant to be entrusted with the franchise." Well, but Sharp and Willliams belonged to that class whom his lordship deems so brutally deficient in intelligence as not to be able to know their own interests or understand their own rights. Then, wherefore strike those two poor ignorant men with the vengeance of the law? Surely, according to Lord John Russell's own showing, they had not intelligence enough to be responsible for their actions. If they were to ignorant to be entrusted with a vote they were likewise too ignorant to be aware that it was wrong to demand it: and they should have been pitied—not punished. Instead of being plunged into a prison, they should have been sent to school.

But even if they were thus deplorably ignorant as Lord John Russell represents their class to be, who was it that kept them in ignorance?—who is it that still keeps the working-class in ignorance? The Government! And then this Government punishes men for that ignorance, or for the results of that ignorance, which itself either studiously maintains or scandalously allows to exist.

But though the plea of "ignorance" be readily caught up by the Government and the Aristocracy when a demand for reform is to be met, it is not considered valid when Political Victims are standing in the dock. No: *them* the Attorney-General represents them as dangerous to the public peace—as men exercising a considerable influence over the multitude—as practised perturbators whose moral power is adequate to raise the masses to rebellion. Almighty God! how can all this tremendous influence be wielded by men too ignorant to be entrusted with the franchise? No: the men who can move the masses, must be clever— intelligent—and eloquent;—and therefore their very position as Political Victims shows that they *are* intelligent enough to enjoy the franchise, and that it was the denial of their just rights which goaded them to despair.

It is well known that Sharp and Williams perished of the cholera, brought on by *starvation,* in the gaol where they were confined. They have left widows and orphans behind them. But has the Government given one shilling to succour these destitute families?—have the authorities of the prison where Sharp and Williams were starved into cholera, and by cholera given unto death,—have these authorities, I say, shown any contrition for the lamentable fate of those men, or any sympathy for the bereaved wives and little ones left behind? The answer is a mournful negative. Yet why should these poor families be thus turned forth destitute upon the world? Even if both Sharp and Williams were as bad as Barabbas the robber, their wives and children must not be crucified with them. The Government permitted a certain system of gaol-discipline to be applied to Sharp and Williams; and under this discipline the men sank and perished. The Government, then, cannot be exonerated from all blame relative to their deaths. Surely as *men*, if not as *ministers*, Lord John Russell and Sir George Grey must feel for those destitute widows—these fatherless children? But no: not a shilling from their purses, either public or private! And yet thousands and hundreds of thousands of pounds are annually lavished upon *titled paupers* and on foreign beggar-princes and mendicant-princesses. Yes—and enormous pensions are annually paid to the Richmond, the Grafton and the St. Albans families because they happen to be descended from certain filthy strumpets who sold their persons to Charles the second. Oh! let the heirs of harlots and the titled progeny of beastly prostitutes fatten upon the luxuries of the land: but spare not a shilling to succor the innocent families of two poor English working men who were murdered by the gaol-discipline of the country!

Universal Suffrage in France

Saturday, December 22, 1849

The experiment of Universal Suffrage has already been tried three times in France, during the last eighteen months. The first occasion was for the election of the National Assembly: the second for that of the President of the Republic;—and the third for that of the Legislative Chamber. I now propose to consider whether the principle of Universal Suffrage has failed to realize in France the hopes and promises of its friends: if it have failed, to what extent the failure has reached and from what causes it has arisen; and whether the past should be allowed to form any criterion for an estimate of prophecy of the future.

First, then, let me examine the condition of the French people at the moment when the glorious Revolution of February, 1848, broke out. The number of persons entitled by their age and property to share in electoral monopoly, was under 200,000;—and yet the male adult population was nearly *eight million*. To secure the votes of those 200,000 franchise-monopolizers, the Minister of the Interior had *sixty thousand places* at his command: thus, what with actual presentations and solemn promises to places, the Cabinet of the day could always reckon, under ordinary circumstances, upon bribing more than a fair half of the electors. But even supposing that this contemptible minority of 200,000 persons had all exercised the franchise worthily, it is quite clear that the enormous majority of male adult population were utterly and lamentably ignorant of what the uses, aims, and objects of the suffrage were. Nor had they any means of enlightenment upon that subject. Under the despot monarchies of the elder and younger Bourbons there was no free press. Newspapers not only had to deposit in the Treasury a large sum as a security in case of political libel; but they were also held under the most rigid censorship; and whole impressions were seized and suppressed if anything obnoxious to the throne or the government appeared in their columns. Unstamped

183

periodicals dared not deal in politics: democratic tracts were only distributed by stealth;—public meetings were not tolerated;—and thus the people were literally without instructors or instruction of any really useful nature. Therefore, with no knowledge of the franchise—with no honest political guides—with no power to hold public assemblies—and with the scandalously demoralizing example of bribable electoral body before their eyes, the people of France were suddenly called upon to exercise the glorious right of Universal Suffrage!

Did ever a nation labour under such deplorable disadvantages? The only teachings they had previously received were execrable: the only examples they could gaze upon, were abominable. The national education was either in the hands of the State or of the Church; and the learning imparted was therefore all in favour of the throne and government. Corruption in every institution communicated a loathsome rottenness to the whole social system; and the public mind was degraded, debased, and demoralised.

Yet it was under the effects of such appalling influences as these, and under such dreadful auspices, that the first experiment of Universal Suffrage was to be made in France. Ledru-Rollin, the honest and far-seeing Minister of the Interior in the Provisional Government, was awake to the deplorable disadvantages under which the glorious principle was to be tested. Therefore was it that he dispatched Commissioners into all the provinces and wrote his famous Circulars, with the view of sending instructors and imparting instruction to the French people. The Republic had been proclaimed: it was the will of France to have a Republic;—and the Provisional Government was therefore bound to teach the nation Republican duties. Had Ledru-Rollin experienced no opposition on the part of some of the "wolves in sheep's-clothing" who were his colleagues in that Provisional Government, the mode of instruction would have succeeded fully and the instructors would have proved completely adequate to the task. But he was thwarted in all his useful plans and statesman-like views by Lamartine, Marrast, Garnier-Pages, Marie, and others; while himself, Louis Blanc, Flocon, and Albert were invariably left in a minority in the Councils of the Provisional Government. Thus the true friends of the Republic were frustrated in the endeavors to counteract the diabolical influences which the system of the ruined Royalty had left behind it;—and millions of men were called upon to exercise all on a sudden a right to which they were utterly unused and for the proper management of which they received at the moment but comparatively little advice.

Again, then, do I say that it was under such menacing auspices the first grand experiment was to be tried. But there was not even a sufficiency of *known and tried men* to set up as candidates. Nine-tenths of the old Chamber were inveterate Monarchists and Corruptionists who did not dare come forward and who would have been hooted off the hustings if they had. In England, the practice of holding public meetings points out good men to the notice of constituencies; but in France no such indications of individual talent and worth had ever transpired because the means to furnish them had been wanting. Where, then, was France to find all on a sudden *nine hundred* "good men and true" to constitute its first Assembly? It was compelled to take the couple of hundred who were already known in public life, and then exercise the best possible discretion with regard to the choice of the remaining seven hundred.

Now, under such circumstances, had the first experiment of Universal Suffrage in France failed altogether – thoroughly, completely, and miserably failed—there would have been little cause for wonder. And in such a case the blame would not have rested with the people—but with that selfish and detestable Royalty which had just been overthrown: for such failure would *not* have been the result of Republican institutions, but the effect of those baleful and diabolical influences which the Monarchy had left behind it. Thus, the failure—if a failure it had been—would have only afforded an additional argument against the demoralizing, franchise-monopolising, ignorance-perpetuating, intelligence-crushing system which had just been kicked out of France,—and likewise a clinching proof of the necessity of Republicanism to cleanse the Augean stable of its foul corruption. In fact, such a failure would have shown that Republicanism should have come much earlier, and *not* that it should be waited for a little longer.

But the first election was no failure at all! No:—despite of all the tremendous disadvantages we have named – despite of all the evil influences we have chronicled, the initiative of the grand experiment of Universal Suffrage in France was no failure. For the Constituent Assembly framed and passed a Constitution which, though characterised by many faults alike of *commission* and *omission*, is nevertheless as transcendently superior to the fiction of a Constitution existing in England as a golden guinea is to a brass farthing. Truly, then, this was a great, and a mighty, and a glorious moment to be raised by those representatives who were embodied results of the first grand experiment made by France in respect to Universal Suffrage.

I shall not pause to detail all that I could have wished the Constituent Assembly to have done;—I shall not here place upon record all that I think it *ought* to have done with regard to the rights of labour and the interests of the working-classses. But I shall unhesitatingly and emphatically proclaim my conviction that, viewing the conduct of the Constituent Assembly *as a whole,* and making all allowances for circumstances and influences, its labours must be regarded as a magnificent guarantee for the work, utility, and intelligence of a body elected on the principles of Universal Suffrage.

One feature in the Constitution formed by that Assembly ought to render the severest democrats lenient in scrutinising its faults. I allude to that clause which not only holds the President of the Republic responsible for his acts, but also expressly, boldly, and plainly provides for his impeachment in case of need, and in a business-like, earnest, and honest manner lays down the judicial procedure by which he is to be rendered amenable to violated laws and to receive condign punishment in the name of an outraged nation. O glorious clause!—it was no failure in the exercise of Universal Suffrage which produced the men who framed and adopted such an enactment!

So much, then, in favour of the *first* test to which the glorious principle was subjected in France. The second occasion on which that principle was called into operation, was in the election of a President of the Republic. The choice fell upon Louis Napoleon Bonaparte. And wherefore? Because he put forth a manifesto in which he not only swore to maintain the Republic, but likewise avowed himself a *Socialist!* Yes—let his admirers or his apologists say what they will of him and his election,—let his success be attributed by some to the magic of the great traditionary name which he bare, and by others to the notion that the French were already sick of the Republic and chose him because they hoped that he would re-establish a Monarchy,—let the English *Times* and the *Chronicle* assert and re-assert as long as they like that his election was the result of a hankering after Princes and Potentates,—and let the enemies of democracy fling that election in our faces as an alleged proof of the inefficiency of Universal Suffrage to aid the cause of Progress,—I say again, and with unabated emphasis, that Louis Napoleon Bonaparte was chosen President of the French nation *because he proclaimed himself a republican and a Socialist!*

Let me here record a few facts to prove that M. Bonaparte gained his election by the pretended adoption of ultra-principles. In the first place, while he was canvassing the public, *ten millions* of hand-bills were struck off by four eminent printers in Paris (Messrs. Firmin Didot, Renouard, Lacampe, and Bourgogne), the contents being to the effect *that Louis Napoleon Bonaparte had been applied to, when a resident in London, to put himself at the head of the English Chartists and Democrats!* These millions of bills inundated all France—carried the damnable lie into the remotest and obscurest nook and corner—and naturally produced a tremendous effect. Then, again, several newspapers were either purchased or subsidised by the Bonapartists; and these prints promulgated the same tale. Furthermore, certain works on Pauperism and Labour which M. Bonaparte had written when in the prison of Ham, and which were as essentially Socio-Communist as the most ultra-thinker could desire, were not only triumphantly appealed to as proofs of his principles, but were also reprinted in the cheapest possible form and circulated by hundreds of thousands. In fine, never was a canvas conducted with more energy—more zeal—more lavish profusion; and never was a sailing under false colours crowned with a more triumphant success. Nine-tenths of the electors were scandalously, flagrantly, wickedly deceived: they thought that they were voting for a true Republican and a Socialist;—and thus was it that Louis Napoleon Bonaparte became President of France.

Who, then, can say that the principle of Universal Suffrage failed in the second experiment? No: it was not the principle which failed—but it was the man who failed to keep his solemn promises. Universal Suffrage cannot undertake to turn a rogue into an honest man, nor yet to prevent an honest man from becoming a rogue. God alone can do this. Sir Robert Peel may carry his election as a Conservative to-morrow; and the next day he may turn round and proclaim himself a Republican. Not only may constituencies, but likewise nations, be deceived by the professions, manifestos, and pledges of individuals. So was it with France. M. Bonaparte was supposed to be an honest and well-meaning man: his word was believed—his pledges were deemed sincere—his apparent frankness inspired confidence on all sides. The millions, in their own integrity of purpose and in their own rectitude of principle, could not for an instant imagine that any man could be base enough to enunciate opinions which in his heart he loathed, and volunteer promises which he never intended to keep: much less could they foresee that a personage who bore a name of which he seemed to be proud and which he might therefore be considered anxious to keep untarnished, would prove utterly lost to all principle—regardless of character—and indifferent to the most solemn vows which any man could possibly have recorded.

The second experiment made in France, relative to Universal Suffrage, was therefore no failure. The third trial of the principle was on the occasion of the general election for the Legislative Assembly. The results of this election showed that a large number of Legitimists were returned—men whose avowed object is the restoration of Monarchy in the person of Henry of Boardeaux: but, on the other hand, there were no less than 250 members of the Mountain party elected. The Cavaignac party, consisting of Moderate Republicans, was likewise large;—and the remainder of the new Chamber was made up of a few Orleanists and men of the old system. But what was the positive result? Why, that the majority of the Chamber consisted of men who would preserve the Republic!

And now be it observed that the Orleanists, the reactionaries, and the men of the old system got into this new Chamber by fraud, falsehood, and hypocrisy. They pretended to "accept" the Republic. In plain terms, they said, "We certainly were not Republicans originally: but as the republic is now an accomplished fact *(un fait accompli)* we take it as it is." Had they not made such professions as these – had they not "accepted" the Republic they would never have been elected at all. They imposed upon their constituencies in the same manner that M. Louis Napoleon Bonaparte imposed upon the nation. This fact, then, proves once more that the principle of Universal Suffrage did not fail—but that certain unprincipled men failed to perform their promises. Such results may happen, and constantly have happened, under systems of the narrowest franchise: they are matters of ordinary occurrence in England;—but there is assuredly less chance of their *recurrence* in electoral districts where Universal Suffrage embraces the whole mass of the intelligence, shrewdness, and caution of the male adult population, than where a limited franchise entrusts the choice of representatives to the "wisdom" of a few.

"But how did the Legitimists deluge the Chamber in such numbers?" our antagonists will inquire. I will explain the anomaly. In the first place be it well understood that millions of men cannot pass *unanimously* all on a sudden from one system to another. Prejudice, ignorance, selfishness, and habit will assert their empire over some portion of a community thus snatched up by the hand of the Revolution and hurled from an obscure and corrupt Past into the destinies of a bright and glorious Future. During the passage from the old extreme into the new, many men will halt—some bewildered, others tenaciously clinging to the abuses on which they fattened, and others again being unable to make up their timid minds to so tremendous a change. These men become the nucleus of a party whose aims speedily define themselves in selfish longings, ambitious views, and reactionary proceedings. They are part and parcel of the detestable influences and execrable results which the wreck of atrocious systems leaves behind. The purity of a true Republic is naturally distasteful to such men; and they accordingly league themselves for the purpose of re-building the Monarchy. Now, gentle reader, can you not understand from what social dunghill the weeds of Legitimacy sprang up even in the climate of a Republic?—but does it not also strike upon your convictions that in proportion as the party which I have just described must irresistibly yield to the continual pressure of Truth, the representatives whom it is at present enable to send into the Chamber will grow in number "small by degrees and beautifully less" until they disappear altogether?

On the other hand, even if there were an alarming influx of avowed Monarchists into the new Chamber, there was likewise a vast increase in the number of true democrats—namely, the Red Republicans of the Mountain. The Legitimists were therefore in a miserable minority; and they would have been powerless for all purposes of evil had the professed Moderates remained faithful to their election-pledges. But it was the perfidy of such men as Odillon Barrot and Leon Faucher that led to so many and such flagrant violations of the Constitution as those which the present Chamber has dared to accomplish. The party that had pretended to "accept" the Republic, threw off the mask the moment they had carried their elections and openly adopted a reactionary system. In vain did the Mountain resist: the unprincipled portion of the Chamber was backed by the equally unprincipled Bonaparte – the republican guarantees were trampled upon—an infamous conspiracy was got up to ruin or expel the best men of the Mountain—and the whole accursed work of perfidy, villainy, deception, and black-hearted treachery was consummated.

But in all this where exists the proof that Universal suffrage has failed as a principle? The same remarks which I just now applied to the election of the President of the Republic, address themselves with equal force to the election of the reactionaries in the Legislative Assembly. The people thought they were electing sheeps whereas when the artificial fleece was thrown off, the chosen ones proved to be wolves. Now had all pledges and promises had been faithfully kept, *three-fourths* of the Legislative Assembly would have been composed of men determined not only to maintain the Republic, but likewise to carry out the meaning and significancy of republican institutions. Well, then, it was upon this that *three-fourths* of the whole body of electors relied: and thus Universal Suffrage would have given *three* Republicans to *one* Monarchist.

And now let us consider what would have been the effect if Universal Suffrage had not existed at all. Had the franchise been limited, the elections would have returned an immense majority ready to overthrow the Republic in an hour and rebuild the Monarchy. But the universality of the franchise amongst the male adult population prevented this lamentable catastrophe;—and it was therefore Universal Suffrage which saved the Republic!

To what conclusion, then, do I come respecting the third experiment which has been made of Universal Suffrage in France? That as a principle it has experienced no failure whatsoever; because if some evil results have transpired, it is quite clear that its existence has prevented consequences ten thousand times more fatal. It has preserved the Republic: and what is more, it will continue to preserve it, unless the sudden exercise of that brute force which is concentrated in an army of 400,000 men should raise up an Empire or restore a Monarchy. At all events it is a myriad times more hazardous for any ambitious man to make such an attempt in the face of a nation enjoying Universal Suffrage, than in a country where a very limited franchise renders it facile to appease, bribe, and win over the electors to a particular cause.

And now, then, what hope has France for the future?—and must the events of the last eighteen months be regarded altogether as criterions for coming years? Everything that is deplorable in those events gives ample promise that France will speedily profit by a bitter experience; while everything that is laudable proves incontestably that she is resolved to work out her freedom in spite of the treachery, the ambition, and the intrigues of despicable adventurers who aim at imperial dignities as the only means of escaping a debtor's prison. To destroy the Republic even for a few years, would be scarcely possible: to destroy it altogether would be more than mortal man can accomplish. The tree of Liberty is planted in the soil of France: it may be out down to the very root—but only to spring up again with a greater strength and in a richer luxuriance, to cover the whole land with its grateful shade.

At the next election France will prove to the world that she has gathered experience from the past. The honest elector will have become intelligent: new interests and despair of success in the old game will induce the hitherto dishonest man to give his vote to Republican candidates. The good that Universal Suffrage has already done, will be increased manifold: the evil it has hitherto succeeded in preventing with some difficulty, it will then counteract with facility. The principle is unquestionable: its merits may be tested in every way – positively and negatively—as a preventive and a cure. The wrong and the misrule which now prevail in France, are not the results of Universal Suffrage—but of that mingled tyranny and treachery which seek to put Universal Suffrage down. The many blows struck at Republicans and Republicanism since the election of Louis Bonaparte, are the consequences—*not* of Universal Suffrage—but of the antagonism to Universal Suffrage. The results of an odious conspiracy against a particular system, must not for a moment be confounded with the working of any one of the principles whereon that system is based. In fact, Universal Suffrage is found to work so well in favour of Progress and against tyranny, that Louis Napoleon Bonaparte has already been thinking of making encroachments upon it as the indispensable stepping-stone to the imperial dignity. This is the highest and grandest tribute which could possibly be paid to the value, utility, and merits of the principle of Universal Suffrage.

Kossuth, Mazzini, and Ledru Rollin

Saturday, December 29, 1849

The newspaper press of this country has become a scandal and a shame throughout Europe. With a few honourable exceptions, the course it has pursued in respect to democratic agitations at home and revolutionary proceedings abroad, has been diabolical, fiend-like, and atrocious to a degree. Not contenting itself with the basest misrepresentations and the most damnable lies that ever were concocted by an unprincipled set of hireling scribes, it has applauded deeds of an atrocity from which savages would shrink and hounded kings and generals on to acts from which cannibals would recoil in horror. By the eternal God! I blush for the whole human species when I reflect that any individuals belonging to it could possibly become so depraved as to lend themselves to the support or justification of some of the greatest monsters as well as some of the vilest hypocrites that ever Satan endowed with human shape and sent upon the earth to curse mankind. A yell of execration throughout the length and breadth of the land ought to salute any journal which dared to publish a syllable in favour of the diabolical butcher Haynau, or those crowned miscreants of Austria and Russia who sent forth the cowardly assassin upon his bloody work. The men who wrote in justification of those monsters must themselves be of the most degraded stamp in respect to principle, although they have good coats upon their backs and gold in their pockets. But the lucre they have acquired by so iniquitous a prostitution of their intellects, can only be classed with the thirty pieces of silver for which Judas betrayed Christ. Freedom is the saving genius of men's physical nature, as Jesus is the divine instrument for the salvation of souls: and therefore the hireling scribes who have dared to write against Liberty, have crucified their Redeemer!

But let us look closely into what has been done by that portion of the press to which I am alluding. These base, venal, and blood-thirsty panderers to the interests of fiends in human shape, have endeavoured to drag the noblest names in Christendom through the mire and filth which the foul imaginations and feculent brains of the slanderers themselves have spawned forth. It is one of the fictions which have been palmed off upon the people, that "gentlemen of the most honourable character as well as of the highest talent, are the conductors of the public press." But if the truth of this assertion were never suspected before, surely recent events must have staggered the national faith in this respect. Indeed, the course adopted by particular newspapers can lead to no other conclusion than that there must be some of the most unprincipled wretches in all England at present holding domination *over,* or having connexion *with,* certain editorial offices. For though men may differ upon points of policy—and honestly differ, too,—though there may be conscientious Tories, sincere Protectionists, and well-meaning Conservatives,—yet it is utterly impossible that any individual can truly and faithfully believe that Kossuth is a swindler, Mazzini an imposter, or Ledru-Rollin a sneaking coward. No: we may believe that Lord John Russell is the most perfect little humbug of a politician that the world ever saw—but we cannot for an instant imagine that he is a burglar;—we may look upon Sir Robert Peel as the craftiest dealer in expedients that ever held the reins of power—but we cannot believe him to be a highwayman;—and we may regard Mr. Benjamin Disraeli as the most trumpery shuffler that ever displayed the chameleon hues of a political turn-coat—but we cannot believe for a moment that he goes about in the disguise of an old-clothes-man, passing off spurious coin. Indeed, were a Hungarian journal to accuse Lord John Russell of being a burglar—a Roman print denounce Sir Robert Peel as a highwayman—or a French Newspaper charge Mr. Disraeli with being a "smasher,"—we should all, as lovers of truth and fair play, feel deeply indignant at such atrocious calumnies being levelled against any of our fellow-countrymen. And yet the names—the glorious names—of Kossuth, Mazzini, and Ledru-Rollin, have been treated by English journals in a manner as scandalous, as vile, and as cowardly as in the case which I have just supposed.

There is no possibility of misunderstanding the characters of the three eminent personages whom I have named. Any evil that is said of them, can be nothing less than sheer calumny and wanton lying. Even those who dissent from their policy, cannot honestly assail their reputation.

Indeed, my firm opinions are—firstly, that any man who accuses Kossuth of embezzlement or fraud, is quite capable of all kinds of rascality and roguery himself;—secondly, that any man who dares to associate the term "impostor" with Mazzini, must be himself the rankest counterfeit and the most impudent humbug that ever lived;—and thirdly, that any man who taxes Ledru-Rollin with cowardice, must himself be the most sneaking poltroon and contemptible nincompoop that ever swaggered under an air of insolent assurance.

The calumniators of Kossuth, Ledru-Rollin, and Mazzini, do not understand what true patriotism is: nor can they comprehend the meaning of laudable ambition. Their own minds are so groveling, so debased, and so utterly unprincipled, that they can understand no feeling save selfishness. Hence is it that they fall back upon the old vulgar, and disgusting expedient of accusing great men of having no other aim than "filthy lucre" in view. The idea of accusing such a man as Kossuth of peculation! Eternal God! how little do those accusers comprehend the magnitude of that hero's mind!—how unworthy are they even to enjoy the right of passing a comment upon his character! Now, if they had confined themselves to such representations as that Kossuth was improperly ambitious—that he aspired to the throne of Hungary—and that he had plunged his country into civil war with a view to work out results favourable to the establishment of a dynasty of his own,—had such been the slanders, I say, there would have been in them something which, if not wearing an aspect of verisimilitude, would at all events have been less impossible than the mean and paltry charge of embezzlement. But to have recourse to the dirtiest of all expedients for the purpose of blackening the name of Kossuth, was a proceeding which only the most cowardly and beggarly-minded of sneaking calumniators could adopt. It is calling into requisition the fish-fag abuse of Billingsgate, because manly argument is wanting: it is ranking in the puddle for filth and on the dunghill for offal to hurl at an enemy from whose armour of proof the legitimate missiles of warfare glance innocuously off.

One newspaper has rendered itself especially infamous in heaping up all the ordures of its foul imagination and all the spawnings of its loathsome venom at Kossuth's door. But why did this print so instantaneously jump to the conclusion that Kossuth was swayed by dirty ideas of pelf? Because its own conduct is based solely on those motives. Indeed, its venality is notorious:—it does not even support a particular party on such honest grounds as its contemporaries—but for money! It is constantly in the market—to be bought and sold like any other good or chattel. At one time 'tis the Carlton Club that bribes: at another the Reform Club. And this is the precious print that dares invest a mote to place in the eye of a hero, when it has so real and unmistakable a beam in its own!

Men who experience an earnest craving to advance the cause of progress,—who oppose tyrants because they hate tyranny, and who war against aristocracies because they detest monopolies,—who burn to rescue their fellow-creatures from serfdom and elevate the nations socially, morally, and politically,—such men as these are above all such vulgar considerations as pelf. They may be ambitious: but their ambition is laudable. They may have their pride: but it is a noble and an admirable sentiment which thus inspires them. In small minds the most paltry and peddling ideas are ever uppermost;—and thus is it that these small minds measure by their own mean and miserable standard the great and glorious minds of such men as Kossuth, Mazzini, and Ledru-Rollin.

The abuse of certain newspapers is the greatest tribute that can possibly be paid to the characters, intellects, and motives of individuals. To be applauded by those prints were to be classed along with the most damnable fiends that disgrace the human species. And inasmuch as these accursed ruffians occupy the extreme point to which the admiration of such journals can extend, the other extreme, which obtains their hatred, is necessarily occupied by the most immaculate and estimable of men.

But after all, what signifies this tremendous labouring on the part of an unprincipled press to run down great men and write down their actions? Does the base attempt succeed? No—ten thousand times No! the thirty-five thousand copies daily issued by the *Times*, and daily renewing the infamous calumnies against Kossuth, cannot crush the truth. Not one soul who reads the slander in the *Times*, believes it. All its subscribers— all who hire it for an hour or who see it at a Club or a coffee-house,—all know that it is propagating the foulest falsehoods. Does the *Times* require a test of its power to ruin by calumny a hero whose deeds shine forth as resplendently as if they were printed upon the noon-day sun? – does the *Times* want to try its strength in this ignoble and wretched endeavour to write men down? Well, it will have that opportunity should Kossuth visit these shores: for in spite of all it has said concerning him, the *Times* may rest assured that never, never will any man have received so grand – so enthusiastic – so fervid a welcome as that which the British people will give to the Hungarian hero!

And if the Times, on the other hand, be anxious to test its own popularity in the country, let its Editor get up a meeting, with himself in the chair, at the London Tavern,—let him there enunciate to the assembly the same slanders against Kossuth which he has dared to promulgate under the protection of the editorial "We" or through the scape-goat medium of "Our Own Correspondent,"—let him do this and see what kind of a reception he would experience.

No: the characters of such men as Ledru-Rollin, Kossuth, and Mazzini, are not to be destroyed by a press devoted to the cause of tyranny and the interests of tyrants. And time will speedily show that I am right in making this assertion. For as assuredly as I am penning these lines at this moment, will the nations of Continental Europe rise again: yes—they will rise in their colossal power and their giant strength;—from the Seine to the Danube will they rise – and the voice of Freedom shall echo from the heights of Montmartre to the Apennine mountains and the Carpathian Hills. Then, whose names will be echoed on every breeze?—who are the exiles that shall first be summoned home? Ledru-Rollin will return to France to assume the reins of office under a veritable Democratic Republic: Mazzini will repair to Rome to accomplish the mighty work of Italian freedom;—and glorious Kossuth will hasten back to unfurl the oriflam of liberty in the land of the Magyar. Then—Oh! then, will the tyrants of Europe tremble and become pale: for with France, Italy and Hungary under the guidance of the noblest spirits of the age, Imperialism and Royalty are as certain to be banished from every nation in Continental Europe, as Democracy is sure to achieve a glorious triumph. The wretched impostor Louis Napoleon Bonaparte,—the cowardly but blood-thirsty and perfidious King of Prussia,—Austria's imperial stripling who has already feasted with such ravenous zest upon human gore,—the cruel, heartless, and hypocritical old Pope, who beneath the garments of sanctity conceals all the worst vices and the most odious passions of Kings,—and then the monster-miscreant of the North, the Emperor Nicholas,—those will be the first potentates of Europe to fall before the popular wrath, when the clock shall strike the hour of retribution!

Be not disheartened, my dear readers, concerning the future. It is as impossible for Continental Europe to remain tranquil, as it is vain for Emperors, Kings, Popes, and Presidents to depend for any length of time upon armies. I would not give five guineas for the purchase of any throne in Continental Europe after the lapse of the next three years. Down they will all tumble the very next time that the din of revolution is heard upon the breeze. Then—back, back, to thy native shores, thou true-hearted patriot, Ledru-Rollin:—back, back to the bosom of a regenerating people, thou fine Italian spirit, Joseph Mazzini;—back, back, thou glorious Kossuth, to receive the fervid welcome which shall greet thee in that native land of thine which thou hast love so well.

A Warning to the Needlewomen and Slopworkers

Saturday, January 5, 1850

A plan has recently been concocted by certain aristocrats and parsons for inducing poor women to become voluntary candidates for transportation. A more scandalous proceeding was never initiated by that patrician class which is so heartless in its oppression and so base in its duplicity towards the sons and daughters of toil. This gilded pill which a parcel of titled and reverend quacks are endeavouring to cram down the throats of starving Englishwomen, is entitled a "Fund for Promoting Female Emigration;" and while the demand for contributions is of course made upon the public generally, the special objects of the pseudo-philanthropic scheme are the poor needlewomen and the slopworkers. I have read the Prospectus—I have conned over the names of the Committee—I have reflected upon the matter in all its bearings—and I can come to no other conclusion than that the whole concern is "a delusion, a mockery, and a snare." Under this impression, I conjure the needlewomen and slopworkers to put no faith in the promises held out: I warn them—emphatically, earnestly warn them against yielding to the representations set forth in such brilliant colours and in such an apparently Christian spirit by the concocters and promoters of this design. Miserable enough ye are in your own country, poor women!—I know it well: but ten thousand times more miserable still would ye find yourselves on board the worthless old emigrant-ships in which it is proposed to pen you up like so many sheep,—ten thousand times more miserable when turned adrift in some colony at the end of the world, with the harrowing conviction that you have been basely juggled into accepting a change of condition only too well calculated to prove that even in the lowest depths of wretchedness there is a lower deep still!

A Warning to the Needlewomen and Slopworkers

The scheme which Mr. Sidney Herbert has initiated, and which has received the sanction of many aristocratic and reverend names, is one involving the most heartless cruelty. It proposes transportation (under the genteel name of "Emigration") as a remedy for a certain amount of female pauperism at home. Without taking the trouble to reflect whether anything can be done to reach the grievances of the poor needlewomen in the land of their birth, the concoctors of the scheme under notice recommend a wholesale deportation. "Banish these poor indigent wretches from the country," exclaim the pseudo-philanthropists: "tear them away from the places they were born and where they wish to die. Separate them from their friends – drag them from the scenes so long familiar to their eyes – bundle them on board a ship – bear them away to the far-off islands of the southern seas – there turn them adrift – and at all events we shall have lessened the number of voices clamouring for bread at home! Nay, more – we shall perhaps be thanked as true friends to the working classes: and we shall peradventure gain popularity. The farce will serve our turn in many ways. While Aristocracies are perishing in every enlightened State, in England our patrician order will sustain itself upon the strength and credit of an alleged philanthropy and an asserted humanity. The Established Church will moreover benefit its tremendous monopoly; inasmuch as parsons are enlisted in this scheme. At all events, it will make the People think we are doing our best for them; and such a belief will do us a great deal of good, in more ways than one."

Upon these principles does the Fund for Promoting Female Emigration appear to be based. In the Committee there is not a single name calculated to inspire the industrious classes with confidence. *Timeo Danaos et dona ferentes* – "I fear the Greeks and those bringing presents:"—in other words, I always mistrust aristocrats when the voluntarily come forward with some alleged boon for the people. There is invariably a trick, a shuffle, or a subterfuge at the bottom of it,—either selfish interest to serve, or an egotistical purpose to achieve. Politicians who deny the male adults of kingdom their natural rights, are no true friends to any section of the community: bishops who coolly pocket twenty or thirty thousand a-year to preach the doctrines of the lowly Jesus, cannot possibly care one fig for starving needlewomen or famishing slopworkers. For who are the upholders—who are the supporters—who are the advocates of that vitiated system which, by keeping all wealth in the hand of a few and consequently spreading pauperism among the masses, creates the very misery into which those needlewomen and those slopworkers are plunged? – who are the upholders of that diabolical system, I ask again? Why, you – all ye Right Honourables, and Most Nobles, and Right Reverends, who have lent your names to the scheme which I am exposing: and you also, ye members of the middle-class – Knights, Reverends and Esquires, whose names fill up the second column in the advertized list of the Committee!

Now in that Committee we have four grades of persons. First, we have Peers of the Realm: Secondly, we have Members of the House of Commons: thirdly, we have Clergymen; and fourthly, we have eminent Merchants. All of these grades are not only interested in maintaining the present vicious, unnatural, and most unjust social system; but are also the very classes which cause, produce, and maintain all the misery, wretchedness, and famine which they deplore. The Peers of the Realm belong to that Aristocracy which has monopolized all the honours and all the lands of the State, and actually made them hereditary in their own families. The Members of the House of Commons belong to that branch of the Legislature which boldly, insolently, and arrogantly denies the right of all the people to be represented, and which has adopted the style and behaviours of the people's masters instead of the people's servants. The Clergymen belong to an establishment which possesses larger revenues than all the other State-Churches in the world put together, but which is nevertheless ever crying out for "more, more!" And the Merchants belong to the class of employers who fatten on the labour of the employed, who thrive by that very competition which ruins the masses and whose constant endeavour seems to be to screw up the human machine to do the greatest possible amount of work at the lowest possible remuneration. Now, then, it is from these four grades that the Committee of the Fund for Promoting Female Emigration is formed; and I ask whether such Committee is calculated to inspire the working classes with confidence in the objects in Society. There maybe two or three well-meaning and conscientious individuals in that Committee: but the majority are not, either by their own personal antecedents or by their social position, at all adapted to satisfy the people at large of the policy of their proposed measure or the purity of their motives.

To speak plainly, I regard it as a scandal, an iniquity, and a shame that any members of the community should be told there is no room for them in their own country and that they must consent to be transported to regions thousands of miles off. For it is a fact – and every promoter of the present scheme knows full well – that if the land-monopoly were abolished in these islands, the laws of primogeniture and entail repealed, the Crown lands properly managed, and the waste lands brought into culture, there would be a sufficiency of food for double the present population of Great Britain and Ireland. The doctrine of surplus-population is a base, wicked, wilful lie; and it is only preached in order to divert men's minds from the pursuit of an investigation into the real causes of the wide-spread pauperism, distress and misery apparent in this country. And let me tell my readers that in proportion as the land becomes the property of fewer owners,—in proportion as the fortunes of aristocrats, capitalists, and monopolists become more colossal,—in proportion, also, as population increases under the present vitiated systems of government and society,— in the same proportion, I say, will distress increase, misery spread more widely, and pauperism work its insidious way throughout these classes which are the bases of the community.

Such will be the inevitable results of landlordism, money-mongering, monopoly, bad government, class legislation, the retention of privileged orders, and the continuous serfdom of the masses. Yes – these will be the tremendous results,—the favoured few becoming more favoured and the starving millions more wretched in circumstances and more extensive in numbers. Then, as the social phases come upon us, will patricians and churchmen stand forward year after year and propose emigration as the remedy? If so, they will in due time drive two-thirds of the whole industrial population into a miserable exile. First it is to the needlewomen these political imposters and reverend quacks address themselves. Oh! The cowards – must they commence the hideous crusade by a campaign against defenceless women? But when they have got rid of these unfortunate workers with the needle, they will tell the tailors to be off. Then the shoemakers must be expected to bundle: next the carpenters will urged into ostracism amongst snakes and cannibals;—and thus will the clearance of human beings go on until only just sufficient labourers will be left as are necessary to supply the luxuries and elegancies of life for the favoured few, and the whole country will be divided into the estates of some two or three hundred thousand land holders, with no more than the requisite number of serfs upon each estate to keep it in order.

Now, then, do my readers comprehend the principle upon which I implore them to place no confidence in this tremendous scheme of wholesale depopulation and multitudinous exile which has been introduced to public notice with such bland patrician smiles and such sanctimonious clerical approvals. Were such proceedings adopted in Russia, the English would contemplate them with horror. "Behold," they would exclaim, "the infamy of that Czar! He wishes to pack off one-third of the industrial population into Siberia, that he and his nobility may have the Russian provinces as vast estates for themselves!" And this is the course which the aristocracy appears to be desirous of adopting in England: the game is to send away to the colonies all who are not absolutely wanted as hewers of wood and drawers of water in the mother-country; and the n there will be no paupermouths to feed – no grumblers to satisfy – no discontent t encounter – no reforms to yield to clamorous multitudes!

It is, therefore, upon principle that I object in the first place to the scheme of the Society for Promoting Female Emigration. I also oppose it on other grounds: namely, that the inducements held out to the needlewomen to emigrate are immensely exaggerated, while the disadvantages and perils are carefully kept in the background. The Society's Prospectus shows that in the Colonies there are more males than females: and this statement, which is true enough, is put forward as a delicate means of saying to the starving needlewomen of London, "Go out to Australia and you will get married the instant you land!" But of what class does a large proportion of the male population of Australia consist? Of the banished felonry from England! And this Society, with Lords, Bishops, Parsons, and Members of Parliament, at its head, actually recommends a respectable though impoverished class of females to transport themselves to New South Wales that they may become the wives of men whom the law has already transported!

I will not dwell longer upon the indelicacy of such a calculation; nor will I do more than just allude to the flagrant insult which it levels against the needlewomen and slopworkers. But I will proceed to explain that the calculation itself is full of delusion: for if the Australian settlements be deluged with females in the manner proposed by this Society, the unmarried male adults will speedily grow very particular in their choice of wives, their nicety and fastidiousness on this point rising in proportion to the increase of candidates from whom the selection may be made. Then, again, as the towns become well supplied with women, the surplus female immigrants will have to turn out upon the tramp, and wander over vast districts in order to seek the rural settlers in hope of finding husbands! God help those who shall be doomed to such crowning ignominy – such perilous wanderings – such heart-breaking alternatives!

Out of every hundred women *transported* by the Society under notice, I will even suppose that thirty shall succeed in forming matrimonial connexions. Twenty more may obtain employment as domestic servants: but what is to become of the remaining fifty? It is false to assert that *any* and *every* woman can succeed in obtaining a livelihood in the colonies. They cannot: the greatest demand is for domestic servants – and no class of persons are so *little* adapted, by previous habits or experience, to undertake those situations as London needlewomen. Let not these poor creatures, then, be deluded by the idea that emigration will prove a panacea for their wretchedness, and that the colonies are so many glorious Edens flowing with milk and honey. Emigration will suit a few:—namely, the young, the strong, and the good-looking;—but the great majority would find themselves miserably disappointed and grossly deceived.

But if these Lords, and Bishops, and Clergymen, and Merchants be really sincere in their professions of sympathy towards a large section of the industrious class, let them set to work to procure the adoption of unequivocal measures and the accomplishment of unquestionable reforms. Let them direct their energies and their influence towards an alteration in the laws which *make* the millions poor, and *keep* them poor too, in order that the few may be rich now and grow richer as time moves on. In the list of the Committee I see the names of the two Cabinet Ministers – Lord John Russell and the Earl of Carlisle (late Lord Morpeth). Why do not these two noblemen propose the reduction of the expenditure by ten or twelve millions? Mr. Cobden has shown how it may be done. The Prospectus before us says, "in the metropolis alone, 33,500 women are engaged in the single business of apparel-making. It is estimated that 28,500 of them are under twenty years of age, and that of these a large portion are subsisting, or attempting to subsist, on sums varying from fourpence-halfpenny to twopence-halfpenny a day." How easily those 33,500 women might be made happy by the smallest parings from some of the incomes of pensioners, placemen, and sinecurists. The late Queen Adelaide's 100,000s. a-year would constitute a neat little item in a fund to be raised for their support, *and to save them from transportation.* Then there are about thirty or forty thousand a-year which the Dukes of St. Albans, Grafton, and Richmond, and some other noblemen, enjoy by virtue of their descent from the strumpets of Charles II: and then there is a sum of 21,000s. a-year to the highly respected and well-beloved King of Hanover – and 50,000*s.* a-year paid to the King of Belgium – and several more thousands annually bestowed upon German beggar-princes and pauper-dukes;—and then, again, there are about sixteen or seventeen thousand pounds which Prince Albert has contrived to suck annually from the nation's vitals, *in addition to* the 30,000*s.* which the Parliament voted him. Surely these little amounts would form a fund to maintain the 33,500 needlewomen in comfort all their lives,—and, as I before said, save them from that penalty which is inflicted upon the felons, scoundrels, and villains who are deemed too bad to be kept in the mother-country. If, then, Lord John Russell and the Earl of Carlisle really care one farthing for those poor needlewomen, let them propose the conversion of the above-named resources to their assistance: and if the Right Honourables, Bishops, Parsons, and Merchants whose names likewise figure in the Committee-list, be also sincere, let them combine their influence to bring about an honest and humane appropriation of those large funds which are now so scandalously misapplied.

But it is in vain to expect anything really useful or good from such quarters. The very establishment of this precious "Fund for Promoting Female Emigration," proves the justice of the impression which the poor entertain – that if they ask the rich and the great for bread, they will receive a stone. Day after day are the masses deluded by bubble schemes and pseudo-charities promulgated by patricians and parsons;–and it is high time that this game of imposture and duplicity should cease. The grievances of the masses are not to propitiated by mock benevolence on the part of aristocratic or ecclesiastical oligarchists:—nor is Pauperism to be met with a decree of banishment abroad instead of an anodyne to be administered at home. Beware, then, ye poor crushed and famishing workers with the needle,—beware how ye suffer yourselves to be deluded by the touter for the emigrant ship and the advocate of transportation: take warning in time and be counselled by the assurance that when the present emigration-humbug shall have proved a failure, the "sympathisers" will do something more real and more truly useful for you.

A Few More Words of Warning to the Needlewomen and Slopworkers

Saturday, January 12, 1850

I am delighted to perceive that the "INSTRUCTOR" does not stand alone in denouncing the infamous scheme devised by Aristocrats, Churchmen, and Merchants, for the wholesale transportation of the needlewomen and slopworkers to Australia. Several newspapers have proclaimed their opposition to the project: and although they have not been bold enough to assist in tearing away the veil of hypocrisy with which the concoctors of the scheme endeavour to hide their real motives, they have nevertheless done good service to the cause of truth, justice, and humanity, by exposing the humbug of this particular emigration movement. Those prints have not ventured to speak upon the utter selfishness which animates the men who are attempting to make a sweeping clearance of thousands of our population: but they have so completely exposed the facilities, errors, and miscalculations upon which the Sidney-Herbert-plan is based, that I confidently expect and sincerely hope the detestable project will perish immediately of pure inanition! At all events, whatever may be the result, the journals to which I am now alluding, and from which I shall presently quote, will have done their duty, as I shall have also performed mine, in warning the needlewomen and slopworkers against a scheme which will only enhance their wretchedness and plunge them into deeper miseries than those which they already experience.

And I will avail myself of this opportunity to tell the Aristocracy that if they really feel themselves to be upon their last legs, as assuredly they are, and if they be solicitous of patching up their worn-out institution by an affectation of sympathy on behalf of the starving millions of these realms, they had better come forward with some plan which will bear the test of closest scrutiny and reflect in itself the merit of sincerity. Let them remember that they have caused nine-tenths of all the hideous miseries now endured by the working-classes of these realms; let them contemplate the damning fact that their privileges constitute the wretchedness of the unprivileged – that their colossal fortunes are built upon the still more gigantic misfortunes of the millions – that their prosperity is enjoyed at the cost of all the workers' and producers' adversity – and that their voluptuous indolence fattens upon the over-tasked industry of the famishing poor. Let them learn and reflect upon all this – and then cease to wonder that they are viewed with mistrust, treated with suspicion, and looked upon with diffidence. Nor can all that they may now do retrieve their characters in the mind of the industrious millions of this country. Their tyranny will never be forgotten – their misrule never pardoned – their greedy avarice never atoned for. They have played the part of despots, monopolists, oppressors, and plunderers so long, that even if they really experienced a sincere contrition, they would not obtain credit for their repentance. The working-classes look upon them as their natural enemies; and they have only themselves to thank for the reputation which they have thus earned. They constitute a stream of pollution which rolls through the social system of these islands: and they can no more disinfect themselves than the most muddy ditch can possibly purify its own waters.

But now let me extract a few of the opinions which the journals above alluded to have passed upon Mr. Sidney Herbert's grand transportation scheme. The *Economist* says, "The slop trade is so overdone by 33,500 workers, that wages are pressed down below the point of subsistence:— their numbers must be lessened by emigration, in order to enable the remainder to command higher wages. But, in the metropolis alone, you have at least as many more at the back of these 33,500 workers at slops who may be classed as needlewomen; and in the country at large, you have, by your own assumption, a surplus of females, amounting to 500,000 who may be said to be all within 24 hours' journey of London. To what extent is it supposed that this emigration must take place in order to supply the colonial deficiency, or to drain off the London surplus – or to which it will be possible, with the funds forthcoming?" And then again, the same journal says, " Suppose these gentlemen with £200,000 at their command, with 12,000 deserving females selected for the voyage, we believe when they came to inquire into the actual condition of our colonies, they would find only one in the whole list, to which they could with any certainty of improving their condition, send any portion of such emigrants. *Let it never be forgotten who and what the class is that they have to deal with. They are fitted only for a town life – are generally totally ignorant of that information and experience which is most valuable in a young country, and in a great majority of cases are not very capable even for ordinary domestic duties.* How can it be otherwise? Their employment from childhood has been their needle. In Sydney, Hobart Town, and most of the chief towns in our Australian colonies, it would be found that of females of this class, seeking to subsist by their needle, the complaint rather is, that there are too many than too few. In South Australia alone, a different state of facts would be found to exist. There, from the sudden growth of wealth, owing chiefly to the remarkable mineral discoveries, a considerable number of respectable young females would be certain of being comfortably settled. But in only South Australia there was in 1847 an entire population of 31,153, including children, about as many as are found in a fifth or sixth-rate English country town. It is quite true that at that time there were nearly 4,000 more males than females; but it would be a most rash conclusion to suppose that, therefore, there exists a demand for 4,000 more adult females."

The lines printed in italic contain an argument which I myself used last week when I said that "no class of persons are so little adapted, by previous habits or experience, to undertake the situation of domestic servants as London Needlewomen." And this argument would be alone sufficient to knock the Sidney-Herbert-plan altogether on the head and give it a well-merited death-blow at once.

"And now," again says the *Economist*, "let us turn to the main object of the undertaking – that of diminishing competition among the slop workers and raising their wages. On the 3rd of this month a meeting was held at Shadwell, which was attended by about 1,100 of these poor slop workers, at which the statistics of their condition and distress were elicited in painful detail. They were told of the great scheme for their improvement. They were told of the great surplus of female population at home and of its great deficiency in the colonies. They were told of the great success which had attended the emigration of a few poor young women by an 'eminent lady;' that one had obtained at once a situation of 20L a-year, and by good conduct had got comfortably married. This meeting was attended by a noble lord and a right honorable gentlemen, and ex-minister, whose names and whose character are a guarantee for the earnestness of all their acts. The account of it was published in a morning paper the next day. Two days afterwards it was succeeded by the letter of Mr. Sidney Herbert, addressed to the morning paper and published as an advertisement in many others. Every possible publicity was given to the undertaking. Without using the words offensively toward the promoters of the scheme, it has been ostentatiously paraded in every possible way. Perhaps this was necessary in order to attract public attention and raise the funds. But what has been the effect already produced, first, on the 1,100 poor women to whom it was propounded at Shadwell personally by Ashley and Mr. Sidney Herbert, then on the whole body of needlewomen in the metropolis and throughout the country, and lastly, on the female labor market of the metropolis itself? How much have these proceedings magnified and embittered the hardships inseparable from this class as it now exists? To what extent have they checked perseverance and self-reliance? How much have hopes been excited and stimulated which can never be realised? How many little opportunities of improving their own condition of husbanding their own means, have been neglected by the excitement of all this stir? And lastly, how many fresh hands have already found their way to London from the country in the hope of being among the lucky number who expect to be so much benefited by this *grand scheme,* as they term it?"

Another newspaper, the *Examiner*, says, "We should like to know the amount of evil which Mr. Sidney Herbert has already been the means of thus unconsciously creating. How many young women have already determined upon seeking their fortune in London by reason of the promulgation of a plan which would make room for them! to say nothing of the hope of being the favoured exiles." And the same journal contains a letter from an enlightened correspondent who thus deals with the precious scheme: "It is not pretended that the female births in the metropolis bear a proportion to the male births different form those in other parts of the kingdom. An examination of the census returns would have shown that, including all females under fifteen years, the proportion in the metropolis is somewhat under the general proportion of the sexes in the kingdom. It must, therefore, be the temptation of bettering their condition that later in life, draws to London from the country more females than males, and we can be at no loss to determine what that temptation is when we see that, in 1841, there were in the metropolis

90,101 more female than male servants; 15,908 more females than males who got their living by washing clothes; an excess of 20,506 female milliners, and of 4,694 nurses. The thronging to London of females to fill these feminine occupations must partake, more or less, of the nature of a lottery, in which all cannot draw prizes; but let the temptation of a free passage to a colony, and patronage to establish them there, with a good chance from obtaining that kind of settlement for life which all women look to gain, be added to the present inducements, and we may expect that the excess of 120,000 females found at the census of 1841 would be swollen to three or five time that number; a result which it must be hopeless to grapple, and the effect of which it must be frightful to contemplate."

The *Spectator* asks, "will not the vacancies be filled up by new comers from the provinces? It is to be feared, indeed, that Mr. Sidney Herbert can hardly keep up the drain so fast as the supply will pour in. it is digging wholes in the sand."

But I have now quoted enough from the above-mentioned journals to show that the plan is as defective in its details as it is inhuman, vile, and unjust in principle.

Three Predictions at London Tavern Meetings

Saturday, January 19, 1850

On three occasions within the last twelve months have I stood upon the platform at the London Tavern at meetings convened by middle-class reformers. The first occasion was that of the inauguration of the National Parliamentary and Financial Reform Association, of the Council of which I am a member; and I then gave utterance to the following prophecy: "If M. Ledru-Rollin and the leaders of the Mountain party be not called upon to assume the reins of power in France, the cause of liberty will be sacrificed all over the world." This prediction provoked a storm of hisses from some of the middle-class gentlemen present; although there were quite enough of the working-class at the meeting to stamp my words with their honest and enthusiastic approval. And the result has fully justified my sad presage; not that I take to myself any credit for having uttered the prediction – because it was nothing more than would have been proclaimed by any man at all accustomed to watch the progress of political events upon the Continent and who dared to express his sentiments with sincerity. But the unthinking, narrow-minded, prejudiced men who bawled out "No," and "Question," upon that occasion, seemed to fancy that Louis Bonaparte and co. would aid the cause of Roman and Hungarian liberty: and if the said bawlers did not really entertain that idea, then they must actually have hoped that the sacred cause itself would be engulfed in ruin. Whatever their real sentiments were, it is quite clear that the prediction which evoked their wrath on the occasion has been fulfilled to the letter. Had Ledru-Rollin and the Mountain risen to power, Rome would be happy and free at this moment,—Hungary would be happy and free at this moment – and all Germany would be enjoying democratic liberty. And, more – Sardinia would have been saved from defeat and Charles Albert from abdication;—and Austrian domination would have melted away like snow from northern Italy. The Mountain would have given effectual aid to the democratic cause wherever such aid was required; and instead of Kossuth being a prisoner in Turkey, and Mazzini a wonderer from his native land, the banner of the Magyar would now be floating freely in the Carpathian breeze and the standard of republicanism continue to occupy the place of the crozier at the Vatican.

My second attendance at the London Tavern was on the occasion of a meeting convened for the purpose of testifying sympathy with Hungary. Mr. David Salomons, an Alderman, occupied the chair; and when I rose to speak, he insolently and arrogantly refused to allow me to address the meeting. But the meeting hissed *him* down – Lord Nugent took my part – and the cause of "freedom of speech" obtained a signal triumph over the intolerance of a narrow-minded man. I then said that it was all very fine for Englishmen to assemble in the London Tavern, make milk-and-water speeches, and string together phrases of maudlin sentimentalism; but that such a proceeding would not afford the slightest practical aid to a gallant nation at the other end of Europe, struggling against the innumerable legions of the leagued tyrants of Russian and Austria. "If," said I, "you are really sincere in you expressed desire that the Hungarians should succeed, then the proper course to adopt is to call upon the Government to declare war in favour of the glorious Magyars: other wise their cause will be lost – tyranny will triumph – and you yourselves will be stultified by this sickly proffer of mere verbal sympathy." Thereupon Mr. Alderman Salomons became furious and declared that if I were Russian spy, I could not possibly do more harm to the Hungarian cause than I had already done by the speech! But who was right after all? And now who looks more like the Russian spy – Mr. Alderman Salomons or myself?

In that same occasion, too Mr. Cobden made a long speech to "prove" that mere sympathy was all that the Hungarians required – and that their cause must triumph immediately inasmuch as the Russians had not a farthing in their treasury to continue the war. I ventured to grapple with those monstrous fallacies also. I said that Russia had means and money to carry on a war against Poland until this noble nation was utterly crushed and its name blotted out of the map of Europe – and that Russia had moreover been engaged for the last fourteen or fifteen years in carrying on a bloody crusade against the glorious mountaineers of the Caucasus. From those facts I drew the inference that Russia would find the same means and money to prosecute it infernal designs against Hungarian liberty;—and in the course of a few months the tidings – the fateful tidings – arrived, that *Russian gold* had bribed the black-hearted villain Georgey to sell his country to foreign invader!

On Monday, the 7th instant I stood for the third time on the platform of the London Tavern;—and on that occasion I ventured a third prediction. I said, "If the middle classes will remain true to the principles which they have now promulgated as the basis of their agitation, and if the working-classes will not only give them all the help in their power, but also maintain an active and concurrent agitation of their own, vast and comprehensive measures of reform must be the *immediate* result – to be followed *closely after* by the People's Charter as the law of the land!" within three years from the present time may this prediction receive its fulfilment, under the circumstances specified. The Ministry is frightened – the Aristocracy trembles from head to foot – the Church is alarmed for its loaves and fishes. Concessions will be made – compromises will be offered by the Government: but if the National Parliamentary and Financial Reform Association will *insist* upon having *all* it asks for, it will obtain *all;*—and I need not say that when once four-fifths of the male adults are emancipated from bondage, they will not leave the reaming fifth many months longer in thralldom. From the possession of that reform which the middle classes are agitating for the attainment of the People's Charter, the step will be comparatively facile and rapid:—and therefore, countenancing the former plan as a means to an end, it assuredly deserves the support of the working classes, who will at the same time be carrying on *their own movement* with a spirit which will show their unflinching determination *never* to rest until the Six Points, whole and entire, be recorded in the Statute-books of Great Britain.

Property

Saturday, January 26, 1850

"Property is robbery," was the maxim which, one day falling from the mouth of a Frenchman, suddenly electrified all Europe. There have been many axioms thus abruptly flung from the lips which have struck upon the comprehension with the vividness of lightning and seared an indelible impress upon the brain: but none ever startled the civilized world with so galvanic a thrill as that of Proudhon. No: not even when, from the French tribune some years ago the memorable dictum was proclaimed, that "the people need not be right to legitimatize their actions;" – nor yet when Cassimir Perier shook the legislative hall with the patriotic cry that "the blood of her children belongs only unto France!" No: never was there a maxim which fell so forcefully upon the universal mind of Christendom, as that which sums up all politico-economical questions in the aphorism – "Property is robbery."

Was it because this maxim suddenly propounded something so monstrous, that it shocked and appalled the strongest minds? No: because even when such minds recovered from their consternation, they could not laugh at their late fears as absurd, nor yet dismiss the cause of terror as something no longer deserving consideration. Was it, then, because the assertion was so pre-eminently ridiculous that every mind instantaneously appreciated it as an exquisite caricature on extreme doctrines of any kind? No: because it struck upon the brain like the solemn note of a bell, and not like the frivolous laugh of a merry-andrew. Why, then, did it produce such an effect? Because it contained in itself a whole cyclopaedia of philosophy, and instantaneously flashed upon the conviction as a key to the reading of present mysteries and the solution of the future questions.

That maxim, indeed, lays open to the mental contemplation the whole arcana of the social system. It compels the reflective mind to examine deeply and minutely into the relative positions of men,—why some feed

213

luxuriously, and others starve—why some sleep upon down, and others upon straw—why some abide in stately mansions, and others have not where to lay their head—why some are clad in purple and fine linen, and others shiver in rags—why some own broad acres, and others cannot take up a grain of dust from the road and call it their own. Why Is all this?—is it God's dispensation?—if so, where is God's justice? Or is it the result of Man's injustice?—if not, what else can it be?

Now, let us look calmly and dispassionately into a few facts which suggest themselves with a logical continuity. God made the earth; and when he had made Man, he said, "Behold, I have given you every herb bearing seed, which is upon the face of all the earth, and every tree in the which is the fruit of a tree yielding a seed: to you it shall be for meat." I am not fond of quoting from the Bible, at any time: but I do so now to convince Aristocrats, Bishops, and Churchmen of all denominations, that there is divine authority for the assertion which I am about to make. And this is, that when Man was first brought into being, the earth was given to him as the garden which was to afford him sustenance. He was ordered to increase and multiply; and this command was issued with the divine fore-knowledge that the earth would yield an abundance to sustain all who might come upon it. The earth was given to the first man to produce him sustenance—to his family, to produce them sustenance likewise—and to all their posterity, to produce them sustenance in the same way. There was no limitation specified with regard to particular individuals: the earth was the general garden, which all had an equal right to till, and the fruits of which all had and equal right to reap. The very first individual, then, that monopolized a piece of this earth to his own special use, and to the detriment of his fellow creatures, committed a theft; and *his* property was robbery!

Now, let us suppose that there was a particular time when the people upon the earth said to each other, "At present the land is in common and each tills, sows, and reaps where he likes. But let us divide it all into equal portions; and then each can do precisely what he chooses with his own." Well, the generation which proposed this scheme and carried it into execution, had a right to do so if they thought fit: but the moment that the members of that generation said to each other, "We will bind the *next* generation to adhere to our system of dividing and appropriating the land,"—at the very instant that they consummated this injustice, *their* property became robbery!

For, let me show you that state of things would inevitably work; and, in order to do so, let me suppose a country containing 100,000 acres and

214

100,000 inhabitants. When the grand division took place, according to the agreement above specified, every individual became the possessor of an acre of ground. But here was A, who had no child at all, B who had one child, and C who had three children. Then, when the generation which divided the land passed away, and the next generation grew up, how stood the matter? Why, C's three sons had to derive their sustenance from one acre of land; whereas B's one son not only inherited his father's acre, but likewise that which A, being childless, had kindly left him in his will. Now, in this case, though B's son could not precisely be designated as a robber, because he was born *into* a particular social system, and did not either make or help to make that social system: nevertheless all the property that he had in disproportionate superfluity above C's three sons, was nothing more nor less than robbery!

From the above supposition, it is apparent that even in the very next generation after the division of the land in the manner supposed, one acre had to afford sustenance to three individuals, while two acres became the property of a single individual. The next generation afterwards would find matters much worse. The three men had married and each left three children—so that there were now nine individuals located on the one acre: whereas fortunate B had only left one son, who consequently inherited his sire's two acres. Then said this rich young man to the nine wretched beings, "You are starving on one acre of land; and I cannot till my two acres with my own hands. But if you will give me your acre, you shall work upon all three acres and have a share of the produce." Thus did the nine poor creatures give up their land to the one rich man; and thenceforth they were entirely at his mercy. He made them rise early and work late—he screwed them down to the meanest pittance—and they became the nucleus of a whole tribe of paupers. But in the advantage which their master took of them, and considering the way in which he subsequently treated them, was not that additional property which he acquired nothing more nor less than a dead robbery?

And now let us return to the starting-point. I stated then that if the particular generation chose to divide all the land, it had a perfect right to do so: but the injustice commenced when they passed laws to render that division imperative upon future generations. This constituted the theft: this made their property a flagrant robbery. They had no right to anticipate the wishes of unborn generations: they received the whole earth free and unshackled as a heritage from their forefathers; and equally free and unshackled were they bound to hand it down to their posterity. The earth was their's only so long as they themselves were upon it; and the moment they went down into their graves, their claim upon any portion of the soil or its fruits clearly ceased. Their rights existed only with themselves, and disappeared when they were removed from the scene. What they should have done, then, was to legislate for themselves, and leave generations free to follow the same or any other course as they thought fit.

Every human being, when he comes into the world, should find a place ready to receive him. The earth is large enough for all who thus come upon it; and no one should be told, "There is not room for you." Because to be told this, is the same as saying, "God has sent you into the world; but God has not provided for your subsistence here;"—which is a foul falsehood and a tremendous impiety. For the earth is capable of maintaining in plenty ten times the number of human beings who are now upon it. Then why is any human being an intruder?—and how happens it that there should be no room for him? Because all the land is in the possession of a few, who monopolize the fruits of the earth; and, under such a system, only just so much labour is required as will produce the luxuries and elegancies of life for these favoured few, and the scanty crusts on which the labourers themselves subsist. But beyond these requirements no labour is wanted; and consequently there are millions who cannot find employment in toiling for others, and who are debarred the opportunity of toiling for themselves. Surely, then, the wretched beings who are thus made to feel that they have no business whatsoever in the world, cannot be far wrong if they turn round upon the favoured few and exclaim, "Your property is robbery; since the fact of your possessing it., and the mode in which you administer it, deprive me of that sustenance which God meant me to derive from the earth when he placed me upon it."

But let me go a step farther. Suppose a country containing 100,000 inhabitants, and producing as much corn as shall produce 100,000 half-quartern loaves a-day. Then, according to the laws and intentions of God as previously quoted, every individual would have a half-quartern loaf a day. But suppose that one individual takes two half-quarterns; and another has consequently none at all? Then the monopolizer's extra half-quartern is a robbery.

Every man should receive a subsistence from the earth, before any individual should be allowed to receive *more* than a subsistence—that is to say, every man must have enough bread to eat, before any ought to be allowed butter with his bread. In a word, all men should have *necessaries*, before any have *luxuries*. Those who have luxuries, while some are without necessaries, are profiting by the robbery of the latter. But how irresistibly striking is the argument, that those who work hard deserve to eat and be well clothed before those who do not work at all should be allowed to touch the bread of idleness or put on the garments of sloth! When the idlers eat and the workers starve, the food of the former is robbed from the latter: when the indolent adorn themselves in silk, while the industrious wrap themselves in rags, the clothing of the rich is robbed from the poor. And herein it is that property is so often robbery.

But how came these social inequalities and these monstrous anomalies to exist? Not by the consent of the majority in every country; for the majority of any given number of persons would not be so foolish as to sell themselves to serfdom, give up their birth-right, and toil in misery all their lives just for the behoof of a favoured few. No: it was robbery which first monopolized the soil and tied up the possession of the land in a few families,—it was the existing generation robbing the future ones—and the rich and the powerful of succeeding generations have perpetuated the injustice!

The laws of fiefs and feudal tenures—of primogeniture, entail, and mortmain—and all the other contrivances which have been adopted to place the land in the possession of a few – to render it a heritage for the families of these few—to make it inalienable for long periods, and thus cause a vast accumulation of wealth in particular quarters, all these laws were at the time so many rascalities making all the *property* which came under their operation nothing more nor less than a dead *robbery*. And the robbery lasts to the present day; although the holders of such property cannot now be justly stigmatised as robbers. This is a remarkable fact— that there is foul robbery everywhere apparent, but you cannot fairly nor properly denounce the men themselves as robbers. And why not? Because if I happened to be descended from a Norman Baron (which, thank God, I am not), or from one of the strumpets of Charles II (which, still more fervently thanking God, I am not), and if in such a case my ancestors had left me an estate, I should assuredly take and keep possessions of it. This would not be my fault. I should see the injustice of the very system which handed down the estate to me: but, being born *into* a social system which I did not make, I could not possibly help myself nor yet be liable to any blame for coming into such a world and finding myself forced to

217

float upon the same tide of circumstances that was bearing all the rest of the community along. Nor would it be requisite, in order to show my abhorrence of such a system, that I should refuse to take possession of an estate which had this descended to me. And therefore, while no one could call me a robber, my property would not be the less of robbery.

When William the Conqueror seized upon some Saxon's estate and gave it to one of his Norman ruffians, this was a theft – and the property thus acquired by the Norman noble was a robbery. The estate may have come down to some peer enjoying it at the present day; the property is still a robbery, although the said peer cannot for a moment be stigmatised as a robber. Tis the same with the pensions bestowed upon the children of Charles the Second's harlots: they were robberies then and are robberies now—but I do not go so far as to call the present recipients of them downright robbers.

From the various facts that have suggested themselves to me, it is quite clear that all property originated in either injustice or robbery, and has been perpetuated in both. But at the same time, we must consider that society has sanctioned this flagrant violation of divine law and human right, because it has permitted it to exist. Therefore, no one would now-a-days be wicked or insane enough to denounce property-holders as robbers, and their property as a legitimate object for spoliation. But what true patriots and earnest reformers must aim at, is the speedy enactment of laws which shall have the effect of dividing and sub-dividing the land and preventing the accumulation of colossal fortunes in the hands of a few. These objects will be accomplished to a great extent by the abolition of primogeniture, mortmain, and entail,—by the facilitation and cheapening of the legal proceedings in conveyancing,—by the equal distribution of a father's property amongst his children at his death,— and by the limitation of testamentary power, so as to ensure the rational, useful, and proper application of each individual's property at his demise. Such enactments, accompanying others to regulate the duties of the employer towards the employed, acknowledging the rights of Labour, recognising it as capital, and providing not only for its fair remuneration but also for its constant employment,—these details of a sound policy would soon alter the face of the land and the aspect of society, and lay a solid foundation for those farther and more complete changes when all property shall be national, and consequently no property be robbery.

The Case of the Journeymen Tailors
Saturday, February 2, 1850

Is it possible that the present system can last? Look at the awful misery which prevails on every side: look at the stern, substantial, unmistakable grounds which exist for discontent throughout the length and breadth of the land. What class of the industrial population is well off? Not one. Which section of the great community of workers can earn enough to live respectably upon? Not one. This is not a question in which a few thousands of individuals are concerned: it regards millions. The agricultural labourers are starving upon four or five shillings a week: the hands in the manufacturing districts are neither fully employed nor adequately paid;—the cutlers and stockingers are famishing;—the miners are in fearful condition;—the needlewomen's case is a scandal to civilization and a practical refutation of England's Christianity;—the coal-whippers may well envy Russian serfs and wish to heaven that they were slaves upon Virginian plantations;—the silk-weavers are driven almost to the very verge of desperation;—and last, though not least, the fraternity of journeymen tailors has been compelled to proclaim its wrongs in the face of day!

The system, then, cannot last. The few are too rich—the many too poor. A thousand pounds a-week, enjoyed by some aristocrat, stand forth in awful contrast to four shillings a-week, which is all that many a hard worker can earn. An Apician luxury on the one hand throws the famine-stricken table on the other into the saddest relief. Destitution is fast breeding desperation: for there are at this moment *millions* of human beings in the British Islands who are proclaiming to the whole world, by various means, that their condition cannot possibly be made worse by anything which may occur.

In the name of heaven, then, let our rulers—let our legislators—let our philanthropists do something to meet the evil. It is useless to denounce

219

as firebrands and revolutionists those men whose only "crime" is their becoming the mouth-pieces of all that tremendous misery whereof I have just spoken. Would to God that these islands could to-morrow be blessed with such measures and such an amount of political reform and social improvement as to render "agitation" utterly unnecessary and turn Chartist halls into lecture-rooms! But such a consummation cannot be hoped for so long as the few shall arrogate to themselves the right of enslaving the millions,—so long as the producers of food are perishing with want, and the makers of costly garments are clothed in rags. Strange and unnatural condition of things!—and yet the man who dares denounce the system is stigmatised as a demagogue, pointed at as a bloody-minded revolutionist, and perhaps thrown into prison as a rebel and a traitor. But, after all, who are the real revolutionists?—the men who proclaim the people's wrongs and demand their redress as a wise precaution—or the men who arrogantly declare that the people are contented and do not want reform?

A recent meeting of Journeymen Tailors at Exeter Hall exposed the frightful condition of no less than 20,000 deserving, industrious, hard-working men in the British metropolis. The first feeling which inevitably seizes upon the mind, on reading the appalling catalogue of wrongs, miseries, privations, and cruelties endured by those persons, is one of astonishment that human patience should be capable of stretching to such inordinate lengths. This is the system adopted:—A great tailor contracts with a middle-man for the work to be done. The average is seven shillings and sixpence for a coat. This middle-man employs a sub-contractor at an average of five shillings the coat; and this sub-contractor gets a still more unfortunate being to make it for three shillings.

Reader, look into the newspapers and see who are the great advertising tailors. *Those* are the men who thus build palaces cemented with the blood of their fellow-creatures, and incrusted with the miseries of twenty thousand families! Just calculate the enormous amount expended by those great clothiers in advertisements alone: one house lays out in this manner as much as 12,000*l*. a-year—another 8000*l*.—a third 5000*l*.—and the others in proportion. *These* are facts which are well known to those who are initiated in the mysteries of the metropolis newspaper offices and who are at all acquainted with the financial details of the advertising system. Look at those enormous amounts, then, thus expended,—add them to the interest of an immense capital sunk in founding these palaces of iniquity and horror,—add again the cost of keeping up those vast establishments—the numerous servitory—the plate-glass—the galaxy of lights—the owners' gorgeous style of living, with carriages, livery-servants, festivals, and country houses, reckon up all these items, and then ask whence comes the colossal income requisite to meet such demands! From the flesh and blood—aye, *the very vitals* of the slop-workers and the journeymen tailors.

At the great meeting above alluded to, Mr. Ellard praised "the system of the old houses of call, which had maintained the principle though it could not always be carried out in practice, that every working man should have sixpence for an hour of labour, in opposition to the new-fangled system of political economy, which declared that there should be no fixed sum as the price of labour, but every man must get what he could—one penny, or two pence, or one halfpenny per hour; while every system of art and chicanery was used, by a system of fines to reduce the prices that were nominally put upon the garments." Mr. Goodfellow, who had himself been confidential man in one of the largest tailoring establishments, said that he had been employed *eighteen hours* every day at *one penny* per hour! And this speaker declared that "if his employer gave nine or ten shillings for a coat, there would be, at the end of the week, certain things, such as being an hour or so behind in time in bringing it into the shop, for which fifteen per cent. would be deducted from the workman in the shape of fines." Mr. Goodfellow likewise mentioned that the middle-man of a certain fashionable tailor, *patronised* by *Royalty* and *Aristocracy,* in Regent Street, rode in his carriage and made 3000*l.* a-year! Are the royal arms over the shop of this fashionable tailor? If so, I sincerely hope that her Majesty will direct Sir George Grey to request that they be taken down with the least possible delay.

Mr. Goodfellow said, in the course of his speech, that "the fact was, that men, women, and children were working from four in the morning till twelve o'clock at night. It was a system of one continued, never-ending slavery. And then to talk of the morality of the question! When the public was told that a certain number of men were required to work in the Post Office on Sunday, they looked upon the matter with horror, as something like sacrilege. But let the clergy go with him to the Tenter Ground next Sabbath-day, and see the amount of work that was given out there on that day, and they would see what was the amount of Sabbath observance produced by this system." What are the parsons about? How

221

will Exeter Hall Saints *dare* to stand forward in may next and ask for money to convert heathens thousands of miles off, when the white slaves of England stand in such awful need of emancipation? What account can the bloated Church give of its twelve million a-year. When such diabolical oppression is practised in this *Christian* country which has the benefit of such a Church?

Mr. Prior, another speaker at Exeter Hall on the occasion referred to, said that "in former years, he knew the condition of their trade was such, that whatever might be the temporary difficulties of the workmen, the parishes never found one of them there: they sustained each other through all the difficulties and necessities to which they were liable, and they subscribed between 6,000*l*. and 7,000*l*. a year, in support of their distressed fellow-workmen. But since the sweating and middle-man systems had come into existence, how had things been reversed! They found tailors now in the most filthy localities of London; and thousands upon thousands of them without so much as the means of appearing in the streets of London by daylight; an extent of misery, in fact, which had seldom been heard of till the *Morning Chronicle* brought it to light." Mr. Prior then proceeded to observe that "if such had been the course of events—if the working tailors had found themselves gradually going down, from the system that was pursued—he would put it down to the meeting whether they did not think it would soon absorb the whole trade? The question then concurred again, who were the parties that were really interested in a continuance of the system? They were the sweaters and the middle-men. The trade—it had been proved by evidence the most incontrovertible—was failing into such depths of misery and poverty, that most awful thoughts had flashed across the minds of many who were the sufferers. They had, for example, asked themselves seriously whether they should become thieves and so qualify themselves for a prison, or whether they should commit self-destruction, in order to escape from their miserable condition. Young men, fresh from the country, had fallen into the hands of sweaters, for whom they worked every day in the week, including Sunday, yet on the Saturday night they were brought in, in debt—positively in debt. Some of these persons, he knew, had felt so disgusted with their unhappy situation, that evil thoughts rose into their minds, and they entertained ideas either of committing theft, or of terminating their existence."

Mr. C. Goodfellow, another speaker at Exeter Hall, said, "he knew well that what he was going to say would be at the expense of a personal sacrifice. Last winter he was suffering greatly, for he had no employment. He was compelled to seek some from Nicoll, who had one establishment in the West-end and another in the City. This employer had the patronage of the Duke and a great number of colonels in the army. He held in his hand a book of the wages he received whilst in this employment, and it would be found from it that he had received five shillings for making a coat which had occupied him full twenty-six hours; and out of that sum he had to pay for trimmings, candle-light, and other charges. He also held in his hand the trade book of Mr.——, of Fleet Street, which had been furnished him by a young man in his employment. By this book nine shillings was paid for a coat, the workman finding trimmings, which would take a tradesman four and a half days to finish."

The grievances of the Journeymen Tailors are thus summed up in a portion of the petition to the House of Commons, adopted on the occasion of the meeting referred to:—"your petitioners beg to inform your honorable house that originally it was the custom of master tailors to employ all their men on their own premises; but of late years a great portion of them have departed therefrom, and now give their work out to be made in the humble habitations of their workmen, whereby the health of those so employed is greatly impaired, their morals affected, and the lives of her Majesty's subjects placed in great jeopardy, through diseases arising from this source, which spreads contagion to a most appalling extent. The system of out-door labour having called into existence a class of persons called "sweaters," who take out large quantities of work, and in order to have a large percentage employ persons in the last stage of destitution, at the lowest possible wages, in the lowest and most miserable neighbourhoods, where ladies' and gentlemen's garments are made in rooms that are used as workshops, bed-rooms, hospital, and kitchen—it being no uncommon thing among this class of workers to see the mother and children confined to their beds with fever, small-pox, or other infectious diseases, and the habits of ladies and coats of gentlemen supplying the covering for their beds—such persons not having the most distant idea of how disease may be conveyed from these miserable places to their own persons and families. Another serious evil of this system is its immoral tendency from the indiscriminate employment of men, women, and children on the same garment in the same room. This system also creates a most flagrant violation of the laws, both of God and man, by causing a profanation of the Sabbath-day, as there is nothing more common than for persons so employed to work as regularly on Sundays as other days."

The remedy, then, as suggested by the petition and as pointed out by the first Mr. Goodfellow who spoke, is this:—"he recommended that all employers should have their work done on their own premises. Parties might say, what were they then to do with female labour? Now he, as connected with that branch of the question, would say that ten shillings a-week for work done on the employer's premises would be better than one pound a week for labour done at home, which was the total destruction of all domestic comfort, as well as the source of most unnatural labour and unhealthy confinement to women." These are Mr. Goodfellow's own words; and in addition to the remedy suggested by the petition and explained by him in his able speech, I should earnestly recommend the immediate formation of a protective Association.

This will be the most effectual means of enabling the poor journeymen to make head against the infamous tyrants who are fattening upon the vitals of crushed men and famine-stricken women, such an Association, by possessing large funds to withstand actions for libel, might boldly print, publish, and hold up to the world's execration the names of the miscreants whose loathed and notorious appellations my fingers are now itching to guide my pen to record. And if the journeymen tailors of the metropolis will form such an Association, one of the first contributors of ten guineas to the fund will be their sincere well-wisher, George W.M. Reynolds.

The "Party of Order" on the Continent

Saturday, February 23, 1850

The police-agents to that despicable mountebank, Louis Bonaparte, have been making an onslaught upon the Trees of Liberty and cutting them down throughout the French metropolis. Some slight disturbances occurred: but no formidable attitude was taken by the Parisian people on the occasion. *They were resolved to bide their time.* One of the features of the trivial commotion which did take place, however, was the somewhat rough handling that the wolf-in-sheep's- clothing, General Lamoriciere, experienced from a knot of individuals, who abused and ill-treated him, so that even his life appeared for a few minutes to be in jeopardy, and now let us see what account the French Correspondent of the *Times* newspaper is compelled to give of the matter. He says, "The whole affair was got up by the Government with a view to a *coup d'etat*—the cutting down the trees was a defiance flung at the people, to bring the matter to an issue; the very men who struck the city-police were paid agents to help it on; and it is even insinuated that the outrage committed on General Lamoriciere was the result of a plan concocted by the police-agents."

And yet it is the "party of order" which practices the rascalities so tersely summed up by the *Times'* correspondent,—that same "party of order" which the *Times* itself supports, lauds, and eulogises on all occasions. My dear readers, whenever you hear of a "party of order" springing up in any country, rest assured that it consists of the most infernal miscreants that ever disgraced the human form,—the most bloody-minded scoundrels that ever wore the shape of a man,—the most sanctimonious, hypocritical, smooth-spoken villains that ever existed as a shame and a scandal to civilization. Look, for instance, at the conduct of the crowned demon, the Emperor of Austria—a mere boy in years, and a veritable fiend in heart. What said Mr. Cockburn in the House of Commons the other day? "After having by means of foreign invasion and domestic treachery overcome the Hungarians, the Emperor of Austria had an opportunity of displaying mercy, if not magnanimity: but instead of taking that course, he had decreed a list of the bloodiest executions that ever disgraced humanity." This detestable stripling-monster—this demon hearted Emperor—feasted his ravenous maw upon the very vitals of the most glorious patriots of eastern Europe; and not contented with the harrowing cruelties and sickening butcheries perpetrated against *men,* his infernal appetite for a gory banquet sought the rest of variety in the blood of murdered *women* and *children*! Oh! ye who are husbands and fathers,—ye who love your wives and your little ones,—ye who can rightly and truly appreciate all that is excellent, humanizing, and angelic in the character of woman, and all that is joyous, innocent, and delightful in the artless prattle of children,—it is for you to hold to execration the name of that imperial miscreant into whose breast Satan had infused his most hellish spirit. Nor let it be forgotten that this Austrian despot, not contented with having committed all the horrors above glanced at, has recently carried out his fiendish hatred of Liberalism and Liberals to such an extent as to employ agents to poison the great, the glorious, the admirable Kossuth! Yes—this statement was fearlessly made by Lord Dudley Stuart last week in the House of Commons; and although a person (for I will neither call him a nobleman or a gentleman) denominated Lord Claude Hamilton, endeavored to laugh away the charge thus publicly made against the Emperor of Austria, there is no reason to doubt the truth of that accusation. Indeed, why should its veracity be suspected, when antecedent circumstances have so fully proven that the imperial butcher is capable of any treachery, however dark—any ruffianism, however vile,—any atrocity, however brutal, ferocious, and bloody. Nor should the public be astonished that such a monster finds a ready champion in a scion of the British Aristocracy: for it is *only* in the aristocratic ranks—or in the columns of the newspapers subsidized by tyrants—that any defence of the Emperor of Austria could possibly be looked for. As a matter of course the imperial butcher has the best and most heartfelt sympathies of the British Aristocracy: there can be no doubt upon *this* point—inasmuch as the *Post, Herald, Standard,* and other newspapers exclusively read *by* the Aristocracy, and written *for* the Aristocracy, all bestow their approval upon the bloody-minded Emperor of Austria and the execrable murderers who have carried out his intentions with such appalling fidelity!

England, therefore, has the nucleus of just such a "party of Order" as that which is busily engaged in breasting the flow of democratic progress on the Continent of Europe. On the memorable 10th of April, 1848, there was no doubt an ardent longing on the part of many of the members of the British Aristocracy to hear that the Iron Duke had mowed down the people wholesale, or cannonaded the half-million of human beings that day assembled on Kennington Common;—and when the result proved the pacific intentions which the Chartists had all along entertained, deep were the regrets in many high quarters that no disturbance had taken place in order to afford the Iron Duke and opportunity of showing how soon he could put the people down! That such were really the sentiments entertained by numerous aristocrats, undeniable proofs can be brought forward. The language held by the Tory newspapers *next day*—the admissions which subsequently slipped into the speeches of certain "noble lords" in both Houses of Parliament—and a variety of other circumstances which could be enumerated if necessary, afford conclusive evidence of the real feeling of the Aristocratic mind towards the working-classes upon the occasion referred to. Can we wonder therefore, that Austrian butcheries and Russian atrocities elicit the applause and awaken the delight of the "upper-classes" of this realm?— can we be astonished if imperial assassins and field-marshal murderers find champions and defenders amongst "noble lords" in this country? Even the splendid exceptions which such men as Lord Dudley Stuart and Lord Nugent constitute with regard to the general rule, cannot rescue the Aristocracy as a class from the imputation of a savage instinct for cruelty in the exercise of political vengeance: on the country, those enlightened noblemen, by thus standing forth as the friends of humanity and of freedom, only throw into a darker and more sinister back-ground the great majority of the title-bearing oligarchs.

The preceding observations have been chronicled with a view to establish the necessity of strengthening the democratic cause wherever its name is known. The "party of order" must be met by an imposing attitude on the side of the people. In France this party is endeavouring to provoke a disturbance, with the hope that matters may thus be precipitated to such an issue as will enable the Mountebank President to change himself into a Ginger-bread Emperor. In Austria the party of order has not quite finished its bloody work: the Emperor whets his appetite from time to time with a few political murders,—while his agents are endeavouring to compass the damnable work of secret assassination! In Rome the party of order has flooded the prisons and restored the Inquisition; in Naples the Lazzaroni are paid by the King to traverse the city *en masse*, shouting "Down with the Constitution!" That miserable old man, the Pope, hesitates to return to the capital which his vile ambition has plunged into so much wretchedness; for his day-thoughts and his night-dreams are haunted by the historical reminiscence that the Rome to which *he* himself has proved so great a curse, is the self-same city which centuries ago produced a Brutus to assassinate Caesar!

Everywhere is the "party of order" pursuing its reactionary policy. The crowned miscreants who stand at the head of the system, have even been thinking of invading Switzerland, for the purpose of hunting out the brave patriots who, driven from their own countries, have found a refuge and a home amidst the republicans of the Alps. In fact, there is no atrocity too heinous—no treachery too fiend-like—no horror too abominable for the "party of order" to perpetrate.

What, then, should the nations do to counteract the influence of this diabolical tyranny? The cause of progress must be strengthened by all imaginable means upon the Continent of Europe;—and the English Democrats must never neglect any opportunity of displaying a heartfelt sympathy with those who are struggling on Freedom's behalf, or suffering for Freedom's sake. Let us boldly and loudly express our ardent hope that the nations of Continental Europe will hasten to rise again, and that they will so manage matters as to make the *next* struggle the *last*. Not that I advocate the political scaffold. God forbid! I am opposed to the punishment of death in any case, and under all circumstances. But I *do* hope and expect that in the coming storm, the brave democrats of the Continent of Europe will seize upon their tyrants and oppressors— hurry them on board ship—and transport them, without delay, to some far distant clime, where they may work *in chains* for the rest of their existence. This is the proper way to treat miscreants:—and by thus clearing the continental nations of the reptiles whose very breath would impart venom even to the purest social atmosphere, the long-persecuted proletarians of Europe may hope to achieve their emancipation.

And while the storm is brewing,—that storm the explosion of which shall overwhelm every throne, break every sceptre, and grind every crown to dust, upon the Continent of Europe;—while the clouds are gathering in the political horizon, and the social elements are amalgamating their power and their energy for the approaching outburst,—let the people of England remain firm to their own moral, peaceful, and bloodless struggle:—and the result shall be that in proportion as the democracy of the continent advances through the tempest and storm to the consummation of its glorious aims, the friends of liberty in the British Isles will progress along the sun-lit and tranquil path of Truth, guided by the hand of Intelligence, unto the everlasting gates of Freedom's Temple.

The Government and the People
Saturday, March 2, 1850

Lord John Russel declares that the people do not want reform,—that they are perfectly happy and contented as they are,—and that only the very lowest murmurings have reached his ears for some time past. To assert that the millions do not desire their rights, is to proclaim a fallacy so glaringly patent and utter an untruth so monstrously absurd, that I wonder any statesman, however brazen-faced, could have had the impudence to volunteer such a declaration even upon his own aristocratic ground in the House of Commons. The averment that the people are contented with their present lot, is a positive insult flung in the face of the toiling slaves and oppressed serfs of these islands: it is the same as telling them that they are a base, servile, wretched crew, hugging the manacles and fetters which aristocratic tyranny has rivetted upon their limbs. But the statement that only the lowest murmurings have recently been wafted to the Ministerial ears, and that the popular satisfaction may thence be inferred, cannot do otherwise than excite feelings of mingled indignation, contempt, and disgust in the heart of every honest reformer.

From the Prime Minister's words we are naturally led to infer two things:—firstly, that if the people wish for reform, they must clamour for it; and secondly, that when their clamours rise to a certain pitch, the Government will listen with respect and yield with readiness. Such is the construction which must be put upon the words of the Prime Minister: but let us see how closely his professions are reconciled with his actions.

In 1848 there was clamour enough. The demand for reform was then loud and general throughout the length and breadth of the land. Monster meetings were held in the metropolis – in all the cities and large towns—in the hamlets—yes, even in the villages. At that time there was not a community of two hundred persons, dwelling anywhere in Great Britain, that had not its Chartist Committee and its Chartist agitation.

230

The representatives of the whole working-class population assembled in London, proclaimed the requirements of their constituencies, and indicated the reforms demanded. So formidable was this agitation, even in its sublime moral aspect,—and it had none other,—that the Government was frightened, the Queen and Prince Albert quitted London, a hundred thousand special constables were sworn in, the metropolis was converted into a vast fortalice, and the Iron Duke received plenary powers to cannonade the people *whenever* and *wherever* he might think fit. Nearly half a million of the proletarian race assembled upon Kennington Common to hold up their hands in favour of the Charter;—and a petition containing quite enough *real* signatures to stamp it with a true political value, was rolled in upon the floor of the House of Commons.

Such was the agitation of 1848. Surely there was something more than "a low murmuring" *then?* At all events, the whole world knows that the Ministers and the Legislature *did* hear *that* clamour for the reform: inasmuch as the voice raised by the British Proletarians shook the entire nation. And not only was reform demanded generally: but *the* reform needed was pointed out specifically. The Minister was left in no manner of doubt as to either the existence of the clamour, or the nature of the object clamoured for: the toiling millions sent up the cry—and the Charters was the remedy insisted upon.

But was the Minister attentive to the wants and requirements thus unmistakably expressed by the wealth-producers of this country?—was the reform thus energetically demanded granted?—or, in a word, was any measure of reform, however slight, conceded at all? No—nothing of the sort! The Aristocracy and its Ministers treated the people with defiance: through the *Times* they almost dared the Chartists to rebellion—pointing significantly to the cannon that was ready to vomit forth death and destruction upon the unarmed masses! And then—because the Chartists would *not* suffer themselves to be even goaded, taunted, bullied, or persuaded into an intemperate policy or violent proceedings—spies were sent among them to practice their damnable arts upon those who were the most enthusiastic in their patriotism or the most desperate in their penury. Thus a few noble spirits were so enmeshed by the designs and schemings of those hellish miscreants, that they were placed in the position where the Government wanted to find them; and a merciless Attorney-General, a partisan Judge, and a middle-class Jury did all the rest!

What, then, is the precise aspect of the case? Why, that if the people do *not* clamour, the Prime Minister argues that they are indifferent to reform: and if they *do* clamour, then they are denounced as spoliators and their leaders are imprisoned or transported.

Surely the true character of the Whig Government must now be known to the nation? Did ever a statesman condescend to more paltry, beggarly, despicable subterfuges than those which are greedily caught up and adopted by Lord John Russell? I will suppose that a deputation of working-men visits him at the Treasury, to represent the condition of the industrious populations and point out the necessity for reform. According to the present tactics of the Government, the following would be the sum and total of the Prime Minister's reply:—"I cannot listen to you as a mere quiet and peaceable deputation. Such a low murmuring cannot possibly produce any effect upon my official ears. The comparative silence of the nation is a proof of satisfaction with regard to existing institutions. If you really wish me to believe that there is a desire in the national breast for reform, you must agitate until the present murmuring shall have swollen into a deafening clamour."—"Very good, my lord," answers the deputation: "we will go away and commence our agitation at once."—"Yes, but take care what you are about," Instantaneously exclaims Lord John Russell: "for if you do go and agitate with energy, I shall set the Attorney-General at you."—"Then how are we to get reform, my lord?" demands the deputation, quite aghast at this most unexpected announcement: "you will not believe that we need reform, because we are too quiet; and you threaten to punish us if we become noisy." But instead of vouchsafing any rejoinder, Lord John shrugs his shoulders, rings the bell, and bows out the deputation. Such are Whig tactics.

But in spite of that shuffling system beneath which so much treachery lurks,—in spite of that double-faced dealing which says, "Agitate to show your sincerity," and then immolates the agitators,—in spite of the marvellous tenacity with which an arrogant Aristocracy, a bloated Church, a dishonest Legislature, and a tyrannical Ministry, cling to old-established feudalisms and long-standing abuses,—in spite of all this, the people *shall*, and *will*, and *must* continue to agitate for the Charter! They will agitate, because they have under-taken a struggle of truth and justice against falsehood and despotism,—and they have become not only interested as mere workers and toilers, but their honour is compromised as patriots, in establishing the triumph of the former upon the ruins of the latter!

Many years have now elapsed since the agitation for the Charter commenced. During the progress of this great movement, the Government has heard both "gentle murmurings" and impatient clamours: yet to neither has any concession been made. Of what use, then, is it for the Minister to demand the "signs of the times," if he will not follow their bidding when they do appear? Such conduct is the veriest trifling which a dishonest Government can practise towards a great people. But Ministers are never at a loss for excuses wherewith to vindicate their own inconsistency, nor wanting in subterfuge whereby to parry the demands made upon them. If the people be as tranquil as the calmest lake on a summer eve, their quietude is assumed as a proof of their felicitous contentment: if they become agitated as the ocean in a storm, the declaration goes forth that a time of excitement is not the proper reason for reform. Whatever be the state of the country, the people must always be in the wrong, and the Ministers in the right.

But how is it possible that such an anomalous condition of things should have sprung into existence? It is because the Ministers, instead of being the people's servants, have become their masters;—no longer the executors of the national will, they have assumed the attitude, demeanour, and conduct of irresponsible dictators. The result is that a constant antagonism exists between the Government and the Nation, the former looking upon the latter as something to be coerced, and the latter regarding the former as something against which all animosities must be levelled. The working classes in England look at the Government as a sort of natural enemy, at whom it is praiseworthy to level as hard a blow as possible, and whose pecuniary exactions it is perfectly legitimate to evade whenever opportunity serves. On the other hand, the Government looks upon the working-classes as dissatisfied grumblers, whom it is necessary to keep down by brute force. Such are the relative feelings: and whence sprang they? The whole fault lies with the Government, which, instead of being the protector of the masses, has become their persecutor—instead of befriending the millions, has betrayed them— instead of conciliating their affections, has won their deadly hatred! Yes—the whole fault lies with the government itself: its injustice towards the many and its truckling towards the few, its own rancorous hate of the millions and its adoration for the oligarchy,—these have been the proofs of its one-sided sympathy, and have naturally placed it in open antagonism with the industrious classes.

Is it not, then, a pretty condition of things when our servants have become our masters, and when the administrators of the whole nation are regarded with abhorrence by seven-tenths of the inhabitants? Surely a radical reform is required somewhere? But it is not that the people require to be more considerate and forbearing: it is that the Government should display more honesty and rectitude. Whatever amount of agitation may now exist, or may shortly be raised, in this country, the masses will deserve no vituperation: the whole blame should be thrown upon the Ministry and the Legislature. But will the middle-classes recognise this fact?—will they be honest for once?—will they, in a word, refuse with indignation evermore to become the agents of vindictive Attorney-Generals and the instruments of partizan Judges? Let them repudiate any future intention of suffering themselves to be made the agents for persecuting, scourging, crushing, ruining, immolating the veritable patriots of the country: and the working-classes will once more place confidence in them.

My Chartist friends, ye must now address yourselves with a renewed energy and a more fervid enthusiasm to the great moral struggle which is at hand. Europe stands upon the verge of a crisis: its condition will shortly be such, that the English Minister, alarmed by the something more than "low murmurings" from across the sea, will not dare refuse timely concessions to your demands. For on the nations of the Continent such a storm is about to burst as the world never saw before,—a storm that will sweep away the relics of feudalism and the elements of serfdom, like chaff upon the wing of the hurricane. And, oh! will it not be a glorious—a blessed—and a thrilling spectacle, to behold the People triumphant at last, and their accursed tyrants all stripped of their gaud and grandeur, and writhing in the chains which thenceforth must be their doom? God grant that when the nations shall rise again, the true Social and Democratic Republic may be proclaimed from the Seine to the Danube—from the Baltic to the Mediterranean;—and then—and *then* only—will there be hope for the Proletarians of the European Continent!

The Good Cause

Saturday, March 16, 1850

Red Republicanism and Socialism are making immense strides upon the continent of Europe—especially in France. The anti-popular journals of both Paris and London affect to ridicule the proceedings of the Red Republicans, and talk magniloquently of "the facility with which a rising will be put down." But if neither Red Republicanism nor Socialism be progressing, nor their disciples to be dreaded, wherefore should such manifold precautions be adopted and such immense preparations made? The truth is that the demon-hearted tyrants and bloody-minded aristocrats of Europe are in such awful terror of democratic propagandism, that they are rendered desperate and driven mad by their fears. Liberalism has even made such progress in Russia, that the incarnate fiend, the Emperor Nicholas, has been frequently attacked, during the last eight or ten months, with paroxysms of fury bordering upon madness; and it is well known that he has intimated to the Emperor of Austria and the King of Prussia his willingness to unite with them in a crusade against the democracy of Europe. The stripling patron of assassins who wears the Austrian crown, would cheerfully consent: but the cowardly, sneaking traitor who calls himself "King of Prussia, by the Grace of God," dares not join in such a scheme. He knows full well that his power already hangs by a thread which the slightest convulsion would snap in twain;— and entirely against his will, is he compelled to decline the proposed alliance. Not but that he possesses to the full all those bloody instincts and satanic predilections which are peculiar to Kings and Aristocracies; and, in obedience to those diabolical promptings, he would gloat over the prospect of a general carnage amongst the votaries of democratic progress. But he is well aware that at the first musket which a Prussian soldier was ordered to fire by his command, in any league that might be concocted between himself and the throned monsters of Russia and

235

Austria, the glorious democrats of Berlin would rise to a man and wreak summary justice not only upon himself but likewise upon all the titled hell-hounds by whom he is surrounded.

In the smaller German States the same fear prevails. The King of Hanover,—a man who receives £21,000 annually from the English Treasury, and whose valet Sellis was some years ago found murdered in so extraordinary and mysterious a way,—would gladly throw himself into the arms of an Austro-Russian crusade against democracy;—and this same willingness is shared by the crowned sneaks of Saxony, Wurttemberg, and Bavaria. But all these ginger-bread puppets, knowing full well that the very next convulsion which occurs in Europe must inevitably hurl them from their seats, tremble at the chance of precipitating by any desperate measure those events which they may perhaps hope to stave off for a time by the "peace-campaigning policy." That is to say, they consider it a safer game to set to work all the usual engines of royal persecution,—the political scaffold, exile, the dungeon, fines, confiscations &c. As if it were possible to stifle truth by such means! The miserable wretches!—they well know that the nations have found them out—that instead of resigning "by the grace of God," they are the instruments of Satan upon earth—and that the accumulated wrongs which centuries and centuries of tyranny and oppression have heaped upon the people of Europe, will speedily redound upon the heads of the tyrants and the oppressors themselves!

In France the most extensive preparations and widely ramified precautions have been adopted to resist the expected outbreak of the Red Republican and Socialist spirit. The partition of the country into four great military divisions, is a measure proving the amount of alarm with which the present crisis is viewed by Monkey Bonaparte and his adherents. For months and months past, no "sign of the times" has presented itself more pregnant with omen than this; and the augury is as cheering for the votaries of Red Republicanism, as it is disheartening to the scoundrel-upholders of tyranny and oppression. It is preposterous— it is almost laughable—for the *Times* to endeavour to persuade its aristocratic and middle-class readers that there is nothing to apprehend in France. Its Paris Correspondence is compelled to have recourse to the most ridiculous expedients to sustain the view which he is *ordered* to take of French affairs; and it is really pitiable to behold the excruciating tortures and spasmodic writhings into which that individual works himself, when endeavouring to give a roseate colour to those clouds which are lowering so darkly and so menacingly upon the hopes of monarchy-worshippers, aristocracy-supporters, and "parties of order," on the continent of Europe. At one time this Paris correspondent "can assure you the General Changarnier is full of confidence and ridicules the idea of a Socialist rising;"—but he does not pause to recollect that "Guizot laughed immoderately," and that "Louis Philippe was never firmer in his saddle," on the eve of the glorious, grand, and adorable revolution which bundled them out of the country. At another time the Paris correspondent of the *Times* has "just completed a visit of several hours to the Faubourg St. Antoine, and nothing could possibly wear the appearance of greater tranquility." Does this precious fool, then, suppose that the brave workmen of Paris are in the habit of posting placards on their doors and windows, to announce the month, the day, and the hour when they intend to rise again? The *Times* is often as asinine as it is mendacious – as foolish as it is false,—and never more so than when it is straining every nerve to mislead its readers relative to foreign affairs. But the favourite "dodge" of the Paris Correspondent of the *Times* is to have "just seen a gentleman who has returned from a tour in the south, and who assures me that there is not the slightest apprehension of any successful rising on the part of the Socialists." Anyone who is accustomed to read the *Times* daily would be astonished at the number of these "gentlemen returning from tours in the south;" and the natural inference is, that the moment they *do* so return, they rush off from the railway terminus to the lodgings of the *Times'* Correspondent in Paris to report to him the impressions received during their travels. Sometimes the Correspondent has "just heard from a gentleman on whose authority he can implicitly rely, that the President is full of confidence and that General Changarnier is acquainted with every movement upon the Socialist chess-board." Why, a child can pen such nonsense as this! What is it, after all? Is it fact—or is it mere assertion? Is it a tangible reason—or only such a statement as any one can fabricate without much fear of contradiction? Most singular indeed is it, that whenever the Paris Correspondent of the *Times* appears to be at a loss for reassuring evidence relative to the condition of France, heaven is sure to send some kind and communicative "traveller from the south," or throw in his way some "gentleman whose authority may be relied upon." Very convenient, indeed, are these "gentlemen" who always arrive at the nick of time, like the hero of romance; and very much like romances, too, are the tales which these *apropos* kind of gentlemen breathe into the willing ears of the *Times'* Correspondent.

The fact is, that no reliance is to be placed upon the Paris Correspondent of the *Times* or any other London daily newspaper. Even the most liberal are so opposed to Red Republicanism and Socialism, that they will not tell the truth. What, then, *is* the truth? Why, the statement made at the outset of this article: namely, that the good cause is making immense strides upon the Continent of Europe. Yes—it is in vain for the newspaper organs of the British Aristocracy and Middle-Classes to attempt to practise the delusion any longer: Red Republicanism *is* progressing—Socialism *is* progressing likewise—and the proof may be seen in the tremendous preparations made to resist the onward march of true democracy. Instead of the Continent of Europe being cursed with kings blasphemously attributing their power to "the Grace of God," the nations, happy and free, will soon enjoy the institutions of pure Republicanism, which may properly and justly be ascribed to "the Grace of God." For as all are equal in the sight of heaven, so must the cause of democracy be the one which the Almighty loves the best: and we know full well that the very fundamental principles of the Christian system are Republican.

The cause of true freedom on the Continent is deriving strength daily and hourly, not only from pure and legitimate proselytism, but likewise from political expediency. While thousands flock, from honest conviction, to the ranks of Red Republicanism, numbers of the Moderates are hastening into the same path because their own milk-and-water party has committed political suicide. The *National* has declared for Red Republicanism: Marrast, Ledru-Rollin's great opponent in the Provisional Government, now confesses his former errors and proclaims his present adhesion to the cause of justice and truth. In a short time the whole Cavaignac party will join the Mountain. What do these changing scenes prove? That the star of Red Republicanism is in the ascendent, and that selfish ambition as well as an earnest and sincere faith are prompting men to worship it. When such political tricksters and time-servers as Marrast and Emile de Girardin kneel to that constellation, there can be no doubt as to the influence which it is already exercising upon the destinies of the world. The proceedings of such men are the straws that show the direction which the wind is blowing.

The Chartist Agitation

Saturday, March 23, 1850

The resuscitated movement in favour of the Charter is daily and hourly gaining ground. In all the cities and principal towns of Great Britain the staunch friends of the cause are rallying around their old standard and are evincing a glorious determination to do their duty. The banner is once more flung forth to the breeze; and the People, if true to themselves, will soon be as free as the air which their flag thus woos. The new combination of the Provisional Committee promises to work well; and it is the resolution of its members to adopt a firm and vigorous policy. They will not only take the necessary steps to conduct the agitation for the Charter to a successful issue along the paths of peace and order; but they will likewise adopt measures to inculcate the necessity and point out the nature of those social reforms which must be proclaimed simultaneously with the demand for political justice. The Charter alone would be comparatively of little avail: it would give political rights; but something more is needed. The whole social system is corrupt and rotten to its very core; and poverty, mendicity, and crime will never disappear from the land until the very framework of society be remodeled. Of these truths the members of the Provisional Committee are well aware; and that knowledge is suggestive of their duties as well as indicative of their experience in the important task of fulfilling them.

An announcement in the advertising columns of the *Instructor* informs the public that an office has been taken for the business of the National Charter Association. The Provisional Committee is unpaid: but its Secretary, who will be in frequent attendance at head-quarters, must receive a salary for his services. At the commencement this remuneration will necessarily be small; and all the details of the administration will be conducted with a view to the strictest economy. But still there are expenses which must be met every Saturday night: the People's work will be done cheaply, but cannot be done for nothing. The rent of the Office, the salary of the Secretary, the printing that is requisite, the cost of public meetings,—in fine, all the little liabilities contingent to the administrative procedure,—these must be regularly and punctually settled. The cause is the People's own: and the People are therefore called upon to support it. A good spirit must be shown at once in taking out the cards of membership: these may be had from the General Secretary by the local committees upon terms of limited credit;—but the proceeds should be sent up to head-quarters as soon and as frequently as possible. If the local committees were only to bestir themselves properly, the cards of membership should alone produce a sufficiency of money to carry on the Association, without actual donations towards a fund for the purpose of aiding the movement. At the same time, where the pecuniary means of individuals will allow them to make such donations, apart from the mere enrolment of membership, the tribute will necessarily be received as a proof of earnest zeal and staunch sincerity in the furtherance of the good cause.

It must likewise be observed that the greater the support the Provisional Committee may experience, the more energetic will the movement be rendered and the sooner will its triumph be ensured. If properly aided by funds, such an agitation may be got up as will indeed convince the Ministry, the Aristocracy, and the Legislature, that the People are anxious to become possessed of their rights and privileges. It therefore behooves every man who loves Democracy and who advocates the Chartist principles, to contribute his mite; and the result is immediately brought within the range of prophecy.

The members of the Provisional Committee are full of hope and confidence. They have taken upon themselves a task which engages much of their time, makes certain demands upon their purse, and involves a considerable amount of personal responsibility. This position they have accepted in the full trust that they will be adequately supported. It would be a most ignominious spectacle to behold the new movement perish through sheer inanition: for such a catastrophe would indeed warrant the Prime Minister to take his stand upon the assertion that the People are indifferent to their rights. That assertion is now a calumny, a falsehood, and an insult: let the Chartists beware how they suffer it to become a truth which the organs and instruments of a selfish Aristocracy may proclaim with all triumph of a characteristic insolence.

What, then, must be done? Every man who reads this article, should be ready to give the response,—aye, and answer it in a practical manner. If he be desirous of obtaining the Charter let him contribute his mite to that fund by aid of which the movement can alone be conducted. Let him at once take out his card of membership; and when he has received it, let him show it to his friends, his neighbours, and fellow-workmen, and enjoin them to "go and do likewise." If at the end of a year,—when the Parliament assembles in 1851,—the Chartist register could prove to the House of Commons that many thousands of men had enrolled themselves as members of the Association, the argument would be a hundred-fold more cogent than all the petitions which might be poured into the Legislative Assembly with the same object in view. The register, if well filled with the names of paying members, would afford a far more *practical* proof of the anxiety and determination of the People to obtain their rights, than could possibly be given by memorials to which signatures may be forged, or by public meetings at which cheering may be ascribed to an evanescent enthusiasm.

Now, then—or never! If the present movement should fail through want of funds, the People will deserve to remain serfs and slaves; and they will have no right to complain hereafter. Wages may be better at present than they have recently been—employment may be more general than it lately was,—but these circumstances should not be permitted to engender apathy. On the contrary, it is precisely at the moment when individuals can afford to pay a shilling for the Chartists cause, that the shilling should be paid. Let no man say, "Oh! there will be enough to give contributions without me!" It is this reliance upon others doing what each one ought to do, that often ruins a good cause. There are too many who reason in that complaisant style; and thus, while each fancies he is singular in adopting such an excuse for failing to do his duty, others are pursuing the same irrational and reprehensible course. No man, then, should trust to others to do what he himself is bound to perform or assist in: everyone should look upon his own individual endeavour as something too important to be lost to aggregate amount of work that is to be done. If there be apathy in struggling to obtain those rights which are now denied, there will be indifference in making use of them when they shall have been obtained;—and no individual is so unimportant an item in the great social mass as to allow a good cause to lose his succor and his support.

"What, then, must be done?" I again ask. The reply is ready at hand, and easily comprehended. Local Committees must exert all their energy; and individual Chartists must manifest all their zeal. Each man should look upon his own effort as if the whole cause depended upon it: each democrat must regard his own individual assistance as if the movement could not possibly be carried on without it. If such a spirit could be aroused—if such a feeling could be excited—the day of triumph would be approximated so closely as to premise a speedy reward for any temporary sacrifice in the shape of money, time, or trouble.

And now let me remind the working-classes that the attainment of the Charter is not a mere question of acquiring certain abstract rights and privileges: it is not a-simple consideration of blooming endowed with the franchise. If it were only this, it would be possible to understand the existence of apathy in many quarters with regard to the Charter. But it is a something far more important than the mere fact of exercising political rights: it is a *wages' question – a labour question – a social improvement question*. The enactment of the People's Charter as the law of the land, will lead to the adoption of measures calculated to place the industrious classes in a comfortable, prosperous, and happy condition. Those measures will give the workers and toilers a fair share of all that they produce: those measures will banish pauperism, extinguish crime, and crush oppression;—those measures will make men's homes happy, and cause smiles to supersede the traces of care and famine upon the countenances of their wives and little ones. This is what the Charter will do: - and now I ask whether it be not worth struggling for?

But I will put a still more practical question,—a question which I will address to every working-man individually. And this is the question:—*"Is the Charter worth a shilling to you?"* Look at your present position— and see what it may become under the operation of the Charter: look at your present wages—and see to what an amount they may be raised under good institutions;—look at your wife and children, as they now are with their pale faces, their scant clothing, their want of education, and their fears for the future—and see how happy they may be rendered under a wise, beneficent, and enlightened system of government. Look at all this, I say—and then tell me whether you will give a shilling (even though you may be scarcely able to afford it at the moment) to obtain the People's Charter. Well, your answer is in the affirmative: you can give no other response. As a man—as a husband—and as a father,—as a member of society, and as one wishing well to the cause of progress and having at heart the interests of your fellow creatures,—in all these capacities you could not say "No" to the question which I have put to you. Then show your sincerity,—you, as an individual, by paying this shilling in aid of the movement which is set on foot to obtain for you that Charter wherein all your hopes and chances of earthly happiness are centred.

The Despot-Ape of France

Saturday, April 6, 1850

The infamous *Times* is constantly expatiating upon what it is pleased to call the anarchical condition of French society: but however unsettled that society may be at the present moment, the cause is to be looked for in the treacherous and diabolical policy pursued by M. Louis Napoleon Bonaparte and the base reactionaries by whom he has surrounded himself. When a man in high office sacrifices a country to his own personal ambition, and selects as his advisers the avowed enemies of the popular cause, what other result can ensue than a wide-spread dissatisfaction? If the French people were to submit tamely to the tyranny of that ape who is now performing his antics on the summit of the governmental tree to which he has managed to climb, they would deserve to wear the most galling chains that a vile despotism could possibly rivet apon their limbs;—and if they do not rise in rebellion again, they will merit the denomination of cowards. But such an opprobrious name will never be merited by the great and glorious French people. They are watching their opportunity—they are measuring their strength—they are taking breath after the fatigues of recent conflicts—and they are studying all the weak points of the enemy. Every day that now passes in tranquility, adds to the strength of the patriots, and diminishes the power of their tyrants. Louis Napoleon Bonaparte, plunging each hour more deeply into pecuniary embarrassments as well as into political perplexities, becomes an object of increasing scorn, mistrust, and hatred. His position is now desperate in the extreme. If he were to resign the Presidency with a view to appeal to the nation and stand as the candidate for re-election, he would instantaneously divest himself of the official immunity which saves him from a debtor's gaol;—and, in addition thereto, he has been assured by his advisers that he stands not the slightest chance of re-election. His debts are goading him on to the maddest experiments; and his destiny trembles between two

244

alternatives, the one representing the sublime, and the other the ridiculous. In plain terms, he must either mount a throne or go to quod!

In every way is *Mister* Bonaparte ruined, he has become an object of contempt, as well as of hatred; and a man who has made himself ridiculous, stands a worse chance of accomplishing his aims in France than a man who is only hated. For the French are the most sensitive people in Europe on that score: they might consent to be ruled by a lion, but never by an ape. A witty sarcasm cuts more deeply amongst the French than the sword. A stern, solemn, and imposing despotism, such as that of Louis Philippe, is calculated to stand on a far firmer foundation in France than the fantastic and mountebank oppression of a contemptible zany. The day that the President's cousin, M. Napoleon Bonaparte, denounced him as "a kite in the eagle's nest," knocked down as much of his original popularity as his own base treachery had already destroyed. For a Frenchman would sooner be lacerated by the claws of a noble lion, than pelted with cocoa-nuts by a grimacing monkey leaping from bough to bough in a lofty tree.

The results of the recent elections have not been fairly dealt with by the *Times* and other English newspapers, it is true that out of those elections, the Moderates have gained ten of the twenty-eight seats previously occupied by Red Republicans. But the fact is that the elections furnished the occasion for the country to pronounce a verdict upon the character and policy of M. Bonaparte, and that verdict has been given against him by an enormous majority. It is quite clear that the nation is two-thirds Red Republican and Socialist. This truth is established beyond all possibility of doubt. Now, a year and a half ago, the *Times* tauntingly said of France, "Behold a Republic without a single Republican in it." Well, granting for a moment that such was the fact, what tremendous progress Red Republicanism and Socialism must have made in order that two-thirds of the entire population should have embraced those doctrines in so short a time! Of a surety, there must be something gloriously vital and irresistibly convincing in Red Republicanism and Socialism, to enable the principles to disseminate themselves at such a wild-fire rate, and if such has been their progress, what immense hope is there for the future! At the same rate, even according to the very showing of the *Times* itself, all France will become proselytised in another six months;—and then what hope can M. Louis Napoleon Bonaparte entertain of saving his carcase from a cell in the debtor's prison of the Rue de Clichy, by donning the imperial purple?

The recent elections, I said, were a verdict pronounced by the particular constituencies acting on the occasion, and must be regarded as the test of the sentiments entertained by the great majority of the nation. I will explain wherefore. If twenty-eight elections were to take place in England, under the present laws, the results would afford no indication of the national opinion: for two reasons—1. Because constituencies of only a few hundreds each (such as Horsham, Thetford, Evesham, Harwich, &c.) might be included in the number: and 2. because no one constituency in any county or borough now represents the true feeling of the whole mass of inhabitants in such county or borough. But in France the case is very different. There all the constituencies are now equal, and every adult gives his vote. Consequently, if twenty constituencies, taken at random in different parts of the country, pronounce all in favour of a certain principles, the inevitable and irresistible inference is that the whole national sentiments have undergone a test.

It is quite clear, then, that there is nothing dangerous nor terrible, nor anarchical in Red Republicanism: otherwise those doctrines would never have been stamped with the approval of many millions of men of all grades of society. The middle-classes would have voted against Red Republicanism and Socialism if these principles had been really pernicious: but it is evident from the result of the elections, that in the great majority of instances the middle joined the working-classes in voting *for* those principles, the opponents of which were only the indolent drones who fatten vampyre-like upon the blood, sinew, and sweat of the industrial millions. It is ridiculous for a miserable minority of men to set themselves up as the only Solons in the nation, and declare that the great majority are all wrong,—especially when the former are interested in maintaining the abuses upon which they grow fat, while the latter are endeavoring to destroy the political infamies and the social wrongs by which they are made to starve. Self-interest constitutes the basis of the policy of the favoured few: intelligence, enlightenment, and justice are the principles which actuate the conduct of the latter.

I know perfectly well that Red Republicanism is subversive—yes, very subversive: aye, and also very destructive. The "Party of Order" in France and the *Times* in England are quite right when they say so. But of what is Red Republicanism subversive? and how is it destructive? It is subversive of the mighty colossus of political tyrannies which France's forty Kings had in succession piled up: it is destructive of the whole net-work of social wrongs which ages of oppression had spread over the greatest and most gallant nation of Continental Europe. Yes—Red Republicanism is a terrible destroyer of the cumulative abuses which centuries of misrule heap up,—a remorseless annihilator of the million injuries which demon-hearted enslavers have inflicted upon the enslaved. And it is because Red Republicanism crushed the accursed throne of Louis Philippe, and will not allow Louis Napoleon to rebuild it,—it is because Red Republicanism swept away the titled Aristocracy, and will not permit a few base politicians to restore it,—it is because Red Republicanism gave the nation universal suffrage, and now watches over that right with a jealous eye,—it is because Red Republicanism is conducting the French mind along the broad and open pathways of truth, and opposes all endeavours to lead it back in to the tortuous and obscure bye-lanes of ignorance,—it is for these reasons that Louis Napoleon dreads it, the tyrant few hate it, and the servile portion of the Press denounce it.

But Mrs. Partington attempting with her broom to keep back the advancing waters of the Atlantic, is not a more ludicrous spectacle than the French President endeavouring to resist the onward-rolling flood of democracy. Mind is always progressing; and therefore no institutions that are influenced by Mind, can ever remain stationary. The Mind of France is now essentially Red Republicanism; and the institutions cannot do otherwise then fall into a plastic comparability therewith. The Party of Order may gather all its forces—may band all is adherents in a serried phalanx—may subsidise the venal portion of the Press in France and England both—may introduce coercive measures—may denounce, gag, persecute, imprison, banish, and even slay,—all this may Louis Napoleon Bonaparte and his creatures do—but the spirit of the French people is as elastic as the steel weapon which will flash forth from the scabbard in vindication of right against wrong, and justice against tyranny.

There never was so contemptible a spectacle in all the world as the figure which the *Times* has cut with regard to the recent elections. For weeks before they took place, the *Times'* Correspondent was incessant and triumphant in its assurances that not a Red Republican would be chosen. Then, as the elections approached, the *Times* began to admit that the Reds were making immense efforts. Next, on the eve of the elections, when all the world could pretty well anticipate the result, the *Times* dropped a hint that one or two Red Republicans *might* be returned—but not more than one or two. Even while the elections were taking place, the French Correspondent of the *Times* was still blatant with his windy assurances in favour of the so-called "cause of order." But, behold! two-thirds of the Reds are returned in triumph;—and for a moment the *Times* admits that it is astounded. A pretty conductor of the public mind is this Journal, which could not see, even at the last moment, that course of events the actual direction of which was weeks previously within the range of prophecy! And this is called the "best-informed newspaper in Europe"—the "leading journal!" Well, but when the result of the elections became an established fact, the poor *Times* manifested all the ludicrous excruciations invariably attendant upon the endeavour to explain away disagreeable concurrences, and invent excuses for unpalatable incidents. Could anything be more ridiculous than to behold the *Times'* Correspondent asserting that the middle-classes only wanted to give the Government a gentle lesson, but did not mean it to be so severe?—could anything be more preposterous than the reiterated declaration made by that self-same wretched scribe, to the effect that the middle-classes repented of the votes they had given the moment the result was known? All this shows how miserable are the subterfuges to which the *Times* is reduced in its endeavours to distort the truth. And what is the truth? Why, that the middle-classes of France voted deliberately, and not rashly,—with a straightforward intention and not a sinister one,—for the purpose of recording their settled convictions in favour of Red Republicanism, and not with a mere view to frighten some very silly persons with a temporary bugbear. It is the *Times* which is supremely silly in this case to believe (or appear to believe) that millions of rational, enlightened, intelligent men could possibly make use of their votes in so idle, reckless, and inconsiderate a fashion.

However, the Red Republicans and Socialists *have* carried the great majority of the elections; and let the *Times* make the best of the result. Yes—and let M. Bonaparte and the whole Party of Order make the best of it likewise. And let them all ponder upon the one grand fact which those elections have established: namely, that the French Army is Red Republican and Socialist. Without an army at his back, a tyrant is powerless: for all tyranny is based upon brute force. It is physical power endeavouring to subdue the influence of Mind. But that power is now wanting to the despot-ape of France: the Army has thrown him off with disgust, contempt, and scorn;—and he will not even fall with the solemnity of the crash which overwhelmed the throne of Louis Philippe—but he will some fine morning quit the ambrosial bowers of the Elysee Palace in the ignominious custody of a sheriff's-officer.

Notes

Abbreviations

LJ = London Journal
MM = Monthly Magazine
RM = Reynolds's Miscellany
RPI = Reynolds's Political Instructor
RWN = Reynolds's Weekly Newspaper

Preface

1. Anon. [online], 'Reynolds, George William Macarthur', *Find-a-Grave*, accessed 12 January 2021. Available at: www.findagrave.com.
2. E.F. Bleiler, 'Introduction to the Dover Edition', in *Wagner the Wehr-Wolf*, ed. by E.F. Bleiler (New York: Dover, 1975), pp. vii–xviii (p. vii).
3. This introduction is from a revised and expanded blog post I wrote for the G.W.M. Reynolds Society: Stephen Basdeo [online], 'Discovering G. W. M. Reynolds', *G.W.M. Reynolds Society*, 17 October 2018, accessed 17 March 2021. Available at: www.gwmreynoldssociety.com.

Thomas Paine has turned the youth's brain: Reynolds's Early Life and Schooling

4. William Henry Ireland, *England's Topographer; or, A New and Complete History of the County of Kent; from the Earliest Records to the Present Time, Including Every Modern Improvement* (London: G. Virtue, 1829), p. 277. The term 'yeoman' emerged during the medieval period when it signified a member of a knight's entourage—the word's military associations are, in fact, still with us today in the office of the British monarch's Yeomen of the Guard. Yet the term's meaning evolved for by at least the sixteenth century it was taken to denote a farmer who belonged to a class lower than the gentry, but who owned and farmed a small plot of land.
5. *England, Births and Christenings, 1538-1975* (Salt Lake City, Utah: FamilySearch, 2013), FHL Film Number: 1736695, item 2, 164.
6. Dick Collins, 'Introduction', in George W.M. Reynolds, *The Necromancer*, ed. by Dick Collins (London: Valancourt, 2009), iii.

7. Ibid., p. iii.
8. Edward Hasted, *The History and Topographical Survey of the County of Kent*, 12 vols (Canterbury: Bristow, 1798), VII, 540–41.
9. Arthur Henry Bullen, 'Barrett, Stephen', in *The Dictionary of National Biography*, ed. by Leslie Stephen and Sydney Lee, 63 vols (London: Smith, Elder, 1885–1900), III, 284.
10. Colin Roderick, ed. *John Knatchbull: From Quarterdeck to Gallows*, (Sydney: Angus and Robertson, 1963), 30–31. This Knatchbull of course is a special case—his account of his school days comes from an autobiography he had written in a gaol cell while he was awaiting execution in Australia for the murder of a chandler named Ellen Jamieson. But his account is nevertheless useful for illuminating some aspects of life at the school.
11. Augustus John Pearman, *History of Ashford* (Ashford: H. Igglesden, 1868), 71.
12. Collins, xi.
13. *Report from Commissioners: Charities in England and Wales: First Report and Appendix* (London: HMSO, 1819), 83.
14. *Report from Commissioners*, 83.
15. WO99/8, Minutes of the Supreme Board of RMC Commissioners, Horse Guards, 23.12.1817, enclosing letter from RMC Governor, Sir Alexander Hope, to Adjutant General, General H Torrens, 13.11.1817, 7. Royal Military College.
16. Sebastian Alexander George Puncher, 'The Victorian Army and the Cadet Colleges, Woolwich and Sandhurst, c.1840-1902' (Unpublished Ph.D. thesis, University of Kent, 2019), 108.
17. Reynolds, George, 1828–30, RMC_WO_151_Vol_1_1806-1864. Royal Military College.
18. Collins, xiv.
19. Anne Humpherys and Louis James, 'Introduction', in *G.W.M. Reynolds: Nineteenth-Century Fiction, Politics, and the Press*, eds Louis James and Anne Humpherys, 2nd edn (London: Routledge, 2019), 1.
20. Collins, xii.
21. Ibid., xv.
22. Reynolds, Edward, 1833–37, RMA_WO_149_Vol_5_1832-1854. Royal Military College Archives.
23. James Grant, *The Newspaper Press: Its Origin, Progress, and Present Position*, 2 vols (London: Tinsley, 1871), I, p. 97: In 1871 James Grant wrote a history of the newspaper press in which he devoted some words to Reynolds's Weekly Newspaper. The editor in 1871 was Edward Reynolds and Grant remarked that 'Mr. Reynolds is a man of family, was educated at one of our great universities, and is in his manners a perfect gentleman'. This quote must refer to Edward instead of George because we know that the latter never attended university.
24. George W.M. Reynolds, 'The Errors of the Christian Religion Exposed', in *The Early Writings of George William MacArthur Reynolds (1814–79): Short Stories, Essays, Translations, and Poetry from The Monthly Magazine, the*

London Journal, and Reynolds's Miscellany, ed. Stephen Basdeo (Leeds: Privately Printed, 2020), 12.

25. Thomas Paine, *The Age of Reason* (New York: Bennett, 1877), 1.
26. Reynolds, *The Errors of the Christian Religion Exposed*, 5.
27. George W.M. Reynolds, 'The Form of Prayer for Charles the First', *RWN*, 15 December 1850, 1.
28. George W.M. Reynolds, *Pickwick Abroad* (London: Willoughby, n.d.), 384; G.W.M. Reynolds, 'Our Glorious Constitution', *RWN*, 17 November 1850, 1.
29. George W.M. Reynolds, 'The French Poets and Novelists', *MM*, May 1837, 524–32.
30. A dossier on Reynolds was compiled by the Home Office in 1848 stated that while in Paris Reynolds had become a French citizen and had also served in the French National Guard (W. Weston to George Grey, 18 April 1848, HO45. OS2410, 345). The reference usually given for the assertion that Reynolds claimed to have been a French citizen and to have fought in the French Revolution of 1830 is *The Modern Literature of France*, 2 vols (London: G. Henderson, 1839), I, i–ii, which Cyril Pearl quoted in *Victorian Patchwork* (London: William Heinemann, 1972), 73. Yet *The Modern Literature of France* quoted by Pearl does not contain any statement by Reynolds to the effect that he fought in the French Revolution.
31. Captain Walmer Vincent of the Royal Navy to Sir George Grey, 9 April 1848, The National Archives, HO 45/2410, Box 1, 337–4.
32. See Old Bailey Proceedings Online (www.oldbaileyonline.org, version 8.0, accessed 15 March 2021), May 1834, trial of Henry Lavery and George Reynolds (t18340515-25).

Reynolds Abroad; or The Tour in France

33. Graham Robb, *Victor Hugo* (London: MacMillan, 1998), 158; W.M. Thackeray [online], *The Paris Sketch Book of Mr M.A. Titmarsh*, accessed 14 March 2021. Available at: www.gutenberg.org.
34. [George W.M. Reynolds], 'Personal Appearance of Eugène Sue', *RM*, 2 January 1847, 136.
35. Reynolds, *The Modern Literature of France*, I, 89.
36. File on 'George William Macarthur Reynolds', Archives Nationales, Cote F.18.2131 cited in Maha R. Atal, 'G.W.M. Reynolds in Paris, 1835–36: A New Discovery', *Notes and Queries*, December (2008), 448–53.
37. Susannah Frances Reynolds, 'Intemperance in Woman', *Teetotaler*, 19 December 1840, 203.
38. Collins, xix–xx.
39. Ibid., xlii.
40. Will of James Brooke Irwin of Stanley Street Brompton, Middlesex, The National Archives, Kew, PROB 11/2238/432
41. UK, Foreign and Overseas Registers of British Subjects, 1628-1969, RG 33: Foreign Registers and Returns, 1627-1960, Piece 065: Paris: Marriages, 1828-1837, 151.

42. Collins, xx.
43. Sophie Raine [online], 'The Youthful Imposter', *G.W.M. Reynolds Society*, accessed 21 January 2020. Available at: www.gwmreynoldssociety.com.
44. 'The Youthful Imposter: A Novel in Three Volumes', *Monthly Magazine*, April (1836), 381.
45. Sara James, 'G.W.M. Reynolds and the Modern Literature of France', in Humpherys and James, 20.
46. G.W.M. Reynolds, *The Youthful Imposter*, 3 vols (London: Longman, 1836). I have not seen this particular edition but its existence is attested to in 'Advertisements', *Morning Post*, 17 October 1835, 1.
47. G.W.M. Reynolds, *The Youthful Imposter*, 2 vols (Philadelphia: Carey and Hart, 1836).
48. A.J.B. Defauçonpret, *Le Jeune Imposteur*, 3 vols (Bruxelles: Wahlen, 1836).
49. 'Art. XXIX.—The Youthful Imposter', *Monthly Review*, April (1836), 594.
50. 'The Parricide', *Pilot*, 14 May 1847, 2
51. 'The Parricide' by George W M Reynolds, Part 4", *Nottingham Review*, 29 June 1847, 3.
52. 'The Parricide', *Leeds Times*, 20 February 1847, 6.
53. 'The Present State of Cheap Literature', *Liverpool Mercury*, 29 June 1847, 3.
54. Captain Walmer Vincent of the Royal Navy to Sir George Grey, 9 April 1848, The National Archives, HO45/2410, Box 1, 337–4.
55. G.W.M. Reynolds, *The Modern Literature of France*, 2nd edn, 2 vols (London: George Henderson, 1841), I, pp. ii–iii.
56. Anne Humphreys, "The Geometry of the Modern City: G. W. M. Reynolds and The Mysteries of London", *Browning Institute Studies*, xi, (1983), 69–70.
57. 'English Literature in France', *Monthly Magazine*, September 1837, 278.
58. Jennifer Conary, 'G. W. M. Reynolds, the *Paris Advertiser*, and the Anglo-Parisian Press', *Victorian Periodicals Review*, 53: 2 (2020), 214–37.
59. It has been asserted that during the mid-1830s Reynolds was the editor of the *Paris Literary Gazette* and also made the acquaintance of, and commissioned essays by, a young art student who lived a few doors down from him named William Makepeace Thackeray. This has been proven by Jennifer Conary to be an incorrect assertion.
60. 'On the Necessity for a New Daily English Newspaper at Paris', *Paris Literary Gazette*, October 27, 1835, 3.
61. Conary, 219–20.
62. George W.M. Reynolds, *Circular* (Paris: Wittersheim, 1835), cited in Conary, 220.
63. Conary, 216.
64. George W.M. Reynolds, 'The Gypsy: A Tale', *Paris Advertiser*, 21 February 1836, 82–84.
65. George W.M. Reynolds, 'The Guardian', *Paris Advertiser*, 24 April 1836, 225–28
66. Conary, 226.
67. 'Advertisement', *Mirror*, 22 October 1836, 272. This lists Reynolds as an agent through whom various texts can be procured.

68. 'English Literature in France', 280.
69. George W.M. Reynolds, 'The Party of Order on the Continent', *RPI*, 23 February 1850, 2.
70. 'Our Library Table', *Athenaeum*, 29 October 1836, 768.
71. Atal, 451.
72. George W.M. Reynolds, *Pickwick Abroad*, cited in Conary, 230.

Taking the Pledge: Reynolds, the *Teetotaler*, and his Early Novels

73. 'Bethnal Green: Building and Social Conditions from 1837 to 1875', in *A History of the County of Middlesex: Vol. 11: Stepney, Bethnal Green*, ed. T.F.T. Baker (London: Victoria Country History, 1998), 120–26.
74. Collins, xxiii.
75. 1841 England Census. Class: HO107; Piece 693; Book 9; Civil Parish: Bethnal Green; County; Middlesex; Enumeration District 31; Folio 40; Page 2; Line 3; GSU roll 438809.
76. Friedrich Engels, *The Condition of the Working Class in England*, ed. Victor Kiernan (London: Penguin, 2009), 73.
77. Enid Gauldie, *Cruel Habitations: History of Working Class Housing, 1780-1918* (London: Allen and Unwin, 1974), 91.
78. 'Dwellings of the poor in Bethnal Green', *Illustrated London News*, 24 October 1863, 4.
79. George W.M. Reynolds, 'Constantina; or, the Importance of its Occupation by the French', *MM*, March 1837, 228–35.
80. Reynolds, 'The French Poets and Novelists', 59.
81. George W.M. Reynolds, 'The Progress of Civilization in Belgium', *MM*, November 1837, 510–14; George W.M. Reynolds, 'The Literature of Hungary', *MM*, July 1837, 33–39.
82. 'Biographical Sketches of Eminent Authors', *LJ*, 29 November 1845, 92.
83. Adam Abraham, 'The Man Who Would be Dickens: Thomas Peckett Prest, Plagiarist', in *Edward Lloyd and his World: Popular Fiction, Politics, and the Press in Victorian Britain*, ed. Sarah Louise Lill and Rohan McWilliam (London: Routledge, 2019), 97.
84. Sarah Louise Lill, 'In for a Penny: The Business of Mass-Market Publishing, 1832–90', in Lill and McWilliam, 22–38.
85. Louis James, ' "I am Ada!": Edward Lloyd and the Creation of the Penny Dreadful', in Lill and McWilliam, 54–70.
86. Ian Haywood, 'The Importance of "Phis": The Role of Imitation in Lloyd's Imitations of Dickens', in Lill and McWilliam, 71.
87. Stephen Knight, *G.W.M. Reynolds and his Fiction: The Man Who Outsold Dickens* (London: Routledge, 2019), 15.
88. Ibid., 15.
89. Reynolds, G. W. M., 1814-1879. n.d. MS Archives of the Royal Literary Fund: Archives of the Royal Literary Fund 957, 2.
90. 'Pickwick Abroad', *Caledonian Mercury*, 5 March 1838, 2.

91. 'Pickwick Abroad', *Carlisle Journal*, 10 March 1838, 4.
92. Reynolds, G. W. M., 1814-1879. n.d. MS Archives of the Royal Literary Fund: Archives of the Royal Literary Fund 957, p. 2.
93. Ibid., p. 4.
94. 'Biographical Sketches of Eminent Authors', 92
95. George W.M. Reynolds, *Grace Darling* (London: George Henderson, 1839), vii.
96. *Observer*, 16 December 1838 cited in Reynolds, *Grace Darling*, vii.
97. *Globe*, 18 September 1838, cited in Reynolds, *Grace Darling*, viii.
98. Jerry White, *Mansions of Misery: A Biography of the Marshalsea Debtors' Prison* (Oxford: Bodley Head, 2016), 83.
99. Reynolds, *Grace Darling*, 6.
100. Ibid., 11.
101. Janet Dunbar, *The Early Victorian Woman: Some Aspects of Her Life, 1837-57* (London: Harrap, 1953), 135.
102. Reynolds, *Grace Darling*, vi.
103. Reynolds, *The Mysteries of London*, III, 293.
104. Reynolds, *Grace Darling*, vi.
105. 'Mr G.W.M. Reynolds and the Jews', *Reynolds's Miscellany*, 20 May 1848, 448.
106. Ancestry [online], 'All four Reynolds children baptised on the same day. Births shown in Registrars book as follows: Blanche b. 23 Feb 1838; Alfred Dowers b. 22 Mar 1840; Edward b. 26 Jan 1842; Frederick b. 20 May 1844', scan of baptismal record uploaded by Josephine Davis and available under George William Macarthur Reynolds listing at: https://www.ancestry.co.uk/
107. Jenny Keating, *A Child for Keeps: the History of Adoption in England, 1918-45* (Basingstoke: Palgrave, 2008), 2.
108. Details of this bankruptcy can be found in Official Assignee's Bankruptcy Files - Christchurch - Reynolds Alfred – 16.04.1885, Archives New Zealand, Christchurch Regional Office.
109. Rohan McWilliam, 'The French Connection: G.W.M. Reynolds and the Outlaw Robert Macaire', in Humpherys and James, 35.
110. 'Review of L'Auberge des Adrets', *Times*, 26 January 1835, 3.
111. Knight, *G.W.M. Reynolds and his Fiction*, 25.
112. McWilliam, 'The French Connection', 45.
113. George W.M. Reynolds, *Robert Macaire; or, The French Bandit in England* (London: John Dicks, 1851), 64.
114. Reynolds, *Robert Macaire*, 64.
115. Knight, *G.W.M. Reynolds and his Fiction*, 25.
116. Collins, xxvii.
117. Susan Zieger [online], 'Temperance, Teetotalism, and Addiction in the Nineteenth Century', *Victorian Web*, 7 September 2002, accessed 25 March 2021. Available at: www.victorianweb.org.
118. George W.M. Reynolds, 'Analysis of the Discussion', *Teetotaler*, 27 June 1840, 5.
119. Ibid.
120. Ibid.

121. Ibid.
122. George W.M. Reynolds, 'Preface to the First Volume', *Teetotaler*, 17 April 1841, i.
123. 'A Warning to Drunkards', *Teetotaler*, 2 January 1841, 222.
124. W.T. Moncrieff, 'Water', *The Teetotaler*, 27 June 1840, 6.
125. George W.M. Reynolds, 'Noctes Pickwickianae', *The Teetotaler*, 27 June 1840, 17.
126. George W.M. Reynolds, 'Noctes Pickwickianae', *The Teetotaler*, 8 August 1840, 54–55 (at 55).
127. 'The Steam Boat: A Tale of the Thames and the Times', *Hull Packet*, 22 October 1841, 4.
128. Knight, *G.W.M. Reynolds and his Fiction*, 30.
129. George W.M. Reynolds, 'The Father: An Episode in the Life of a Nobleman', *The Teetotaler*, 14 November 1840, 163.
130. Susannah Frances Reynolds, 'Sonnet', *The Teetotaler*, 26 December 1840, 212.
131. Susannah Frances Reynolds, 'The Galley Slave', *The Teetotaler*, 29 May 1841, 44–46.
132. George W.M. Reynolds, 'Farewell to the Public', *The Teetotaler*, 25 September 1841, 277.
133. Collins, xxvii.
134. Reynolds, 'Farewell to the Public', 277.
135. 'Master Timothy's Bookcase by G.W.M. Reynolds', *The Era*, 3 October 1841, 4.
136. George W.M. Reynolds, *A Sequel to Don Juan* (London: Paget, 1843), 10.
137. Collins, xxviii.

In 'the city of strange contrasts': *The Mysteries of London* and the Urban Underworld

138. Berry Chevasco, 'Lost in Translation: The Relationship between Eugène Sue's *Les Mysteres des Paris* and G.W.M. Reynolds's *The Mysteries of London*', in *G.W.M. Reynolds: Nineteenth-Century Fiction, Politics, and the Press*, ed. by Anne Humpherys and Louis James, 2nd edn (Abingdon: Routledge, 2019), 135–47 (at 135).
139. Richard C. Maxwell, 'G. M. Reynolds, Dickens, and the *Mysteries of London*', *Nineteenth-Century Fiction*, 32: 2 (1977), 188–213 (at 213).
140. Chevasco, 137.
141. Alfred Crowquill, 'Outlines of Mysteries', *Bentley's Miscellany*, 17 May 1845, 529.
142. Eugène Sue, *The Mysteries of Paris* (London: E. Appleyard, 1844), 52.
143. Ibid.
144. Ibid.
145. Alyxandra Mattison, 'The Execution and Burial of Criminals in Early Medieval England, c.850-1150: An Examination of Changes in Judicial Punishment Across the Norman Conquest' (Unpublished PhD thesis, University of Sheffield, 2016), 40

146. James Greenwood [online], 'The Seven Curses of London' (London, 1869), accessed 10 July 2020. Available at: https://www.victorianlondon.org.
147. Guy Dicks, *The John Dicks Press* (Published by the Author, 2005), 9.
148. This section is republished from a peer-reviewed academic paper of mine: Stephen Basdeo, ' "That's Business": Organised Crime in G.W.M. Reynolds' *The Mysteries of London* (1844-48)', *Law, Crime and History*, 8: 1 (2018), 53-75.
149. Anon. '[untitled article]', *The Times*, 9 December 1864, 6.
150. Reynolds, *The Mysteries of London*, II, 187.
151. Ibid., II, 218.
152. Stephen Knight, *The Mysteries of the Cities: Urban Crime Fiction in the Nineteenth Century* (Jefferson, NC: McFarland, 2012), 2.
153. Ibid., I, 69-70.
154. Ibid., I, 5.
155. Reynolds, *The Mysteries of London*, I, 149.
156. Ibid., 4.
157. Ibid., 6.
158. Ibid., 5.
159. Clive Emsley, *Crime and Society in England, 1750-1900*, 2nd Edn. (London: Longman, 1996), 234.
160. Reynolds, *The Mysteries of London*, I, 60.
161. Ibid., I, 60.
162. Ibid., II, 83.
163. Ibid., I, 127.
164. Ibid., II, 238.
165. Ibid., I, 149.
166. Ibid., II, 253–54.
167. Ibid., II, 271.
168. Helen Macfarlane, Trans. 'Manifesto of the German Communist Party', *The Red Republican*, 9 November 1850, 162.
169. Reynolds, *The Mysteries of London*, II. 149.
170. *Ibid.*, I, 150.
171. *Ibid.*, I, 51.
172. *Ibid.*, I, 99-101.
173. *Ibid.*, I, 93.
174. Ibid., II, 418.
175. Ibid., I, 304-10.
176. Ibid., I, 192.
177. Ibid., I, 196.
178. Ibid.
179. Emsley, *Crime and Society in England*, 56.
180. William Augustus Miles, *Poverty, Mendicity, and Crime* (London, 1839), 45.
181. Reynolds, *The Mysteries of London*, II. 95.
182. Ibid.

183. George Robb, *White-Collar Crime in Modern England: Financial Fraud and Business Morality, 1845-1929* (Cambridge: Cambridge University Press, 1992), 31-32.

184. Anne Humpherys, 'An introduction to G.W.M. Reynolds's "Encyclopedia of Tales"', in Humpherys and James, 127.

185. Louis James, 'Time, Politics, and the Symbolic Imagination in Reynolds's Social Melodrama', in Humpherys and James, 189.

186. George W.M. Reynolds, *Faust: A Romance of the Secret Tribunals* (London: John Dicks, 1884), 159.

187. James, 'Time, Politics, and the Symbolic Imagination in Reynolds's Social Melodrama', in Humpherys and James, 189.

188. Letter from G.W.M. Reynolds to the Post Office, 16 November 1846, Stephen Basdeo Personal Collection. This letter reads: '11 Powell Street West, Goswell Road. Sir, I shall be much obliged to you if you will direct all letters addressed to me in either of the following ways, be forwarded to me at my own private residence above:— Mr G.W.M. Reynolds, 13 or 12 Warwick Square; To the Editor of Reynolds's Magazine, 13 Warwick Square. Your very obedient servant, George W.M. Reynolds. Nov. 16th. 1846.'

189. Herbert History [online], 'London, 204/206 Goswell Road', accessed 8 July 2021. Available at: http://www.herberthistory.co.uk/

190. 'Published at the Office', *RM*, 7 November 1846, 16.

191. 'To Our Readers', *RM*, 7 November 1846, 16.

192. George W.M. Reynolds, *Wagner the Wehr-Wolf* (London: John Dicks, 1884), 7.

193. Reynolds, *Wagner the Wehr-Wolf*, 7.

194. *The Daily News* (1847), quoted in 'The Infamous Literature of the Lower Orders', *The Hampshire Advertiser*, 6 November 1847, 3.

195. Reynolds, *Mysteries of London*, IV, p. 75.

196. Ibid., IV, p. 74.

'Universal suffrage in the hands of the people': Reynolds's Political Activism

197. Reynolds, *A Sequel to Don Juan*, 35.

198. Reynolds, *The Mysteries of London*, IV, 232–34.

199. Ibid., 202–04.

200. George W.M. Reynolds, 'Foreign Intelligence', *Weekly Dispatch*, 20 February 1848, 1.

201. R.G. Gammage, *A History of the Chartist Movement* (London, 1894), 294.

202. Ibid.

203. W. Weston to Sir George Grey, 18 April 1848, HO45. OS 2410, p. 345 cited in Humpherys and James, 3.

204. Antony Taylor, "Commons-Stealers', 'Land-Grabbers' and 'Jerry-Builders': Space, popular radicalism and the politics of public access in London, 1848– 1880', *International Review of Social History*, 40: 3 (1995), 388.

205. 'Meeting on Kennington Common—Monday', *The Freeman's Journal*, 15 March 1848, 1.
206. Ibid.
207. George W.M. Reynolds, 'The Editor's Speech at the Monster Meeting on Kennington Common', *RM*, 1 April 1848, 326.
208. 'Meeting', *Morning Chronicle*, 15 March 1848, 4.
209. 'Chartist Convention, Yesterday', *Morning Chronicle*, 8 April 1848, 5. For details on Lord Stanley's diary entry see Chris Anderson [online], 'Lord Stanley's diary and the riddle of Reynolds', *G.W.M. Reynolds Society*, December 2020, available at: www.gwmreynoldssociety.com.
210. George W.M. Reynolds, 'The Drones and the Bees in Britain's Hives', *RWN*, 27 July 1851, 1.
211. 'The Great Chartist Demonstration, The Annual Register, 1848', in *British Working-Class Movements: Select Documents, 1789–1875*, ed. by G.D.H. Cole and A.W. Wilson (London: MacMillan, 1967), 404–05.
212. Dorothy Thompson, *The Dignity of Chartism*, ed. by Stephen Roberts (London: Verso, 2015), 180–81
213. Richard Whiting quoted in Dorothy Thompson, *The Chartists: Popular Politics in the Industrial Revolution* (Aldershot: Wildwood House, 1986), 325.
214. George W.M. Reynolds, 'The Government and the People', *RPI*, 2 March 1850, 2.
215. George W.M. Reynolds, 'Property', *RPI*, 26 January 1850, 2.
216. George Julian Harney, 'Manifesto of the Red Republicans of Germany', *Democratic Review*, July 1849, 67–70.
217. George Julian Harney [L'Ami du Peuple, pseud.], 'The Charter and Something More', *Red Republican*, 22 June 1850, 1–2.
218. John Saville, 'Introduction', in *Red Republican and Friend of the People*, ed. by John Saville, 2 vols (London: Merlin, 1966), I, i, iii–v.
219. Charles Marx and Frederic Engels, 'Manifesto of the German Communist Party', *Red Republican*, 9 November 1850, 161–63.
220. Helen Macfarlane, 'Remarks on the Times—Apropos of Certain Passages in No.1 of Thomas Carlyle's Latter-Day Pamphlets, April, May, and June 1850', in *Helen Macfarlane: Red Republican—Essays, Articles, and her Translation of the Communist Manifesto*, ed. by David Black (London: Unkant, 2014), 1–22.
221. George Julian Harney, 'Birthday of Maximilian Robespierre', *Democratic Review*, May 1850, 463.
222. See George Julian Harney, 'Political Postscript', *Democratic Review*, April 1850, 439 and George Julian Harney, 'Political Postscript', *Democratic Review*, March 1850, 400.
223. This tavern was actually on Queen Street in Hull and not in London, even though the news report (cited below) of Reynolds's appearance might lead modern readers to think that the report is about a meeting held in London. See: Edward Baines, *History, Directory & Gazetteer, of the County of York*, 2 vols (Leeds: Office of the Leeds Mercury, 1823), II, 323.

224. 'Town Council Meeting', *Hull Packet*, 27 July 1849, 2.
225. 'Notabilia', *Examiner*, 20 April 1850, 3.
226. Albert R. Schoyen, *The Chartist Challenge: A Portrait of George Julian Harney* (London: Heinemann, 1958), 196.
227. 'Preliminary Word', *Household Words*, 30 March 1850, 1
228. 'The Mountain', *Supplement to RPI*, 5 January 1850, 73–74.
229. Edwin F. Roberts, 'A New History of England', *RPI*, 10 November 1849, 10.
230. 'Some Scraps of Verse and Prose by Dante Gabriel Rossetti', *Pall Mall Magazine*, December (1898), 492.
231. 'Dips into the Diary of Barabbas Bolt, Esq.' *The Man in the Moon*, vol. 3 (1848), 236–44 (at 236).
232. Ibid.
233. Gammage, 358.

'A diseased, corrupt, and sink-like mind': *The Mysteries of the Court of London, Reynolds's Weekly Newspaper*, and the Road to Wealth

234. Louis James, 'Reynolds, George William MacArthur', in *The Oxford Dictionary of National Biography*, ed. by H.C.G. Matthew and Brian Harrison, 63 vols (Oxford University Press, 2004), XLVI, 537.
235. Thomas Clark, *A Letter Addressed to G.W.M. Reynolds Reviewing his Conduct as a Professed Chartist* (London: T. Clark, 1850), 16.
236. 'Annual Dinner of Mr Reynolds's Establishment', *RWN*, 18 July 1852, 3.
237. George W.M. Reynolds, 'An Address to the Public', *RM*, 29 July 1848, 48.
238. Andrew King, 'Reynolds's Miscellany, 1846–1849: Advertising Networks and Politics', in Humpherys and James, 60.
239. Dicks, *The John Dicks Press*, 17.
240. Reynolds, *Mysteries of London*, IV, 416.
241. Dicks, 19.
242. King, 'Reynolds's Miscellany, 1846–49', 65.
243. Dicks, 19.
244. 'Now Publishing in Weekly Numbers', *RM*, 29 December 1850, 368.
245. This information is taken from a history book written by one of John Dicks's descendants. See Dicks, *The John Dicks Press*, 1–60.
246. Dicks, *The John Dicks Press*, 63.
247. G.W.M. Reynolds, *The Mysteries of the Court of London*, 8 vols (London: John Dicks, 1849–56), VIII, 412.
248. Henry Mayhew, *London Labour and the London Poor*, 4 vols (London, 1861), I, accessed 1 May 2021. Available at: www.gutenberg.org.
249. James Greenwood [online], 'The Seven Curses of London (1869)', *Dictionary of Victorian London*, ed. by Lee Jackson, accessed 21 May 2021. Available at: https://www.victorianlondon.org/publications/seven8.htm
250. G.W.M. Reynolds, *The Mysteries of the Court of London*, 8 vols (London: John Dicks, 1849–56), I, 253–54.

251. Chevasco, 138.
252. 'Charles Dickens and the Democratic Movement', *RWN*, 8 June 1851, 7.
253. Clark, *A Letter Addressed to G.W.M. Reynolds*, 21.
254. Ibid, 36.
255. W.M. Thackeray, *The Complete Works of William Makepeace Thackeray*, 22 vols (Boston, MA: Houghton, 1889), XXII, 457.
256. Collins, xxxix.
257. 'Death of Mr Reynolds's Eldest Son', *RWN*, 29 September 1850, 12.
258. George W.M. Reynolds, 'The Crowned Miscreants and Harlots of Europe', *RWN*, 9 June 1850, 1.
259. Antony Taylor, 'Some Little or Contemptible War upon her Hands: Reynolds's Newspaper and Empire', in Humpherys and James, 100.
260. George W.M. Reynolds, 'The Selfish and Rapacious Oligarchy', *RWN*, 8 September 1850, 1.
261. George W.M. Reynolds, 'The People's Rights', *RWN*, 13 April 1851, 1
262. George Julian Harney, 'Samuel Kydd', *in George Juilan Harney: The Chartists were Right: Selections from the Newcastle Weekly Chronicle*, ed. by David Goodway (London: Merlin, 2014), 34–39 (at 35).
263. Harney, 'Samuel Kydd', p. 35: Harney specifically remembers that it Kydd was the Gracchus who worked for *RPI* and *RWN*, even though some historians have attributed this to Edward Reynolds.
264. Stephen Roberts, 'Samuel Kydd', in *Radical Politicians and Poets in Early Victorian Britain*, ed. by Stephen Roberts (Lewiston, NY: Edwin Mellen Press, 1993), 107–27.
265. Will Gray [online], 'The Parliamentary Reform Association, 1849', *Forgotten Victorians*, 23 August 2017, accessed 3 May 1850. Available at: https://williamgray101.wordpress.com/.
266. George W.M. Reynolds, 'The Revival of a Working-Class Agitation', *RPI*, 10 November 1849, 1–2.
267. F.E. Gillespie, The Political History of the English Working Classes, 1850-1867 (Chicago University Press, 1923), 77.
268. Reynolds, 'The Revival of a Working-Class Agitation', 1.
269. Malcolm Chase, *Chartism: A New History* (Manchester University Press, 2007), 335.
270. Clark, *A Letter Addressed to G.W.M. Reynolds*, 1.
271. Reynolds, 'The Revival of a Working-Class Agitation', 1.
272. Clark, *A Letter Addressed to G.W.M. Reynolds*, 4.
273. Ibid., 5.
274. George Julian Harney, 'To the Democrats of Great Britain and Ireland', *Democratic Review*, June 1850, 32–40.
275. Clark, *A Letter Addressed to G.W.M. Reynolds*, 36.
276. George W.M. Reynolds, 'To the Borough Electors of Finsbury', *RWN*, 26 May 1850, 1.
277. George W.M. Reynolds, 'Lord Harrowby's Pugilism and Mr Henry's Law', *RWN*, 16 June 1850, 1.

278. Ibid.
279. James McMullen Rigg [online], 'Ryder, Dudley Francis Stuart', in *The Dictionary of National Biography*, ed. by Leslie Stephen and Sidney Lee, 63 vols (London: Smith, Elder, 1885–1900), accessed 9 September 2021. Available at: https://en.wikisource.org
280. Reynolds, 'Lord Harrowby's Pugilism and Mr Henry's Law', 1.
281. Ibid.
282. Ibid.
283. 'Mr G.W.M. Reynolds', *Lancaster Gazetteer*, 15 June 1850, 4.

Seamstresses, Soldiers, and Statues: Reynolds's 'Memoirs' and Historical Novels Series

284. Reynolds, *The Mysteries of London*, IV, 254.
285. James, 'Time, Politics, and the Symbolic Imagination', in Humpherys and James, 191.
286. Knight, *G.W.M. Reynolds and his Fiction*, 176.
287. George W.M. Reynolds, *Canonbury House; or, the Queen's Prophecy* (London: John Dicks, 1884), 174.
288. G[eorge] W.M. R[eynolds], 'To a New-Born Child', *RM*, 1 April 1854, 12.
289. 'Annual Dinner of Mr Reynolds's Establishment', *RWN*, 13 July 1856, 9.
290. 'Annual Dinner of Mr Reynolds's Establishment', *RWN*, 17 July 1853, 17.
291. Karl Marx and Friedrich Engels, *On Britain* (Moscow: Progress Publishers, 1971), 459–63.
292. 'Annual Dinner of Mr Reynolds's Establishment', *RWN*, 23 July 1854, 4.
293. 'Annual Dinner of Mr Reynolds's Establishment', *RWN*, 12 July 1857, 5.
294. 'Paid Leave' [online], *Striking Women: Rights and Responsibilities*, accessed 2 June 2021. Available at: https://www.striking-women.org/
295. 'Annual Dinner of Mr Reynolds's Establishment', *RWN*, 13 July 1862, 5.
296. 'Annual Dinner of Mr. Reynold's Establishment', *Reynold's Weekly Newspaper*, 12 July 1857, 5
297. 'Penny Novels', *MacMillan's Magazine*, June 1866, 96-105
298. Lynn M. Alexander, 'Creating a Symbol: The Seamstress in Victorian Literature', *Tulsa Studies in Women's Literature*, 18: 1 (1999), 29–38 (at 29).
299. George W.M. Reynolds, *The Seamstress; or, The White Slave of England* (London: John Dicks, 1853), 19.
300. Karl Marx, *Capital: A New Abridgment*, ed. by David McLellan (Oxford University Press, 1995), 42–50.
301. 'Advertisement', *RM*, 15 November 1851, 272.
302. George W.M. Reynolds, *The Soldier's Wife* (London: John Dicks, 1852–53), 10.
303. Reynolds, *The Mysteries of London*, IV, 293.
304. 'Sedition in the Ranks', *RWN*, 25 September 1853, 4.
305. 'Exposure of Tyranny and Cruelty in the Army', *RWN*, 25 September 1853, 4.
306. George W.M. Reynolds, 'To the Editor', *Standard*, 18 December 1866, 3.

307. Sucheta Bhattacharya, 'G.W.M. Reynolds: Rewritten in Nineteenth-Century Bengal', in Humpherys and James, 249.

308. Greatandhra Bureau [online], 'Nostalgia: The Costliest Silent Film Made In India', *Greatandhra: Dare to Write*, 26 January 2021, accessed 11 June 2021. Available at: https://www.greatandhra.com/

309. Collins, xxxix.

310. Gammage, 392.

311. Ernest Jones, *Libel Exposed: Being a Full Report of the Action for Libel, Ernest Jones. G.W.M. Reynolds, Tried in the Queen's Bench* (London, 1859), 7

312. Karl Marx, 'Marx to Engels, January 14, 1858', cited in John Saville, *Ernest Jones: Chartist* (London: Lawrence and Wishart, 1952), 242.

313. Karl Marx, 'Marx to Engels, October 21, 1858', cited in Saville, 243.

314. Karl Marx, 'Marx to Engels, October 8, 1858', cited in Saville, 242.

315. 'Ernest Jones', Saturday Review, 16 July 1859, 72; 'Ernest Jones', *Leeds Mercury*, 12 July 1859, 4.

316. Gammage, 392.

317. James B. Herrick, 'Certain Textbooks on Heart Disease of the Early Nineteenth Century', *Transactions of the Seventeenth Annual Meeting of the American Association of the History of Medicine*, 10: 2 (1941), 136–47.

318. Bleiler, 157.

319. London, England, Church of England Marriages and Banns, 1754-1936; Westminster; St Marylebone; 1847–76, Entry 331, 166.

320. Asa Briggs, *Victorian People: A Reassessment of Persons and Themes, 1851-67* (University of Chicago Press, 1955), 227.

321. Angus Hawkins, *Parliament, Party and the Art of Politics in Britain, 1855–59* (Basingstoke: Palgrave, 1987), 158.

322. Leaflet issued by the National Reform Union (n.d.) [1866–67] cited in G.D.H. Cole and A.W. Filson, *British Working-Class Movements: Select Documents 1789–1875* (London: MacMillan, 1967), 531–32 (531).

323. George W.M. Reynolds, 'Kossuth, Mazzini, and Ledru-Rollin', *RPI*, 29 December 1849, 1.

324. K. T. Hoppen, *The Mid-Victorian Generation: England, 1846–886* (Oxford University Press, 1998), 250.

325. "Reform Fete and Banquet," *The Beehive*, 5 October 1867, 1.

326. Mark Hovell, *The Chartist Movement*, ed. by T.F. Prout (Manchester University Press, 1943), 299.

'Kind Reader, who have borne with me so long': Reynolds's Later Life and Death

327. R. Wherry Anderson, 'Reynolds's: 1850–1900', *RWN Jubilee Supplement: 1850–1900*, 27 May 1900, 1.

328. Humpherys and James, 'Introduction', 7.

329. Collins, li.

330. London, England, Church of England Marriages and Banns, 1754-1936; Westminster; St Marylebone; 1847–76, Entry 331, 166.
331. 1881 England Census, London; Islington; Islington East; District 4b RG11/250, 36.
332. Andrew King, *The London Journal, 1845-83: Periodicals, Production and Gender* (London: Routledge, 2004), 69.
333. Collins, lii.
334. England & Wales, National Probate Calendar (Index of Wills and Administrations), 1858-1995, 1879, 86.
335. Dicks, *The John Dicks Press*, 54.
336. 'The Death of a London Journalist', *Aberdeen Journal*, 29 January 1894, 3.
337. New York, U.S., Arriving Passenger and Crew Lists (including Castle Garden and Ellis Island); 1881-06-01 [not paginated].
338. Anon. 'Penny Fiction', *Quarterly Review*, July (1890), 151; Kathryn Tynan, 'The Book-Lover', *The Speaker*, 30 September 1893, 355.
339. Anon. 'Some Scraps of Verse and Prose by Dante Gabriel Rossetti', *Pall Mall Magazine*, December (1898), 480–96 (p. 492).
340. A.W. Thompson, *Democratic Readings* (London: John Dicks, 1896), pp. 200–14.
341. G.D.H. Cole, *Chartist Portraits* (London: MacMillan, 1943), 254, 262, 340.
342. James Ramsay MacDonald, 'Reynolds, George William MacArthur', in *The Dictionary of National Biography*, ed. by Leslie Stephen, 63 vols (London: Smith, Elder, 1885–1900), XLVIII, 44–45.
343. George W.M. Reynolds, 'Political Rights and Social Reforms', *RWN*, 15 September 1850, 1.

Reynolds's Political Instructor

344. 'Advertisement', *RM*, 31 November 1849, 304.
345. 'William Cuffay', *RPI*, 13 April 1850, 1.

Further Reading

Readers will find references listed in the 'Notes' section. This list, however, is essential reading for anybody who would like to become better acquainted with the life and work of G.W.M. Reynolds. I encourage you to subscribe to updates on the G.W.M. Reynolds Society's website (https://gwmreynoldssociety.com/); the society's website also contains an extensive bibliography of every scholarly work on Reynolds's life and fiction.

Atal, Maha R. 'G.W.M. Reynolds in Paris, 1835–36: A New Discovery', *Notes and Queries*, December (2008), 448–53.

Basdeo, Stephen, ed. *English Rebels and Revolutionaries* (Barnsley: Pen and Sword, 2022)

Bhattacharya, Sucheta, 'G.W.M. Reynolds: Rewritten in Nineteenth-Century Bengal', in *G.W.M. Reynolds: Nineteenth-Century Fiction, Politics, and the Press*, ed. by Anne Humpherys and Louis James, 2nd edn (Abingdon: Routledge, 2019), 247–58.

Bleiler, E.F. ed., *Wagner the Wehr-Wolf* (New York: Dover, 1975)

Carver, Stephen James. 'The Wrongs and Crimes of the Poor: The Urban Underworld of *The Mysteries of London* in Context', in *G.W.M. Reynolds: Nineteenth-Century Fiction, Politics and the Press*, ed. by Anne Humpherys and Louis James, 2nd edn (Abingdon: Routledge, 2019), 149–62.

Chevasco, Barry, 'Lost in Translation: The Relationship between Eugène Sue's *Les Mysteres des Paris* and G.W.M. Reynolds's *The Mysteries of London*', in *G.W.M. Reynolds: Nineteenth-Century Fiction, Politics, and the Press*, ed. by Anne Humpherys and Louis James, 2nd edn (Abingdon: Routledge, 2019), 135–47

Cole, G.D.H., *Chartist Portraits* (London: MacMillan, 1943)

Collins, Dick, ed. *The Necromancer* (New York: Valancourt Books, 2007)

Conary, Jennifer, 'G. W. M. Reynolds, the *Paris Advertiser*, and the Anglo-Parisian Press', *Victorian Periodicals Review*, 53: 2 (2020), 214–37

Diamond, Michael, 'From Journalism and Fiction into Politics', in *G.W.M. Reynolds: Nineteenth-Century Fiction, Politics, and the Press*, ed. by Anne Humpherys and Louis James, 2nd edn (Abingdon: Routledge, 2019), 91–99

Dicks, Guy, *The John Dicks Press* (Published by the Author, 2005)

Gammage, Robert George, *The History of the Chartist Movement* (London: Holyoake, 1854)

Hackenberg, Sara 'Romanticism Bites: Quixotic Historicism in Rymer and Reynolds', in *Edward Lloyd and his World: Popular Fiction, Politics, and the Press in Victorian Britain*, ed. by Rohan McWilliam and Sarah Lill (London: Routledge, 2020), 164–82

Haywood, Ian, 'The Importance of "Phis": The Role of Imitation in Lloyd's Imitations of Dickens', in *Edward Lloyd and his World: Popular Fiction, Politics, and the Press in Victorian Britain*, ed. by Sarah Louise Lill and Rohan McWilliam (London: Routledge, 2019), 54–70

———, *The Revolution in Popular Literature: Print, Politics and the People, 1790–1860* (Cambridge University Press, 2004)

Humphreys, Anne, "The Geometry of the Modern City: G. W. M. Reynolds and The Mysteries of London", *Browning Institute Studies*, xi, (1983), 69–70.

Humpherys, Anne and Louis James, eds. *G.W.M. Reynolds: Nineteenth-Century Fiction, Politics, and the Press*, 2nd edn (London: Routledge, 2019)

James, Louis, *Fiction for the working man, 1830–1850* (Oxford University Press, 1963)

———, ' "I am Ada!": Edward Lloyd and the Creation of the Penny Dreadful', in *Edward Lloyd and his World: Popular Fiction, Politics, and the Press in Victorian Britain*, ed. by Sarah Louise Lill and Rohan McWilliam (London: Routledge, 2019), pp. 54–70

———, James, Louis, 'Reynolds, George William MacArthur', in *The Oxford Dictionary of National Biography*, ed. by H.C.G. Matthew and Brian Harrison, 63 vols (Oxford University Press, 2004), XLVI, p. 537.

———, 'Time, Politics, and the Symbolic Imagination in Reynolds's Social Melodrama', in *G.W.M. Reynolds: Nineteenth-Century Fiction, Politics, and the Press*, ed. by Anne Humpherys and Louis James, 2nd edn (London: Routledge, 2019), 181–209

James, Sara, 'G.W.M. Reynolds and the Modern Literature of France', in *G.W.M. Reynolds: Nineteenth-Century Fiction, Politics, and the Press*, ed. by Anne Humpherys and Louis James, 2nd edn (London: Routledge, 2019), 19–32

King, Andrew, *The London Journal, 1845–83: Periodicals, Production and Gender* (London: Routledge, 2004)

———, 'Reynolds's Miscellany, 1846–1849: Advertising Networks and Politics', in *G.W.M. Reynolds: Nineteenth-Century Fiction, Politics, and the Press*, ed. by Anne Humpherys and Louis James, 2nd edn (Abingdon: Routledge, 2019), 53–75

Knight, Stephen, *G.W.M. Reynolds and his Fiction: The Man Who Outsold Dickens* (London: Routledge, 2019)

———, *The Mysteries of the Cities: Urban Crime Fiction in the Nineteenth Century* (Jefferson, NC: McFarland, 2012)

Law, Graham, 'Reynolds's "Memoirs" Series and the Literature of the Kitchen', in *G.W.M. Reynolds: Nineteenth-Century Fiction, Politics, and the Press*, ed. by Anne Humpherys and Louis James, 2nd edn (London: Routledge, 2019), 199–211

Leger-St.-Jean, Marie [online], *Price One Penny*, available at: www.priceonepenny.info

MacDonald, James Ramsey, 'Reynolds, George William MacArthur', in *The Dictionary of National Biography*, ed. by Leslie Stephen, 63 vols (London: Smith, Elder, 1885–1900), XLVIII, 44–45.

Maxwell, Richard C., 'G. M. Reynolds, Dickens, and the *Mysteries of London*', *Nineteenth-Century Fiction*, 32: 2 (1977), 188–213

——, 'G. M. Reynolds, Dickens, and the Mysteries of London', *Nineteenth-Century Fiction*, 32: 2 (1977), 188–213

——, *Mysteries of Paris and London* (University Press of Virginia, 1992)

McWilliam, Rohan, 'The French Connection: G.W.M. Reynolds and the Outlaw Robert Macaire', in *G.W.M. Reynolds: Nineteenth-Century Fiction, Politics, and the Press*, ed. by Anne Humpherys and Louis James, 2nd edn (Abingdon: Routledge, 2019), 33–53

Pearl, Cyril, *Victorian Patchwork* (London: William Heinemann, 1972)

Shannon, Mary, *Dickens, Reynolds and Mayhew on Wellington Street: the Print Culture of a Victorian Street* (Abingdon: Routledge, 2015)

Taylor, Antony, 'Some Little or Contemptible War upon her Hands: Reynolds's Newspaper and Empire', in *G.W.M. Reynolds: Nineteenth-Century Fiction, Politics, and the Press*, ed. by Anne Humpherys and Louis James, 2nd edn (Abingdon: Routledge, 2019), 99–123

Index

abolition of slavery, 35, 36
Ainsworth, William Harrison, xvi, 17
Algeria, 26
American Civil War, 135
American Revolution, 9, 10
annual parliaments, 77, 79, 155, 158
Antier, Benjamin, 36
Arbroath, 111
anarchism, 171, 173, 174, 246
apprentices, 102, 180
Armand, Jean, 37
aristocracy, 11, 26, 50, 54, 55, 60, 62,
    63, 66, 77, 79, 85, 86, 104, 106,
    107, 110, 113, 116, 117, 128, 129,
    145, 150, 152, 156, 159, 161, 165,
    175, 182, 202, 205, 212, 221, 226,
    227, 231, 232, 237, 238, 240, 247
Atal, Maha, xviii
Athenaeum, 22
Australia, 12, 126, 202, 205, 207
Austria, 120, 172, 174, 192, 196, 211,
    226, 227, 228, 235, 236

Baines, Edward, 136
Bank of England, 80
Barrett, Stephen, 4
Baudry, Louis Claude, 19, 21
Beales, Edward, 136, 139
Beehive, 139
Belgium, 15, 88, 204
Bennis, George, 15, 16, 20
Bentley's Miscellany, 51
Birmingham, 136, 181
Blanc, Louis, 91, 184

Bleiler, E.F., xviii
blinding as punishment, 53, 54
Black Death, 69
Black Forest, 70
Bolton, 155
Bow Bells, xiv, 141
breakdown of feudalism, 63
Breton, Rob, ix
Bright, John, 136, 138
Brighton, 107
British Empire, viii, 35, 110
Bronterre O'Brien, James, 91, 94. 97
Brunel, Isambard Kingdom, xvi
Burke, Edmund, 10, 11
Bulwer Lytton, Edward, 17
Byron, Lord George Gordon, 47

Cade, Jack, 87
Caleb Williams, 17
Carlile, Richard, 8
Cave, Edward, 4
Census (1841), 25, 36, 208, 209
Chambers' London Journal, 142
Chapman and Hall, 29
Chapponier, Alexis, 37
Charles II, 204, 217, 218
Charles X of France, 12
Chartism, xii, 49, 90, 91, 97, 114,
    132, 133, 136, 137, 150, 152–56,
    157–62, 227, 230, 231, 234, 239–43;
    Chartist Movement (Hovell), 146;
    Chartist Portraits (Cole), 146;
    History of the Chartist Movement
    (Gammage), 82; Kennington

267